Advanced
Modula-2

Advanced Modula-2

Herbert Schildt

Osborne **McGraw-Hill**
Berkeley, California

Osborne **McGraw-Hill**
2600 Tenth Street
Berkeley, California 94710
U.S.A.

For information on translations and book distributors outside of the U.S.A., write to
Osborne **McGraw-Hill** at the above address.

A complete list of trademarks appears on page 369.

Advanced Modula-2

1234567890 DODO 89876

ISBN 0-07-881245-3

C O N T E N T S

INTRODUCTION

I have been fortunate to be able to write the kind of programming book that I always wanted. Years ago, when I began to program, I tried to find a book that presented algorithms for such tasks as sorts, linked lists, simulations, and expression parsers in a straightforward way with their underlying theory. I also wanted a book that would give insights into many of the common problems that I might find in programming. I never found exactly the book that I was looking for; now, I have written that book.

This book covers a wide range of subjects and contains many useful algorithms, procedures, functions, and approaches that are written in the Modula-2 language. There are many Modula-2 compilers available for virtually all microcomputers. I used the Logitech Modula-2 compiler for the examples in this book; however, with few exceptions, these examples will compile and run on any of the Modula-2 compilers, including the Interface Technologies M2SDS system.

Chapter 1 begins with a short overview of the language. Chapter 2 covers sorting—including arrays and disk files. Chapter 3 deals with stacks, queues, linked lists, and binary trees. This may seem like a lot to cover in one chapter, but the subjects form a solid unit.

Chapter 4 discusses dynamic allocation methods. Chapter 5 presents an overview of operating-system interfacing and assembly language linkage. Chapter 6 covers statistics and includes a complete statistics program. Chapter 7 is about codes, ciphers, and data compression; it includes a short history of cryptography. Chapter 8 describes several random number generators and then discusses how to use them in two simulations: a check-out line in a store and a random-walk portfolio management program.

Chapter 9, my personal favorite, contains the complete code to a recursive descent parser. (Years ago, I would have given just about anything to have had that code!) The chapter is for those who need to evaluate expressions. Chapter 10 covers converting programs from other languages into Modula-2. Chapter 11 discusses Modula-2's support of coroutines and concurrent procedures. Chapter 12 finishes the book with a discussion of debugging.

If you would like to obtain an IBM PC-compatible diskette that contains all of the programs and algorithms in this book, please complete the order form and mail it with your payment enclosed. If you are in a hurry, call (217)586-4021 to place your order.

—**H.S.**

Disk Order Form

Please send me _____ copies, at $29.95 each, of the programs in *Advanced Modula-2*. *Foreign orders*: add $5.00 for shipping and handling.

_____

Name

_____

Address

_____

City   State   ZIP

_____

Telephone

Method of payment: Check _____ VISA _____ MC _____

Credit card number: _____

Expiration date: _____

Signature: _____

Send to: Herbert Schildt
            RR 1, Box 130
            Mahomet, Illinois 61853

A Review of
Modula-2

CHAPTER 1

This book uses a problem-solving approach to illustrate advanced concepts in the Modula-2 programming language. The book examines various common programming tasks, and develops solutions with an emphasis on style and structure. Each chapter covers a different area of programming and presents one or more solutions. Through this approach, the text covers various Modula-2 topics and nuances, as well as the general programming theory behind the algorithms.

It is assumed that you have a working knowledge of Modula-2, and have access to a compiler and a computer. If you are an experienced Modula-2 programmer and anxious to get to the "meat" of the book, you should skip to Chapter 2 at this time; the rest of this chapter gives a quick review of Modula-2, including origins, syntax, and library procedures. The final section is a brief discussion of the key differences between Modula-2 and Pascal.

The Development
of Modula-2

Modula-2 is one of the most important programming languages of this century. In a world filled with many computer languages and hundreds of dialects of each language, this statement sounds fairly strong—and it is. Only a handful of languages rank as milestones in programming history. Each has succeeded because it offered the programmer an easier, more flexible, manageable tool with which to work. Modula-2 is such a tool.

The development of computer languages has been an evolutionary process where the survival of a language is based on the number of programmers actually using it. The languages that have survived have been the ones that people liked to use. Modula-2's heritage goes all of the way back to the beginnings of computer languages. When professional programmers discuss

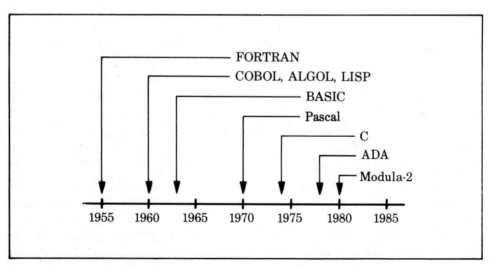

Figure 1-1. A time line of important programming languages

breakthroughs in computer languages, the following languages keep cropping up: FORTRAN, ALGOL, LISP, BASIC, Pascal, C, and Modula-2. Figure 1-1 shows a time line of these and other important languages. As Figure 1-1 shows, Modula-2 is the most recent language in this progression. In many ways, Modula-2 combines the best ideas that are found in its predecessors.

Modula-2's Beginnings

Virtually everyone that has worked with computers knows—or at least has heard of—a language called Pascal. Many programmers know that Niklaus Wirth created it. Because of Pascal, Professor Wirth has become a famous figure in contemporary computer science. In 1970, Pascal was invented because Professor Wirth was dissatisfied with the languages that were generally available to teach programming. For example, at that time, FORTRAN, the first high-level language, provided the DO statement as its only built-in loop, which forced programmers to use GOTOs when they needed other types of loops. FORTRAN also had several peculiarities that made it difficult to learn quickly and that could easily mislead both beginners and professionals. On the other extreme, while easy to learn, BASIC did not lend itself to the clear presentation of algorithms, and only had the FOR loop for iteration. Pascal solved these and other problems by offering good loop constructs, a simple yet elegant syntax, and good error checking.

Pascal succeeded beyond Professor Wirth's expectations. Around the world, many major colleges and universities have adopted it for teaching programming, and thus there are many programmers who are fluent in Pascal. Because of Pascal's use in colleges and universities and because of the available pool of programmers, industry began to use Pascal as a general-purpose programming language for research and development. Even though designed as a teaching language, Pascal has become so popular that it is one of the most important general-purpose programming languages in current use.

The fact that Pascal moved from the classroom to research and development is part of the reason that Professor Wirth began work on a language to succeed Pascal. Because Pascal was designed as a teaching language, it lacked several important features that a general-purpose language needs. For example, it does not have strings, random access disk files, and separate compilation and linking. How to handle these extensions—if they were handled at all—was left up to the programmers who implemented the language. Thus, every implementation was somewhat different. (Remember that, while Professor Wirth *designed* the language, many companies, universities, and individuals have created implementations to run on a variety of different computers.) The problem with having different implementations is that programs that were written on one enhanced Pascal compiler were not necessarily *transportable* to another. A *transportable program* will compile and run on different compilers without needing changes. The reason that this is so important is that commercial software houses spend millions of dollars on developing programs, so they want the programs to run on the widest possible variety of computers and operating systems.

Although pleased with the success of Pascal, Professor Wirth was troubled that so many enhanced versions of the language existed, and that many of these versions were not in line with Pascal's original concept. Why Wirth did not create his own enhanced Pascal is unclear; however, there seem to be three main reasons. First, the range and acceptance of the enhanced versions were so great that it might not have been possible to "pull them into line"—thus, a true "enhanced Pascal" may have been only another version. Second, it is possible that Professor Wirth wanted to keep Pascal as simply a teaching language. Third, and perhaps most important, as Professor Wirth began to think about an enhanced version of Pascal, multiprocessing languages were beginning to appear in experimental form and it was generally acknowledged that future languages would need multiprocessing capability. Unlike the type of programs that you have probably written or used, a *multiprocess program* contains two or more equally important, interactive but discrete processes. Sometimes called *coroutines*, these processes in theory execute simultaneously. So, instead of simply enhancing Pascal, Professor Wirth elected to define a new language that would both be a "better Pascal" and support a multiprocess-program environment. In 1975, Professor Wirth defined and implemented an experimental language that he called *Modula* (MODUlar LAnguage). By 1979, Professor Wirth finished an enhanced version called Modula-2. Since its release, the use of Modula-2 has grown steadily.

The Modula-2 Philosphy

In general, language influences the way that people think. This statement is true for human languages, the language of mathematics, and programming languages. For example, it has been said that French is a poetic language, that German is an engineering language, and that English is a poor blend of these! More seriously, consider the language of calculus. Both Isaac Newton and Gottfried Leibniz independently developed the basis for calculus. However, Leibniz's notation, or language, was easier to understand and use than was Newton's. Hence, it is Leibniz's notation that is still used today. Even though both Newton's calculus and Leibniz's calculus could solve the same problems, *Leibniz's language made it easier to solve them*. The same type of situation exists in programming.

Computer science is still a young endeavor. As such, not only programming languages are evolving and progressing, but also the way that people think about problems and their solutions is changing. When Professor Wirth created Modula-2, he actually also defined an approach to problem-solving. The essence of this method is *modularity*, which is embodied in the Modula-2 language. A modular approach to problem-solving suggests that every problem consists of either two or more subproblems, or a solution. Therefore, any problem either can be reduced into its parts, or can be solved.

In programming, you can break every programming problem down into smaller pieces, or subproblems. You can then separate these smaller pieces into even smaller pieces, or into individual statements or subroutines (solutions). There are two advantages to reducing a problem into its parts. First, it lets you see all elements and facets of the task more clearly — in essence, it allows you to understand the problem more easily. Second, it enables you to code and debug pieces of the program a little at a time. This advantage is important because debugging time seems to be an exponential relationship that is based on the size of the routine or program. Therefore, the smaller the pieces are that you are working with, the less trouble you will have.

The Modula-2 language strongly promotes the concept of task reduction by allowing you to create separate logical routines easily that you later combine to make your program. Therefore, you can think of a Modula-2 program as being a collection of small pieces, as shown in Figure 1-2. The form of a normal BASIC program is included for comparison.

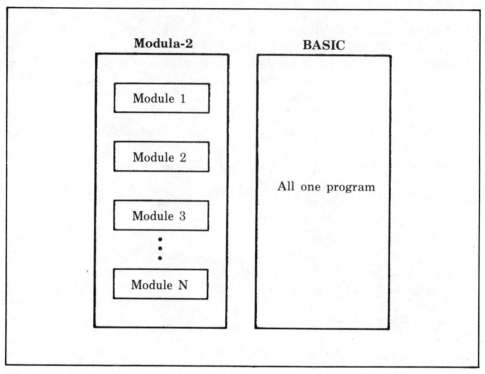

Figure 1-2. A Modula-2 program compared to a BASIC program

Syntax Summary

Modula-2 has 40 reserved words that form the language and that may not be used for any other purpose. They are as follows:

AND	DEFINITION	EXIT
ARRAY	DIV	EXPORT
BEGIN	DO	FOR
BY	ELSE	FROM
CASE	ELSIF	IF
CONST	END	IMPLEMENTATION

IMPORT	**POINTER**	**TO**
IN	**PROCEDURE**	**TYPE**
LOOP	**QUALIFIED**	**UNTIL**
MOD	**RECORD**	**VAR**
MODULE	**REPEAT**	**WHILE**
NOT	**RETURN**	**WITH**
OF	**SET**	
OR	**THEN**	

This section will describe each of these reserved words.

AND

The logical operator **AND** combines two **BOOLEAN** expressions. The outcome of the operation is **TRUE** if and only if both expressions are **TRUE**; it is **FALSE** if not. For example,

> **TRUE AND TRUE**
> is **TRUE** while

> **TRUE AND FALSE**
> is **FALSE**.

ARRAY

You use **ARRAY** to form an array declaration. The general form of a single-dimension array declaration is

> *VarName*: **ARRAY** [*low..high*] **OF** *type*;

where *VarName* is the name of the array variable, *low* and *high* are the lower and upper bounds of the array, and *type* is the base data type.

Multidimensioned array declarations have this general form:

> *VarName*: **ARRAY** [*low1..high1*],
> [*low2..high2*],...[*lowN..HighN*] **OF** *type*;

Here, the lower and upper bounds of each dimension are explicitly declared.

BEGIN

BEGIN signals the beginning of either a **MODULE**'s code or a **PROCE-DURE**'s code.

BY

BY specifies the increment in the **FOR** statement. For example, the following fragment will count from 10 to 0:

```
FOR x:=10 TO 0 BY -1. DO
    .
    .
    .
END;
```

CASE

The **CASE** statement is a multiway decision path. The computer compares the object of the **CASE** against each case and, if it finds a match, then it executes the code that is associated with that case. If it does not find a match, then it executes the code that is associated with the optional **ELSE** case, if that case exists. In the **CASE** statement, vertical bars separate cases, and only constants may be used in the case list. The general form of the **CASE** statement is

```
CASE VarName OF
    const1: statement sequence |
    const2: statement sequence |
    const3: statement sequence |
            .
            .
            .
    constN: statement sequence
    ELSE: statement sequence
END;
```

CONST

CONST declares a constant in a **MODULE** or **PROCEDURE**. For example, the following declares **MaxEvent** to be a constant that is equal to 100.

```
CONST
   MaxEvent = 100;
```

Notice that a constant declaration uses an equal sign and not a colon.

DEFINITION

DEFINITION declares a **DEFINITION MODULE**. It is placed directly before the reserved **MODULE**, and indicates that the **MODULE** describes only the definition of what will be done. The actual code to do the work is in the **IMPLEMENTATION MODULE**, which is described later. Together, these modules support separate compilation and linking.

DIV

DIV is the **INTEGER** and **CARDINAL** division operator. You can only use the / sign with **REAL** numbers.

DO

DO is used with the **FOR**, **WITH**, and **WHILE** statements. (See the description of each of these statements for specific information about **DO**.)

ELSE

ELSE helps to form the optional else clause of the **IF** and **CASE** statements. The computer executes the statement sequence that follows the **ELSE** only if the **IF** condition and any **ELSIF** conditions are **FALSE** or if none of the **CASE** statements are satisfied. (See **IF** and **CASE** for more information on the role of **ELSE**.)

ELSIF

ELSIF is an optional clause to the **IF** statement that takes the place of the traditional **IF/THEN/ELSE/IF** compound statements. (See **IF** for more information on **ELSIF**.)

END

END terminates statement sequences, **PROCEDURE**s, and **MODULE**s.

EXIT

EXIT forces the exit from a **LOOP** loop. When the computer encounters **EXIT**, it terminates the loop and resumes execution at the first line of code after the **LOOP**'s **END** statement. (See **LOOP** for examples of using **EXIT**.)

EXPORT

EXPORT allows other **MODULE**s to have knowledge of and access to **PROCEDURE**s and **TYPE**s that another **MODULE** may contain. There may only be one **EXPORT** statement for each **MODULE**. The most common use of **EXPORT** is with separately compiled **MODULE**s: the modifier **QUALIFIED** is required to ensure that conflicts between names do not occur. For example, this fragment **EXPORT**s **Counter**, **Payee**, and **YTD**.

```
DEFINITION MODULE AccountPayable;

EXPORT QUALIFIED Counter, Payee, YTD;
:
:
END AccountPayable;
```

FOR

The **FOR** loop will repeat a statement sequence for a predetermined number of times. Its general form is

> **FOR** *ControlVar:=expression* **TO** *expression*
>   **BY** *expression* **DO**
>   *statement sequence*
> **END;**

The **BY** is optional: if it is not present, then the computer increments the **ControlVar** each time that the loop repeats; if it is present, the computer increments or decreases **ControlVar** by the value of the **BY** expression. In this way, you can count by increments other than one, or you can run the loop backwards by using a negative value.

This example prints the number 1 to 10 on the screen:

```
FOR x:=1 TO 10 DO
  WriteInt(x, 3);
END;
```

This code will print the numbers 10 through 1:

```
FOR x:=10 TO 1 BY -1 DO
  WriteInt(x, 3);
END;
```

If you program in Pascal, you should note that Modula-2 does not use **DOWNTO**.

FROM

FROM indicates in which library a specified **PROCEDURE** or **TYPE** is found. (See **IMPORT** for more information on finding **PROCEDURE**s and **TYPE**s.)

IF

The **IF** statement has three basic forms. The simplest form is

> **IF** *expression* **THEN** *statement sequence* **END;**

If the *expression* is **TRUE**, then the computer will execute the *statement sequence*. Otherwise execution resumes with the first line of code following the **END**.

You can add the optional **ELSIF** so that the computer will check for one or more alternatives. The general form of the **IF/ELSIF** is

> **IF** *expression* **THEN** *statement sequence*
> **ELSIF** *expression* **THEN** *statement sequence*
> **ELSIF** *expression* **THEN** *statement sequence*
> **ELSIF** *expression* **THEN** *statement sequence*
>
> .
> .
> .
>
> **END**;

If the **IF** *expression* is **TRUE**, then the computer executes its *statement sequence* and skips all of the **ELSIF**s. If the **IF** *expression* is **FALSE**, then the computer executes the **ELSIF**s until it finds one that is **TRUE** and executes its *statement sequence*. If none of the expressions are **TRUE**, then the computer takes no action.

The final option is the **ELSE**, which provides for a *statement sequence* that the computer will execute if the **IF** and **ELSIF**, if any, conditions are **FALSE**. The general form for the **ELSE** is

> **IF** *expression* **THEN** *statement sequence*
> **ELSIF** *expression* **THEN** *statement sequence*
> **ELSIF** *expression* **THEN** *statement sequence*
> **ELSIF** *expression* **THEN** *statement sequence*
>
> .
> .
> .
>
> **ELSE** *statement sequence*
> **END**;

IMPLEMENTATION

IMPLEMENTATION declares an **IMPLEMENTATION MODULE,** which holds the actual code that performs the functions that are described in the corresponding **DEFINITION MODULE**. These two modules create libraries and allow for separate compilation and linking.

IMPORT

IMPORT tells the compiler where to find certain **TYPE**s and **PROCE-DURE**s. The most common form of the **IMPORT** statement is

FROM *library* **IMPORT** *identifier list*

where *library* is the name of the library that holds the identifiers specified in the *identifier list*. For example, in order to use **WriteLn** from **InOut**, you must have this **IMPORT** statement:

```
FROM InOut IMPORT WriteLn;
```

IN

IN is a set operator that determines whether a specified element is a member of a set. The general form is

element **IN** *set*

IN evaluates **TRUE** if *element* is a member of *set* and **FALSE** if not.

LOOP

LOOP creates an endless loop. No provision for termination is built into the statement. The only way the compiler can leave a **LOOP** is if you use the **EXIT** command, which causes the compiler to terminate the loop immediately when it encounters **EXIT**. The general form of the **LOOP** statement is

LOOP *statement sequence*
END;

For example, the following loop will run until you type a **q**.

```
LOOP
  Read(ch);
  IF ch='q' THEN EXIT END;
END;
```

MOD

The **MOD** operation computes the remainder of an integer division. For example, 10 DIV 3 equals 3 with a remainder of 1. Therefore, **10 MOD 3** equals 1.

MODULE

The **MODULE** is central to Modula-2 because all program activity occurs in **MODULE**s. There are four kinds of **MODULE**s:

- program
- **DEFINITION**
- **IMPLEMENTATION**
- local

It is beyond the scope of this review to cover each of these fully. However, they all have a general form that is similar to that of the program **MODULE** (except that **IMPLEMENTATION MODULE**s have no code body). The general form of a program **MODULE** is shown here:

```
MODULE name;
    IMPORT list
    CONST definitions
    TYPE definitions
    VAR declarations
    PROCEDURE declarations

BEGIN
    statement sequence
END name.
```

NOT

NOT is a logical operator that reverses the state of a **BOOLEAN** expression: that is, **NOT TRUE** is **FALSE** and **NOT FALSE** is **TRUE**.

OF

OF is used in an array declaration. (See **ARRAY** for examples of the way that **OF** is used.)

OR

OR is the logical **OR** operator. The outcome of an **OR** operation is **TRUE** if at least one operand is **TRUE**. For example, **TRUE OR FALSE** is **TRUE**, but **FALSE OR FALSE** is **FALSE**.

POINTER

POINTER declares pointer variables. A pointer variable is simply a variable that holds the address of another variable. The following code declares a **ptr** to be a pointer to an **INTEGER**.

```
VAR
    ptr: POINTER TO INTEGER;
```

PROCEDURE

You use **PROCEDURE** to declare a procedure. There are two types of **PROCEDURE**s: those that return values and those that do not return values. The general form of a **PROCEDURE** with no return value is

> **PROCEDURE** *name*(*parameter list*);
>   **CONST** *list*;
>   **TYPE** *list*;
>   **VAR** *declarations*
>   **PROCEDURE** *declarations*
> **BEGIN**
>   *statement sequence*
> **END** *name*;

As you can see, it is possible to have **PROCEDURE**s inside **PROCEDURE**s.

In general, everything that is declared inside a **PROCEDURE** is known only within that **PROCEDURE**. This helps make stand-alone subroutines possible.

To enable a return value, you only need to change the first line of a **PROCEDURE**, as shown here:

PROCEDURE *name(parameter list)*: *type*;

Here, *type* is the type of value that the **PROCEDURE** will return. You must explicitly specify the return value by using the **RETURN** statement.

QUALIFIED

You use the **QUALIFIED** modifier with the **EXPORT** statement to link the **MODULE** name with the **EXPORT**ed identifiers. Its use is mandatory for separately compiled **MODULE**s, and is optional for local **MODULE**s.

RECORD

A **RECORD** is a conglomerate data type that allows you to link several different variables together and access them as a unit. The general form of a **RECORD** is

```
RecName = RECORD
        Var1: type;
        Var2: type;
        Var3: type;
          .
          .
          .
        VarN: type;
END;
```

You access individual elements of a record by using the dereferencing operator ., which is a period. For example, given

```
TYPE
  Rec = RECORD
          I: INTEGER;
          R: REAL;
  END;

VAR
  x: REC;
```

the following assignments are valid:

```
x.I:=10;
x.R:=10.10;
```

REPEAT

The **REPEAT** loop is the only loop in Modula-2 that will always execute at least once. This occurs because the test condition is at the bottom of the loop. The general form of the **REPEAT** loop is

> **REPEAT**
>   *statement sequence*
> **UNTIL** *expression*;

The *expression* following the **UNTIL** must evaluate to a **BOOLEAN** value. The loop will run until *expression* becomes **TRUE**. For example, this loop will repeat until you type a **q**.

```
REPEAT
   Read(ch);
UNTIL ch='q';
```

RETURN

RETURN returns a value from a **PROCEDURE**. The general form of **RETURN** is

> **RETURN** *expression*;

where the *expression* must be the same type as specified in the **PROCE-DURE** declaration. (See **PROCEDURE** for more information on **RETURN** and return values.)

SET

SET declares a **SET** type. A *set* is a group of values of a subrange or an enumeration. Only the set operators and procedures can operate on **SET** variables. For example, the following code creates a **SET** of digits:

```
TYPE
   digits = [0..9];
   DigSet = SET OF digits;
```

THEN

See **IF** for examples of using **THEN**.

TO

See **FOR** for examples of using **TO**.

TYPE

TYPE tells the compiler that **TYPE** definitions will follow in the code. A **TYPE** definition either creates a new type of data, or gives a new name to an existing type.

UNTIL

See **REPEAT** for examples of using **UNTIL**.

VAR

VAR tells the compiler that variable declarations will follow in the code.

WHILE

The **WHILE** loop has the general form

> **WHILE** *expression* **DO**
> *statement sequence*
> **END**;

Here, *expression* must evaluate to a **BOOLEAN** value. The **WHILE** loop will run while *expression* is **TRUE**. For example, this loop will repeat until you type a **q**.

```
Read(ch);
WHILE ch<>'q' DO
  Read(ch);
END;
```

WITH

WITH automatically dereferences a **RECORD**, thus eliminating the need for the dereferencing operator. The general form of **WITH** is

> **WITH** *RecName* **DO**
> *statement sequence*
> **END**;

The following code fragment illustrates the use of **WITH**:

```
TYPE
  RecType = RECORD
              index: INTEGER;
              ratio: REAL;
  END;

VAR
  rec: RecType;

BEGIN
  WITH rec DO
    ratio:=10.1;
    index:=1;
  END;
  .
  .
  .
```

The Modula-2 Standard Procedures

As you know, most of Modula-2's standard procedures are not built into the compiler itself, but rather are found in various library modules that are supplied with the compiler. Although Modula-2 compiler implementors have the right to provide whatever library routines they want, most will supply at least those libraries that Professor Wirth described. Therefore, this section summarizes these libraries and their procedures. However, remember that your compiler may use different names for both the libraries and the procedures.

Conversions

The **Conversions** library contains the routines to convert **INTEGER**s and **CARDINAL**s to strings.

PROCEDURE ConvertCardinal(number, width: CARDINAL;
                           VAR str: ARRAY OF CHAR);

ConvertCardinal will convert the **CARDINAL number** into a string that has a minimum width of **width**, and will place the result in **str**.

PROCEDURE ConvertInteger(number: INTEGER; width:
                          CARDINAL;
                          VAR str: ARRAY OF CHAR);

ConvertInteger will convert the **INTEGER number** into a string that has a minimum width of **width**, and will place the result in **str**.

FileSystem

FileSystem contains the procedures and types that are necessary to perform both ASCII and binary disk file I/O.

TYPE

> Response = (done, notdone, notsupported,
>   callerror, unknownmedium,
>   unknownfile, paramerror, toomanyfiles
>   eom, userdeverror);

Response determines the outcome of the various disk file operations, as shown here.

Response	Meaning
done	successful completion
notdone	an error not specified by the other fields
notsupported	internal use
callerror	file in improper state for requested operation, such as trying to write to a read-only file
unknownmedium	drive does not exist
unknownfile	file specified for deletion cannot be found
paramerror	invalid parameter
toomanyfiles	attempted to open more files than supported by the system
eom	end-of-medium reached
userdeverror	internal use

TYPE

> File = RECORD
>
> .
> .
> .
>
> eof: BOOLEAN;
> res: Response;
>
> .
> .
> .

END;

File creates file descriptor variables. The only fields of general use to the programmer are **eof**, which indicates that the compiler has reached the end-of-file, and **res**, which indicates the status of each operation.

PROCEDURE Again(VAR f: File);

Again causes the next read operation to read the same character again from the specified file.

PROCEDURE Close(VAR f: File);

Close flushes the specified file's buffer, writes an EOF mark, and closes the file.

PROCEDURE Create(VAR f: File; medium: ARRAY OF CHAR);

Create creates a temporary file. Here, **medium** is the name of the disk drive and **f** is a file descriptor. Most applications seldom use **Create**.

PROCEDURE Delete(VAR f: File; FileName: ARRAY OF CHAR);

Delete removes a file from the medium. **FileName** is the name of the file to delete and **f.res** holds the outcome of the operation.

PROCEDURE GetPos(VAR f: File; High, Low: CARDINAL);

GetPos returns the current byte location of the specified file. The location is returned in **High** and **Low**, which represent the high-order and low-order words of a long integer. The location is computed by using this formula:

$$position = (High*2^{16})+Low$$

PROCEDURE Length(VAR f: File; High, Low: CARDINAL);

Length returns the length in bytes of the specified file. The computer returns the length in **High** and **Low**, which represent the high-order and low-order words of a long integer. The length is computed by the formula

$$length = (High*2^{16})+Low$$

PROCEDURE Lookup(VAR f: File; FileName: ARRAY OF CHAR;
new: BOOLEAN);

Lookup opens a file named **FileName** and initializes the file descriptor **f**. If the file does not exist and **new** is **TRUE**, then the computer will create the file; if the file exists, the computer does not create it and returns an error in **f.res**.

PROCEDURE ReadByte(VAR f; File; VAR wd: BYTE);

ReadByte reads one byte from the current position of the specified file and places it in **wd**. The file's current position is then advanced to the next byte. You generally use this procedure on binary files.

PROCEDURE ReadChar(VAR f: File; VAR ch: CHAR);

ReadChar reads one character from the current position of the specified file and places it in **ch**. The file's current position is then advanced to the next character. You generally use this procedure on ASCII files.

PROCEDURE ReadNBytes(VAR f: File; buffer: ADDRESS;
numbytes: CARDINAL;
VAR numread: CARDINAL);

ReadNBytes reads **numbytes** of bytes from the specified file and places them into the buffer that **buffer** points to. The computer returns the actual number of bytes read in **numread**. You generally use **ReadNBytes** on binary files.

PROCEDURE ReadWord(VAR f; File; VAR wd: WORD);

ReadWord reads one word from the current position of the specified file and places it in **wd**. The file's current position is then advanced to the next word. You generally use this procedure on binary files.

PROCEDURE Rename(VAR f: File, NewName: ARRAY OF CHAR);

Rename changes the name of a file. The file descriptor **f** must reference a valid file, and **NewName** is the name to change to.

PROCEDURE Reset(VAR f: File);

Reset sets the specified file to open, and positions the file pointer to the top of the file.

PROCEDURE SetModify(VAR f: File);
PROCEDURE SetOpen(VAR f: File);
PROCEDURE SetRead(VAR f: File);
PROCEDURE SetWrite(VAR f: File);

The procedures **SetModify**, **SetOpen**, **SetRead**, and **SetWrite** set the type of operations that can be performed on the specified file. **SetModify** enables read-write operations. **SetOpen** sets a file to "idle"—no operations are allowed, but the file is still open. **SetRead** enables read-only operations and **SetWrite** enables write-only operations.

PROCEDURE SetPos(VAR f: File; High, Low: CARDINAL);

SetPos supports random access file I/O. The specified file will be positioned at the byte location specified by **High** and **Low**, which represent the high-order and low-order words of a long integer. The location is computed by using this formula:

$$position = (High*2^{16})+Low$$

PROCEDURE WriteByte(VAR f: File; b: BYTE);

WriteByte writes the byte in **b** to the specified file, and advances the current file position to the next byte. You generally use **WriteByte** with binary files.

PROCEDURE WriteChar(VAR f: File; ch: CHAR);

WriteChar writes the character in **ch** to the specified file, and advances the current file position to the next character. You generally use **WriteChar** with ASCII files.

PROCEDURE WriteNBytes(VAR f: File; buffer : ADDRESS;
$\qquad\qquad\qquad$ **numbytes: CARDINAL;**
$\qquad\qquad\qquad$ **VAR written: CARDINAL);**

WriteNBytes writes to the specified file **numbytes** of bytes from the buffer that **buffer** points to. The computer returns the number of bytes that is actually written in **written**. You generally use this procedure with binary files.

PROCEDURE WriteWord(VAR f: File; wd: WORD);

WriteWord writes the word in **wd** to the specified file and advances the current file position to the next word. You generally use **WriteWord** with binary files.

InOut

InOut contains the standard, high-level procedures to perform console I/O on strings, characters, and integers. It also supports the redirection of I/O to disk files.

VAR
   Done: BOOLEAN;

Done indicates the success or failure of certain routines.

PROCEDURE CloseInput;

CloseInput closes the current input file and returns input back to the console.

PROCEDURE CloseOutput;

CloseOutput closes the current output file and returns output back to the console.

PROCEDURE OpenInput(extension: ARRAY OF CHAR);

OpenInput redirects input to a user-specified file. If **extension** is not null and the user does not specify an extension explicitly, then **extension** will be the extension to the specified filename. If the computer finds the file, the computer sets **Done** to **TRUE**, and then takes all input from the specified file until a call to **CloseInput** is executed.

PROCEDURE OpenOutput(extension: ARRAY OF CHAR);

OpenOutput redirects output to a user-specified file. If **extension** is not null and the user does not specify an extension explicitly, then **extension** will be the extension to the specified filename. If the computer finds the file, the computer sets **Done** to **TRUE** and then sends all output to the specified file until a call to **CloseOutput** is executed.

PROCEDURE Read(VAR ch: CHAR);

Read reads the next character from the current input device. **Done** is **TRUE** unless the computer encounters the EOF marker.

PROCEDURE ReadCard(VAR i: CARDINAL);

ReadCard reads a **CARDINAL** from the current input device.

PROCEDURE ReadInt(VAR i: INTEGER);

ReadInt reads an **INTEGER** from the current input device.

PROCEDURE ReadString(VAR str: ARRAY OF CHAR);

ReadString reads a string from the current input device. The read is terminated when the computer encounters any character with an ASCII value of a space (32) or less.

PROCEDURE Write(ch: CHAR);

Write writes a character to the current output device.

PROCEDURE WriteCard(c, width: CARDINAL);

WriteCard writes the **CARDINAL** c of a minimum field width of **width** to the current output device. The computer outputs leading blanks if necessary.

PROCEDURE WriteHex(c, width: CARDINAL);

WriteHex writes the **CARDINAL** c of a minimum field width of **width** to the current output device in hexadecimal format. The computer outputs leading blanks if necessary.

PROCEDURE WriteInt(i: INTEGER; width: CARDINAL);

WriteInt writes the **INTEGER i** of a minimum field width of **width** to the current output device. The computer outputs leading blanks if necessary.

PROCEDURE WriteLn;

WriteLn writes a carriage return/linefeed sequence to the current output device.

PROCEDURE WriteOct(c, width: CARDINAL);

WriteOct writes the **CARDINAL c** of a minimum field width of **width** to the current output device in octal format. The computer outputs leading blanks if necessary.

PROCEDURE WriteString(str: ARRAY OF CHAR);

WriteString writes a string to the current output device.

MathLib0

MathLib0 contains several routines that perform special mathematical functions, such as sine and cosine. It also contains procedures to convert between **REAL**s and **INTEGER**s.

PROCEDURE arctan(r: REAL): REAL;
PROCEDURE cos(r: REAL): REAL;
PROCEDURE exp(r: REAL): REAL;
PROCEDURE ln(r: REAL): REAL;
PROCEDURE sin(r: REAL): REAL;
PROCEDURE sqrt(r: REAL): REAL;

The routines **arctan**, **cos**, **exp**, **ln**, **sin**, and **sqrt** return the values that their names imply.

PROCEDURE entier(r: REAL): INTEGER;

The **entier** procedure returns the **INTEGER** equivalent of **r**. Truncation may occur.

PROCEDURE real(i: INTEGER): REAL;

The **real** procedure returns the **REAL** equivalent of **i**.

NumberConversions

NumberConversions contains the necessary routines to convert between strings and **CARDINAL**s and **INTEGER**s.

PROCEDURE CardToString(c: CARDINAL;
VAR str: ARRAY OF CHAR;
width: CARDINAL);

CardToString converts the **CARDINAL c** into a string of a width of **width**, and places the result in **str**.

PROCEDURE IntToString(i: INTEGER;
VAR str: ARRAY OF CHAR;
width: CARDINAL);

IntToString converts the **INTEGER**, **i**, into a string of a width of **width**, and places the result in **str**.

PROCEDURE StringToCard(str: ARRAY OF CHAR;
VAR c; VAR OK: BOOLEAN);

StringToCard converts the number in **str** into a **CARDINAL**, and places the result in **c**. **OK** is **TRUE** if the conversion is a success.

PROCEDURE StringToInt(str: ARRAY OF CHAR;
                     VAR i; VAR OK: BOOLEAN);

StringToInt converts the number in **str** into an **INTEGER**, and places the result in **i**. **OK** is **TRUE** if the conversion is a success.

Processes

Processes has many of the routines that support Modula-2's concurrent programming environment. In **Processes**, the type **SIGNAL** is defined, which allows communication between processes.

PROCEDURE Awaited (sig: SIGNAL): BOOLEAN;

Awaited determines whether there is any process that is waiting for the specified signal **sig**. It will return **TRUE** if a process is waiting; it will return **FALSE** if not.

PROCEDURE Init(VARsig: SIGNAL);

Init intializes a signal. You must do this before you can use the signal.

PROCEDURE SEND(VAR sig: SIGNAL);

SEND sends the specified signal **sig**. If no process is waiting for **sig**, then **SEND** has no effect; if a process is waiting, the waiting process will resume execution.

PROCEDURE StartProcess(p: PROC; workspace: CARDINAL);

StartProcess starts the new process **p** with a certain number, **workspace**, of bytes of work space. Control is transferred to the process after the call.

PROCEDURE WAIT(VAR sig: SIGNAL);

WAIT suspends execution of the current process and waits for the specified signal. If no other processes are running, then a call to **WAIT** will terminate the program.

RealConversions

RealConversions contains the two routines that allow **REALs** to be converted into strings and strings to be converted to **REALs**.

PROCEDURE RealToString(r: REAL;
       numdig, width: INTEGER
       VAR str: ARRAY OF CHAR;
       VAR OK: BOOLEAN);

RealToString converts the **REAL r** to a string with a certain number, **numdig**, of digits to the right of the decimal point and a maximum field width of **width**. **OK** returns **TRUE** if the conversion succeeds, and the result will be placed in **str**.

PROCEDURE StringToReal(str: ARRAY OF CHAR;
       VAR r: real;
       VAR OK: BOOLEAN);

StringToReal converts the number in **str** to a **REAL** value, and places the result in **r**. If the conversion succeeds, **OK** will have the value **TRUE**.

RealInOut

RealInOut contains the procedures to read and write **REAL** numbers to the current I/O device—which is generally the console. These routines are not found in **InOut**.

PROCEDURE ReadReal(VAR r: REAL);

ReadReal reads a real number from the current input device, and places the result in **r**.

PROCEDURE WriteReal(r: REAL; width: CARDINAL);

WriteReal writes **r** to the current output device. The **width** specifies the minimum field width.

Storage

Storage contains the necessary procedures to support dynamic allocation. All memory is allocated from the heap, which conceptually lies between the program memory and the stack.

PROCEDURE ALLOCATE(VAR ptr: ADDRESS; size: CARDINAL);

The **ALLOCATE** procedure allocates a certain number, **size**, of bytes from the heap. The address of the first byte is returned in **ptr**.

PROCEDURE Available(size: CARDINAL): BOOLEAN;

Available returns **TRUE** if there are at least a certain number, **size**, of free bytes of memory that are left in the heap.

PROCEDURE DEALLOCATE(VAR ptr: ADDRESS; size: CARDINAL);

DEALLOCATE releases a certain number, **size**, of bytes that **ptr** points to.

Strings

The **Strings** library contains several routines that allow easy manipulation and comparison of strings. Keep in mind that all strings are arrays of characters and must begin their indexing at zero.

PROCEDURE Assign(VAR source, dest: ARRAY OF CHAR);

Assign copies the contents of **source** into **dest**.

PROCEDURE CompareStr(str1, str2: ARRAY OF CHAR);

CompareStr compares two strings. It returns 0 if they are equal, 1 if **str1** is greater than **str2**, and −1 if **str1** is less than **str2**.

PROCEDURE Concat(str1, str2: ARRAY OF CHAR;
VAR dest: ARRAY OF CHAR);

Concat concatenates **str1** and **str2**, and places the result in **dest**.

PROCEDURE Copy(source: ARRAY OF CHAR;
index, len: CARDINAL;
VAR dest: ARRAY OF CHAR);

Copy copies a substring of **len** characters, starting at **index**, from **source** into **dest**.

PROCEDURE Delete(VAR str: ARRAY OF CHAR;
index, len: CARDINAL);

Delete removes from **str** a substring of length **len** that starts at **index**.

PROCEDURE Insert(substr: ARRAY OF CHAR;
                     VAR str: ARRAY OF CHAR;
                     index: CARDINAL);

Insert inserts at **index** the string **substr** into **str**.

PROCEDURE Length(str: ARRAY OF CHAR): CARDINAL;

Length returns the length of **str**.

PROCEDURE Pos(substr, str: ARRAY OF CHAR): CARDINAL;

Pos returns the position of **substr** in **str**. If **substr** is not in **str**, then the value that is returned is greater than **HIGH(str)**.

System

SYSTEM contains various types and procedures that are necessary to do system-level programming. The actual contents of **SYSTEM** will vary widely between implementations, but the types and routines that are presented here should be common to all.

TYPE
BYTE;
WORD;
ADDRESS = POINTER TO WORD
PROCESS;

BYTE and **WORD** mean essentially what their names imply. They represent 8-bit and 16-bit quantities on most 16-bit computers. **ADDRESS** is simply a memory address. These three types create variables that directly access the computer's hardware — bypassing Modula-2's normal type-checking facilities. You use **PROCESS** for concurrent process handling.

PROCEDURE ADR(VarName): ADDRESS;

ADR returns the address of any variable.

PROCEDURE IOTRANSFER(VAR ISR, from: PROCESS;
 IntVectNum: CARDINAL);

IOTRANSFER transfers control to the interrupt service routine **ISR**. The current process is **from** and the interrupt vector number is **IntVectNum**.

PROCEDURE LISTEN;

LISTEN temporarily lowers the priority of the current process, and allows other lower-priority processes to execute.

PROCEDURE NEWPROCESS(proc: PROC;
 ProcessAddr: ADDRESS;
 WorkSpace: CARDINAL;
 VAR process: PROCESS);

NEWPROCESS creates a new process. Here, the procedure **proc** will become the process, **ProcessAddr** is the address of **proc**, **WorkSpace** is the number of bytes that the process requires, and **process** is a variable that transfers control between processes.

PROCEDURE SIZE(VarName): CARDINAL;

SIZE returns the size in bytes of the specified variable.

PROCEDURE TRANSFER(VAR from, to: PROCESS);

TRANSFER transfers program control between processes.

PROCEDURE TSIZE(TypeName): CARDINAL;

TSIZE returns the size in bytes of the specified type.

Terminal

Terminal contains a subset of **InOut** with the following additions that are described here.

PROCEDURE KeyPressed( ): BOOLEAN;

KeyPressed returns **TRUE** if the user presses a key at the console; it returns **FALSE** if not.

PROCEDURE ReadAgain;

ReadAgain causes the last character that was read to be read again on a subsequent call to **Read**.

Differences Between
Modula-2 and Pascal

Overall, Modula-2 and Pascal appear to be very similar. Both are structured languages with similar program-control statements. Because Modula-2 succeeded Pascal, most of the differences between the two languages fall into two major categories: enhancements and improvements. Enhancements include features that did not exist in Pascal, such as libraries and system-dependent routines, which broaden the types of problems that you can solve. Improvements include minor changes that were intended to clean up loose ends, such as the development of the **ELSIF** statement and the more-consistent use of **BEGIN** and **END**. A minor category contains features that are just different—not necessarily better—such as the changed functions of

Write and **WriteLn**. This section will compare the major differences between Modula-2 and Pascal.

MODULEs and Linking

Standard Pascal does not support the separate compilation of source files or linking. Modula-2 not only supports these things, but also virtually demands them! In Modula-2, you can think of programs as modular with each module being only a piece of the total program. Linking all of the pieces together creates the final executable version of the program. In Modula-2, these pieces are called **MODULE**s. The program **MODULE** is the first module that is executed when your program runs. For example, here are two identical programs—the one on the left is in Modula-2, and the one on the right is in Pascal:

```
MODULE Test;          PROGRAM Test;

   VAR                    VAR
     a:INTEGER;             a:INTEGER;

   BEGIN                 BEGIN
     a:=10;                 a:=10;
   END Test.            END.
```

As you can see, the first words in the programs differ. In Modula-2, you do not use the keyword **PROGRAM**; instead, you use the reserved word **MODULE** to begin a program **MODULE**.

Two other types of **MODULE**s are **IMPLEMENTATION MODULE**s and **DEFINITION MODULE**s. You use them to create separately compiled pieces of your program, which you will link together to create the final executable program. A **DEFINITION MODULE** defines what a separately compiled **MODULE** will do, and its corresponding **IMPLEMENTATION MODULE** actually performs the operations.

Given the **MODULE** scenario, you can see that it is possible to have separate programmer teams write large programs in pieces. This makes managing large projects much easier, and is one of Modula-2's major advantages over Pascal. In fact, Professor Wirth thought that **MODULE**s were the single most important difference between Modula-2 and Pascal. In Modula-2 terminology, the separate modules are sometimes called *library modules*, or simply *libraries*.

Import

Before you can use a library procedure, you must explicitly request it by using the **IMPORT** statement. The **IMPORT** statement causes the specified procedures to be linked into your program. The procedure includes not only those procedures that you write that need to be **IMPORT**ed, but also most of the standard library procedures, such as **WriteLn**, because most of Modula-2's standard procedures are in libraries. In short, only a handful of Modula-2's standard procedures are built into the compiler. This differs greatly from Pascal, where the standard procedures are built in.

Data Types

Besides having all of Pascal's built-in data types, Modula-2 has two important additions. First, the new type **CARDINAL** is defined as being a positive integer. For most 16-bit Modula-2 implementations, the range of **CARDINAL** values will be between 0 and 65,535. Because of certain technical reasons, arithmetic on **CARDINAL**s is faster than arithmetic on **INTEGER**s. Hence, programmers often use **CARDINAL**s as loop counters to make their code execute faster.

Second, **BITSET** is a predefined set type that generally has the same number of elements as the number of bits in a word.

Case Sensitivity

Unlike many Pascal implementations, Modula-2 is *case sensitive* with regard to identifiers: that is, uppercase letters and lowercase letters are different. This means that **INIT**, **Init**, and **init** are distinct and separate names. All Modula-2 reserved words must be in uppercase.

Modula-2 identifiers may consist of only letters and digits—you cannot use special characters. This differs from Pascal, which allows the underscore.

Comments

Modula-2 comments are placed between the symbols (∗ and ∗). To denote sets, Modula-2 uses the curly braces { }, which Pascal uses for comments.

Unlike Pascal, in Modula-2 you may nest comments. This means that you can have comments within comments. This makes it easy to "comment out" large pieces of code—even if they already contain comments. This is especially helpful during debugging.

The Standard Procedures

Frankly, there is little similarity between Modula-2's standard procedures and Pascal's standard procedures. You may become confused because many names are the same in both languages, even though the functions of the procedures are different.

The most common example is that of **Write** and **WriteLn**. In Pascal, you can use these procedures to display characters, strings, and numbers to the screen. However, in Modula-2, you use **Write** to display a character, and **WriteLn** simply outputs a carriage-return/linefeed combination—it cannot take any arguments. When you need to print an entire string, you must use the procedure **WriteString**. **WriteString** does not issue a carriage-return/linefeed sequence. Because you cannot use **WriteString** to output numeric values, Modula-2 has specific procedures that are for this purpose, including **WriteInt**, **WriteCard**, and **WriteReal**. For example, in Pascal,

```
WriteLn('This is ');
Write('the number ',1);
```

must be written in Modula-2 as

```
WriteString('This is ');
WriteLn;
WriteString('the number');
WriteCard(1,1);
```

In addition to the differences in **WriteLn** and **Write**, Modula-2's disk I/O has no relationship to Pascal's disk I/O.

Perhaps the most important difference between Pascal's and Modula-2's standard procedures is that Pascal's are strictly defined, whereas Modula-2's primarily depend on the implementation. This means that the actual procedures that are included with a Modula-2 compiler are at the discretion of the implementor to some extent. However, the libraries that Professor Wirth created for his initial implementation provide a de facto standard that most implementations generally adhere to.

Code Blocks

There is a subtle but important structure difference between the program-control statements in Modula-2 and program-control statements in Pascal. This difference has to do with blocks of code. These statements include the loops **FOR**, **WHILE**, and **REPEAT**, and the **CASE** and **IF** statements. In Pascal, you must use **BEGIN** and **END** around a group of statements to create a code block, as shown here.

```
WHILE X<100 DO
   BEGIN
        .
        .
        .
   END;
```

In Modula-2, however, the object of the **WHILE** (and all control statements) is assumed to be a block that contains one or more statements. Therefore, the same code looks like this in Modula-2:

```
WHILE X<100 DO
   .
   .
   .
END;
```

An **END** terminates all of the loop-control statements except for the **REPEAT** loop, which uses **UNTIL**. Both the **CASE** and **IF** statements also work in a similar fashion. The only places that the Pascal-like **BEGIN/END** structure is used is starting and ending procedure code, and the main program code.

The FOR Loop

Modula-2's **FOR** loop has been expanded to allow an optional increment factor. For example, the following code will print the numbers 0 to 10 in increments of 2 on the screen:

```
FOR X=0 TO 10 BY 2 DO
   WriteCard(X,2);
END;
```

Because the increment factor may also be a negative number, Modula-2 does not have the **DOWNTO**. For example, to print the numbers 10 through 0 on the screen, you would write

```
FOR X=10 TO 0 BY -1 DO
   WriteCard(X,2);
END;
```

The CASE Statement

There are two differences between the **CASE** statement in Modula-2 and the **CASE** statement in Pascal. First, as stated earlier, each case is assumed to be a block; therefore, you may enter multiple lines for each case without using a **BEGIN/END** block. Instead, you use a new operator, |, to separate the cases from each other.

Second, Modula-2 includes an **ELSE** condition, which is executed if none of the cases match. For example, the following code performs the menu-selection portion of a spelling checker.

```
Read(choice);

CASE choice OF
   '1': CheckSpelling; |
   '2': Reset;
        Save;          |
   '3': Reset;
        Load;          |
   '4': Quit;
ELSE
   Error;
END;
```

If the user types any number other than 1 through 4, the computer executes the **Error** routine. Notice that the | does not follow the last case prior to the **ELSE**.

The IF Statement

Modula-2 has an improved version of the **IF** statement over the one that Pascal has, because Modula-2 includes the optional **ELSIF** test. **ELSIF** replaces the cumbersome **IF/ ELSE IF** compound statement pair. The general form of the **IF** statement is

> **IF** *condition* **THEN** *statement sequence*
> **ELSIF** *condition* **THEN** *statement sequence*
> .
> .
> .
> **ELSIF** *condition* **THEN** *statement sequence*
> **ELSE** *default statement sequence*
> **END;**

As you can see, you can have any number of **ELSIF** conditions. However, remember that the computer will execute one and only one statement sequence, and that it will execute the **ELSE** only if all of the conditions have been false.

If you are converting code from Pascal into Modula-2, you can still use the less structured **IF/ELSE IF** form—but you should definitely not use it for any new programming.

Evaluation of BOOLEAN Expressions

An important but sometimes overlooked difference between Modula-2 and Pascal is in the way that **BOOLEAN** expressions are evaluated. In Modula-2, the computer evaluates compound expressions from left to right until it can make a determination about the outcome. In some cases, this means that the computer may not evaluate all of the expressions. For example, in

```
IF (x<>0) AND (y DIV x = 15) THEN WriteCard(y,3) END;
```

if **x** equals 0, the expression is **FALSE** and the computer will not execute the second expression **y DIV x = 15**. In this way, you can avoid using an extra line of code to prevent a divide-by-zero error.

LOOP and EXIT

Modula-2 contains a new loop construct called **LOOP**, which is not in Pascal. **LOOP** causes the computer to execute a sequence of statements continuously—

that is, **LOOP** actually causes an infinite loop! The only way that you can terminate a **LOOP** is by using the **EXIT** command, which can be located anywhere in the loop. For example, the following example will print the ASCII number of the characters that are typed at the keyboard until you press **q**:

```
LOOP
   Read(ch);
   WriteCard(ORD(ch),3);
   IF ch='q' THEN EXIT END;
END;
```

You can use many **EXIT**s inside one **LOOP**. This would allow the **LOOP** to have multiple exit points.

At first glance, the **LOOP** statement of Modula-2 may seem destructured because it does not have a clearly defined exit point. However, there are many programming situations that do not fit nicely into the other three loop statements. If you use it properly, **LOOP** is an important addition to Modula-2.

Arrays as Procedure Parameters

One of Pascal's most glaring problems is its restriction that array dimensions of an argument to a procedure must be the same as declared in the procedure's parameter list. This restriction makes it impossible for you to have truly general routines that use arrays as parameters. In Modula-2, this situation has been remedied through the use of *open array parameters*. An open array parameter is a parameter that has only the type of its elements defined, and not the actual dimensions or boundaries. With these open array parameters, you can pass arrays of various sizes into the same procedure. For example,

```
PROCEDURE String(str: ARRAY OF CHAR);
```

declares **str** as an array of characters, but does not specify how long it is or what its boundaries are.

Functions and Return Values

Modula-2 has dropped the reserved word **FUNCTION**, which Pascal uses to denote a procedure that returns a value. In Modula-2, regardless of whether a procedure returns a value or not, the procedure is still called a **PROCEDURE**.

If you are converting a program from Pascal to Modula-2, to make a procedure into a function, you must specify what data type will be returned. You do this in exactly the same way that you did in Pascal. To return a value, you *do not* assign it to the procedure name (as in **Pascal**), but rather you use the **RETURN** statement. For example, the following procedure returns **TRUE** or **FALSE**.

```
PROCEDURE Sample(count: CARDINAL): BOOLEAN;
BEGIN
   IF count<100 THEN RETURN TRUE
   ELSE RETURN FALSE
   END;
END Sample;
```

Concurrency

Modula-2 supports coroutines and concurrent processes, while Pascal does not. Modula-2 concurrency allows you to write sophisticated systems programs, which you could not write by using Pascal. Although not applied to most programming tasks, concurrency support is an important addition to Modula-2.

Sorting and Searching

C H A P T E R   2

In the world of computer science, perhaps no other tasks are more fundamental or as extensively analyzed as the tasks of sorting and searching. Virtually all database programs, compilers, interpreters, and operating systems use these routines. Generally, the point of sorting data is to make searching that data easier and faster. For this reason, this chapter will examine sorting first.

Sorting

Sorting is the process of arranging a set of similar information into an increasing or decreasing order. Specifically, in a sorted list i of n elements,

$$i_1 <= i_2 <= \ldots <= i_n$$

There are two general categories for the sorting of algorithms: first, the sorting of arrays, both in memory and in random-access disk files; and second, the sorting of sequential disk files or tape files. This chapter will be concerned primarily with the first category because it is of the most interest to the microcomputer user. However, the chapter will discuss the general method of sorting sequential files.

The main difference between sorting arrays and sorting sequential files is that each element of the array is always available. This means that you may compare or exchange any element with any other element at any time. With a sequential file, only one element is available at any particular time. For this reason, the sorting techniques of arrays and the sorting techniques of sequential files differ greatly.

When you sort information, generally you use only a portion of that information as the *sort key*. You use this key in the comparisons, but when you must make an exchange you transfer the entire data structure. For example, in a mailing list, the ZIP-code field might be used as the key, but the entire address is sorted. For simplicity, this chapter will be sorting character arrays while developing the various sorting methods. Later, you will learn how to adapt any of these methods to any type of data structure.

Classes of Sorting Algorithms

You may use three general methods to sort arrays:

- By exchange
- By selection
- By insertion

To understand these three methods, imagine a deck of cards. To sort the cards by using *exchange,* you would spread the cards on a table, face up, and then proceed to exchange out-of-order cards until the deck is in order. To sort by using *selection,* you would spread the cards on the table, select the lowest-value card, take it out of the deck, and hold it in your hand. Then, from the remaining cards on the table, you would select the lowest-value card and place it behind the one already in your hand. This process would continue until all cards are in your hand. Because you always selected the lowest card from those on the table to place at the end of cards in your hand, when the process finishes, the cards in your hand will be sorted. To sort the cards by using *insertion*, you would hold the cards in your hand and take one at a time. As you take cards from the deck in your hand, you would place them into a new deck on the table, always inserting them in the correct position. The deck on the table will be sorted when you have no cards in your hand.

Judging Sorting Algorithms

There are many different algorithms for each sorting method. They all have some merits, but the general criteria for judging a sorting algorithm use the following items as their foundation:

1. How fast can it sort information in an average case?

2. How fast is its best case and its worst case?

3. Does it exhibit *natural* or *unnatural* behavior?

4. Does it rearrange elements with equal keys?

Clearly, how fast a particular algorithm sorts is of great concern. It can be shown that the speed with which you can sort an array is directly related to the number of comparisons and the number of exchanges—with exchanges taking more time. As you will see later in this chapter, some sorts require an exponential amount of time to sort each element, and some require logarithmic time.

The best case and worst case run times are important if you expect to encounter this situation frequently. Often, a sort will have a good average case but a terrible worst case.

A sort exhibits *natural* behavior if it "works" least hard when the list is already in order, harder as the list becomes less ordered, and hardest when a list is in inverse order. How hard a sort works is based on the number of comparisons and exchanges that are executed.

To understand why rearranging elements with equal keys may be important, imagine a database that is sorted on a main key and a subkey, such as a mailing list with the main key being the ZIP code and the subkey being the last name within ZIP codes. When you add a new address to the list and re-sort the list, you do not want the subkeys to be rearranged. To guarantee this, a sort must not exchange main keys of equal value.

You will look first at representative sorts from each category to analyze the efficiency of each. Later, you will study improved sorting methods. Each of the sorts will use the two user-defined types shown here:

```
TYPE
    DataItem = CHAR;
    DataArray = ARRAY [1..100] OF CHAR;
```

Therefore, to change the type of data that each sort will use requires that you change only these two type definitions. The array dimension is arbitrary and you are free to change it as necessary.

The Bubble Sort   The best-known and most infamous sort is the *Bubble sort*. It derives its popularity from its catchy name and its simplicity. For reasons that will become evident, it is one of the worst sorts ever conceived.

The Bubble sort is part of the exchange category of sorting. The general concept behind the Bubble sort (and the way that it got its name) uses repeated comparisons and, if necessary, exchanges of adjacent elements. It is similar to bubbles in a tank of water with each bubble seeking its own level. The simplest form of the Bubble sort is shown here:

```
PROCEDURE  Bubble(VAR item: DataArray; count:CARDINAL);
VAR
   i,j: CARDINAL;
   x: DataItem;
BEGIN
   FOR i:=2 TO count DO
     FOR j:=count TO i BY -1 DO
       IF item[j-1]>item[j] THEN
         (* now swap the elements  *)
         x:=item[j-1];
         item[j-1]:=item[j];
         item[j]:=x;
       END
     END
   END
END Bubble;
```

Here, **item** is the array of **DataItem**s to be sorted and **count** is the number of elements in the array. Two loops drive the Bubble sort. Given that there are **count** elements in the array, the outer loop causes the array to be scanned **count**−1 times. This is necessary to ensure that, in the worst case, every element is in its proper position when the procedure terminates. The inner loop actually performs the comparisons and exchanges.

This version of the Bubble sort can sort a character array into ascending order. For example, the following short program will sort a string read from a disk file called **test**. You can use this same program with the other sort routines in this chapter by changing the sort procedure.

```
MODULE SortDriver;

  FROM InOut IMPORT Read, Write, WriteLn;

  FROM FileSystem IMPORT File, Response, Lookup,
        SetRead, Close, ReadChar;
  TYPE
    DataItem = CHAR;
    DataArray = ARRAY [1..100] OF DataItem;

  VAR
    i,j: CARDINAL;
    data: DataArray;
    F1: File;

PROCEDURE  Bubble(VAR item: DataArray; count:CARDINAL);
VAR
  i,j: CARDINAL;
  x: DataItem;
BEGIN
  FOR i:=2 TO count DO
    FOR j:=count TO i BY -1 DO
      IF item[j-1]>item[j] THEN
        (* now swap the elements  *)
        x:=item[j-1];
        item[j-1]:=item[j];
        item[j]:=x;
      END
    END
  END
END Bubble;


BEGIN
  REPEAT   (* open text file to be sorted *)
    Lookup(F1,"test",FALSE); (* must be there *)
  UNTIL F1.res = done;

  SetRead(F1);

  i:=1;
  REPEAT   (* read in up to 100 characters *)
    ReadChar(F1,data[i]);
    INC(i);
  UNTIL F1.eof AND (i<=101);
  DEC(i);   (* don't count eof *)

  Close(F1);
```

```
Bubble(data,i);

FOR j:=1 TO i DO      (* display the sorted data *)
  Write(data[j])
END;

END SortDriver.
```

To illustrate the way that the Bubble sort works, here are the passes used to sort the array **dcab**:

Initial	d	c	a	b
Pass 1	a	d	c	b
Pass 2	a	b	d	c
Pass 3	a	b	c	d

When you analyze any sort, you must determine how many comparisons and exchanges will be performed for the best, average, and worst cases. With the Bubble sort, the number of comparisons is always the same because the two **FOR** loops will still repeat the specified number of times, whether the list is initially in order or not. This means that the Bubble sort will always perform

$$1/2(n^2-n)$$

comparisons, where n is the number of elements to be sorted. This formula is derived from the fact that the outer loop executes $n-1$ times and the inner loop executes $n/2$ times. Multiplying these quantities together produces this formula.

The number of exchanges is zero for the best case — an already sorted list. The number for the average case is $3/4(n^2-n)$, and the number for the worst case is $3/2(n^2-n)$. It is beyond the scope of this book to explain the way to derive these numbers, but you can see that as the list becomes less ordered, the number of elements that are out of order approaches the number of comparisons. (Remember that there are three exchanges in a Bubble sort for every element out of order.) The Bubble sort is said to be an *n-squared algorithm* because its execution time is a multiple of the square of the number of elements. This is bad for a large number of elements because execution time is directly related to the number of comparisons and exchanges. For example, if you ignore the time that the Bubble sort takes to exchange any out-of-position element, you can see that if each comparison takes 0.001 seconds, then sorting 10 elements will take about 0.05 seconds, sorting 100 elements

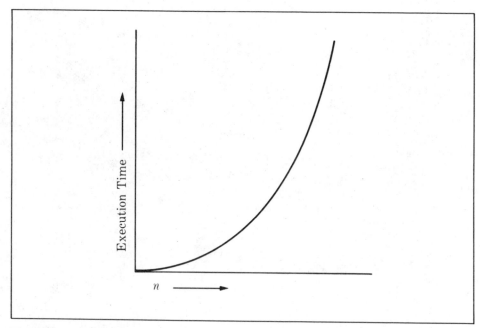

Figure 2-1. Execution time of an n^2 sort in relation to array size

will take about 5 seconds, and sorting 1000 elements will take about 500 seconds. A 100,000-element sort—the size of a small telephone book—would take about 5,000,000 seconds, or about 1,400 hours (about two months of continuous sorting)! The graph in Figure 2-1 shows how execution time increases in relation to the size of the array.

You can make some improvements to the Bubble sort to speed it up—and to help its image a bit. For example, the Bubble sort has one peculiarity: an out-of-order element at the large end, such as the **a** in the **dcab** example, will go to its proper position in *one* pass, but a misplaced element in the small end, such as the **d** in the example, will rise slowly to its proper place.

Instead of always reading the array in the same direction, subsequent passes could reverse direction. In this way, elements that are greatly out of place will travel quickly to their correct position. This version of the Bubble sort is called the *Shaker sort*, after its "shaking" motion over the array:

```
PROCEDURE  Shaker(VAR item: DataArray; count:CARDINAL);
(* this is an improved version of the Bubble sort *)

VAR
```

```
      j,k,l,r: CARDINAL;
       x: DataItem;
  BEGIN
    l:=2; r:=count; k:=count;
    REPEAT
      FOR j:= r TO l BY -1 DO
        IF item[j-1]>item[j] THEN
          (* swap *)
          x:=item[j-1];
          item[j-1]:=item[j];
          item[j]:=x;
          k:=j;
        END;
      END;

      l:=k+1;

      FOR j:=l TO r DO
        IF item[j-1]>item[j] THEN
          (* swap *)
          x:=item[j-1];
          item[j-1]:=item[j];
          item[j]:=x;
          k:=j;
        END;
      END;

      r:=k-1;
    UNTIL l>r
  END Shaker;
```

Although the Shaker sort does improve the Bubble sort, it still executes on the order of n^2 because the number of comparisons is unchanged and the number of exchanges is only reduced by a relatively small constant.

The Selection Sort   A *Selection sort* selects the element with the lowest value and exchanges that element with the first element. Then from the remaining $n-1$ elements, the sort finds the element with the least key and exchanges it with the second element, and so forth, to the last two elements. For example, if you used the Selection sort on the array **bdac**, each pass would look like this:

Initial	b	d	a	c
Pass 1	a	d	b	c
Pass 2	a	b	d	c
Pass 3	a	b	c	d

The basic Selection sort is shown here:

```
PROCEDURE  Select(VAR item: DataArray; count:CARDINAL);
VAR
   i,j,k: CARDINAL;
   x: DataItem;
BEGIN
   FOR i:=1 TO count-1 DO
     k:=i;
     x:=item[i];
     FOR j:=i+1 TO count DO    (* find smallest element *)
       IF item[j]<x THEN
         k:=j;
         x:=item[j];
       END;
     END;
     item[k]:=item[i];    (* swap  *)
     item[i]:=x;
   END;
END Select;
```

Unfortunately, like the Bubble sort, the outer loop executes $n-1$ times and the inner loop $1/2(n)$ times. This means that the Selection sort requires

$$1/2(n^2-n)$$

number of comparisons, which makes it too slow for a large number of items. The number of exchanges for the best case is $3(n-1)$, and the number of exchanges for the worst case is $n^2/4+3(n-1)$. For the best case, if the list is in order, then the sort needs to move only $n-1$ elements, and each move requires three exchanges. The worst case approximates the number of comparisons. The average case is difficult to determine and is beyond the scope of this book to develop. However, the number of comparisons for the average case is $n(\ln n+y)$, where y is Euler's constant, which is about 0.577216. Although the number of comparisons for both the Bubble sort and the Selection sort are the same, the number of exchanges in the average case is far less for the Selection sort.

The Insertion Sort   The *Insertion sort* is the third and last of the simple sorting algorithms. The Insertion sort initially sorts the first two members on the array. Next, the algorithm inserts the third member into its sorted position in relation to the first two members. Then, the sort inserts the fourth element into the list of the three elements. The process continues until all elements have been sorted. For example, for the array **dcab**, the Insertion sort would look like this:

Initial	d	c	a	b
Pass 1	c	d	a	b
Pass 3	a	c	d	b
Pass 4	a	b	c	d

A version of the Insertion sort is

```
PROCEDURE  Insert(VAR item: DataArray; count:CARDINAL);
VAR
  i,j: CARDINAL;
  x: DataItem;
BEGIN
  FOR i:=2 TO count DO
    x:=item[i];
    j:=i-1;
    WHILE (j>0) AND (x<item[j]) DO
      item[j+1]:=item[j];
      j:=j-1;
    END;
    item[j+1]:=x;
  END
END Insert;
```

Unlike the Bubble sort and the Selection sort, the number of comparisons that occur when you use the Insertion sort will depend upon how the list is initially ordered. If the list is in order, then the number of comparisons is $n-1$. If it is out of order, then the number of comparisions is $1/2(n^2+n)-1$, while the number of comparisons for the average case is $1/4(n^2+n-2)$.

The number of exchanges for each case is as follows:

Best	$2(n-1)$
Average	$1/4(n^2+9n-10)$
Worst	$1/2(n^2+3n-4)$

Therefore, for worst cases, the Insertion sort is as bad as the Bubble sort and the Selection sort; for average cases, it is only slightly better. However, the Insertion sort does have two advantages. First, it behaves *naturally:* it works the least when the array is already sorted, and it works the hardest when the array is sorted in inverse order. This quality makes the Insertion sort excellent for lists that are almost in order. Second, it does not change the order of equal keys. This means that if a list is sorted by using two keys, then it remains sorted for both keys after you use an Insertion sort.

Even though the comparisons may be fairly good for certain sets of data, the fact that the array always must be shifted down means that the number of moves can be significant. However, the Insertion sort still behaves naturally, with the fewest exchanges occurring for an almost-sorted list and the most exchanges for an inversely ordered array.

Improved Sorts

All of the algorithms given so far had the flaw of executing in n^2 time. This means that, for large amounts of data, the sorts would be slow — in fact, at some point, too slow to use. Every computer programmer has heard or told the horror story of the "sort that took three days." Unfortunately, these stories are often real. Generally, when a sort takes too long, it is the fault of the underlying algorithm. However, a sad commentary is that the first response is often, "Let's write it in assembly code." Although assembly code will sometimes speed up a routine by a constant factor, if the underlying algorithm is bad, the sort will still be slow — no matter how optimal the coding. Remember that, when the time of a routine is in relation to n^2, increasing the speed of the coding or the computer will only cause a slight improvement because the rate at which the run time increases is exponential. (In essence, the graph in Figure 2-1 given earlier is shifted to the right slightly, but the curve is unchanged.) Remember that if the routine is not fast enough written in Modula-2, then it will not be fast enough when you write it in assembler! The solution is to use a better sorting algorithm.

This section will develop two excellent sorts. The first is the Shell sort and the second is the QuickSort, which is generally considered the best sorting routine. These sorts run so fast that if you blink, you will miss them!

The Shell Sort   The Shell sort is named after its inventor, D.L. Shell. However, the name seems to have stuck because its method of operation actually resembles sea shells that are piled one upon another.

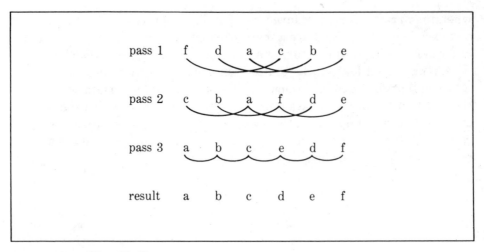

Figure 2-2. The Shell sort

The general method, which is derived from the Insertion sort, is based on diminishing increments. Figure 2-2 shows the Shell sort when applied to an array **fdacbe**. First, the routine sorts all elements that are three positions apart. Then, it sorts all elements that are two positions apart. Finally, it sorts all those adjacent to each other.

It may not be obvious that this method yields good results, or that it even will sort the array, but it does both. The algorithm is efficient because each sorting pass involves either relatively few elements or elements that are already in reasonable order, so that each pass increases order in the array.

You can change the exact sequence for the increments. The only rule that you must follow is that the last increment must be 1. For example, the sequence

$$9, 5, 3, 1$$

works well and is used in the Shell sort, which is shown here. You should avoid sequences that are powers of 2 because, for mathematically complex reasons, they reduce the efficiency of the sorting algorithm (but the sort will still work).

```
PROCEDURE Shell(VAR item: DataArray; count:INTEGER);
CONST
  t = 5;
VAR
  i,j,k,s,m: INTEGER;
  h: ARRAY[1..t] OF INTEGER;
  x: DataItem;
BEGIN
  h[1]:=9; h[2]:=5; h[3]:=3; h[4]:=3;  h[5]:=1;
  FOR m:=1 TO t DO
    k:=h[m];
    s:=-k;
    FOR i:=k+1 TO count DO
      x:=item[i];
      j:=i-k;
      IF s=0 THEN
        s:=-k;
        s:=s+1;
        item[s]:=x;
      END;
      WHILE (j>0) AND (x<item[j]) AND (j<=count) DO
        item[j+k]:=item[j];
        j:=j-k;
      END;
      item[j+k]:=x;
    END;
  END;
END Shell;
```

The inner **while** loop has three test conditions. The **x<item[j]** is a comparison that is necessary for the sorting process. The tests **j>0** and **j<=count** keep the sort from overrunning the boundary of the array **item**. These extra checks will degrade the performance of the Shell sort to some extent. Slightly different versions of the Shell sort employ special array elements called *sentinels*, which are not actually part of the information to be sorted. Sentinels hold special termination values, which indicate the least possible element and the greatest possible element. This method makes the bounds checks unnecessary. However, using sentinels requires a specific knowledge of the data, which limits the generality of the sort procedure.

The analysis of the Shell sort presents some difficult mathematical problems, which are far beyond the scope of this discussion. However, the execution time of the Shell sort is proportional to $n^{1.2}$ for sorting n elements. This is a significant improvement over the n^2 sorts given earlier. To understand how great an improvement this sort presents, study Figure 2-3, which shows both an n^2 graph and an $n^{1.2}$ graph. However, before you decide to use the Shell sort, you should know that the QuickSort is even better.

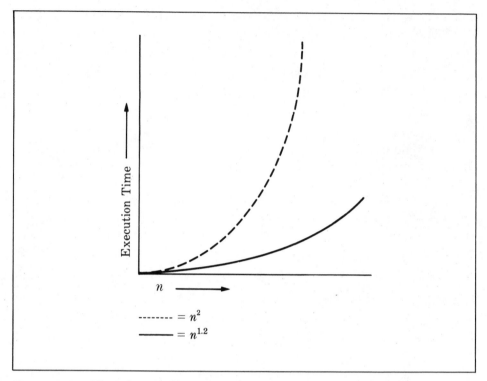

Figure 2-3.   The n^2 and $n^{1.2}$ curves

The QuickSort   The QuickSort, invented and named by C.A.R. Hoare, is generally considered to be the best sorting algorithm currently available, and its performance is superior to all others in this book. The QuickSort is based on the exchange method of sorting. This is surprising when you consider the terrible performance of the Bubble sort—the simplest version of an exchange sort!

The QuickSort is based on the idea of partitions. The general procedure is to select a value called the *comparand* and then partition the array into two parts with all elements greater than or equal to the partition value on one side and those values less than the partition value on the other. The QuickSort repeats this process for each remaining part until it sorts the array. For example, for the array **fedacb**, if you use the value **d** as the partition value, then QuickSort would rearrange the array like this:

Initial	**f**	**e**	**d**	**a**	**c**	**b**
Pass 1	**b**	**c**	**a**	**d**	**e**	**f**
Pass 2	**a**	**b**	**c**	**d**	**e**	**f**

In the second pass, this process is repeated for each part, **bca** and **def**. The process is essentially recursive in nature; the cleanest implementations of QuickSort are recursive algorithms.

You can select the middle comparand value in two ways: either at random or by averaging a small set of values that are taken from the array. For optimal sorting, it is best to select a value that is precisely in the middle of the range of values. However, this is not easy to do for most sets of data. In the worst case, the chosen value is at one extremity. Even in this case, QuickSort still performs well. The Modula-2 code for the QuickSort shown here selects the middle element of the array, in essence at random.

```
PROCEDURE QuickSort(VAR item: DataArray; count:CARDINAL);
   PROCEDURE qs(l,r:CARDINAL; VAR it:DataArray);
     VAR
       i,j: CARDINAL;
       x,y: DataItem;
   BEGIN
     i:=l; j:=r;
     x:=it[(l+r) DIV 2];
     REPEAT
       WHILE it[i] < x DO i:= i+1 END;
       WHILE x < it[j] DO j:=j-1 END;
       IF i<=j THEN
         y:=it[i];
         it[i]:=it[j];
         it[j]:=y;
         i:=i+1; j:=j-1;
       END;
     UNTIL i>j;
     IF l<j THEN qs(l,j,it) END;
     IF l<r THEN qs(i,r,it) END;
   END qs;

BEGIN
     qs(1,count,item);
END QuickSort;
```

In this version, the procedure **QuickSort** sets up a call to the main sorting procedure called **qs**. This enables you to maintain the common interface of **item** and **count**.

Deriving the number of comparisons and exchanges that QuickSort performs requires mathematics beyond the scope of this book. However, you can assume the number of comparisons to be $n \log n$ and that the number of exchanges is about $n/6 \log n$. These numbers are significantly better than any of the sorts given earlier.

The equation

$$N = a^x$$

can be rewritten as

$$x = \log_a N$$

This means, for example, that if you needed to sort 100 elements, then QuickSort would require 100 ∗ 2, or 200, comparisons because log 100 is 2. Compared with the Bubble sort's 990 comparisons, this number is quite good.

There is one nasty aspect to QuickSort that you should be aware of. If the comparand value for each partition happens to be the largest value, then QuickSort degenerates into *slowsort* with an n^2 run time. However, generally, this does not happen.

You must choose a method of determining the value of the comparand carefully. Often, you can determine this by the actual data that you are sorting. In large mailing lists where the sorting is often by ZIP code, the selection is simple because the ZIP codes are fairly evenly distributed and a simple algebraic procedure can determine a suitable comparand. However, in certain databases, the keys may be so close in value that a random selection is often the best method available. A common and fairly effective method is to sample three elements from a partition and then take the middle value.

Sorting Other Types of Data

Until now, the chapter has only been sorting arrays of characters because these make it easy to present each of the sorting routines. You may sort arrays of any of the built-in data types by simply changing the type definition of **DataItem**. However, it is generally complex data types like strings or groups of information like **RECORD**s that need to be sorted. Remember that most sorting involves a key and information linked to that key. To adapt the algorithms to sort other structures, you may need to alter the comparison section, the exchange section, or both. The algorithm itself will remain unchanged.

Because QuickSort is one of the best general-purpose routines available at this time, the rest of this chapter will use it in the examples, but the same techniques will apply to any of the sorts that were described earlier.

Sorting Strings

The easiest way to sort strings is to create an array of strings. This implies that you can change the type definition of **DataItem** to an array of characters. This allows you to maintain easy indexing and exchanging, and does not change the basic QuickSort algorithm. The version shown here will sort the strings into alphabetical order:

```
TYPE
    DataItem = ARRAY [0..80] OF CHAR;
    DataArray = ARRAY [1..100] OF DataItem;

FROM Strings IMPORT CompareStr;   (* needed to compare
                                     strings *)

PROCEDURE QuickSort(VAR item: DataArray; count:CARDINAL);
    PROCEDURE qs(l,r:CARDINAL; VAR it:DataArray);
       VAR
          i,j: CARDINAL;
          x,y: DataItem;
    BEGIN
       i:=l; j:=r;
       x:=it[(l+r) DIV 2];
       REPEAT
          WHILE CompareStr(it[i],x)=-1 DO i:= i+1 END;
          WHILE CompareStr(x,it[j])=-1 DO j:=j-1 END;
          IF i<=j THEN
             y:=it[i];
             it[i]:=it[j];
             it[j]:=y;
             i:=i+1; j:=j-1;
          END;
       UNTIL i>j;
       IF l<j THEN qs(l,j,it) END;
       IF l<r THEN qs(i,r,it) END;
    END qs;

BEGIN
    qs(1,count,item);
END QuickSort;
```

Notice that **CompareStr** must be imported from **Strings** to perform the string comparisons. String comparisons take longer than character comparisons because several elements must be tested in each case.

Sorting Records Most application programs that require a sort will probably need to sort a group of data. In Modula-2, these compound data types are called **RECORD**s. A mailing list is an excellent example, because a name, street, city, state, and ZIP code are all linked together. When this conglomerate unit of data is sorted, a sort key is used, but the entire record is also exchanged. To understand this process, you first need to create a **RECORD** to hold the information. If you use the mailing address as an example, a convenient **RECORD** to hold the information is

```
TYPE
   address = RECORD
           name : ARRAY [0..30] OF CHAR;
           street: ARRAY [0..40] OF CHAR;
           city: ARRAY [0..20] OF CHAR;
           state: ARRAY [0..2] OF CHAR;
           zip: ARRAY [0..9] OF CHAR;
   END;
```

After you define **address**, you must change the type definition of **DataItem** to be

```
DataItem = address;
```

After you have made these changes, you will need to change the comparison sections of **QuickSort** based on the field that you are sorting. The version of **QuickSort** shown here uses the **zip** field. This means that the mailing list will be sorted in ascending order based on the ZIP code of the address.

```
PROCEDURE RecordQuickSort(VAR item: DataArray; count:CARDINAL);
   PROCEDURE qs(l,r:CARDINAL; VAR it:DataArray);
      VAR
        i,j: CARDINAL;
        x,y: DataItem;
   BEGIN
      i:=l; j:=r;
      x:=it[(l+r) DIV 2];
      REPEAT
        WHILE CompareStr(it[i].zip,x.zip)=-1 DO i:= i+1 END;
        WHILE CompareStr(x.zip,it[j].zip)=-1 DO j:=j-1 END;
        IF i<=j THEN
          y:=it[i];
          it[i]:=it[j];
          it[j]:=y;
          i:=i+1; j:=j-1;
        END;
```

```
    UNTIL i>j;
    IF l<j THEN qs(l,j,it) END;
    IF l<r THEN qs(i,r,it) END;
  END qs;

BEGIN
    qs(1,count,item);
END RecordQuickSort;
```

Sorting Disk Files

There are two types of disk files: sequential and random-access. If either type of disk file is small enough, it may be read into memory and sorted by using the array-sorting routines given earlier. However, many disk files are too large to be sorted easily in memory and require special techniques. The specific technique that you use depends upon whether the disk file may be accessed randomly or sequentially. Since most microcomputer database applications use random-access files, they will be examined first.

Sorting Random-Access Disk Files   Used by most microcomputer database applications, random-access disk files have two major advantages over sequential disk files. First, they are easy to maintain. You may update information without having to copy the entire list over. Second, you can treat them like a large array on disk, which greatly simplifies sorting and searching. Using random-access disk files means that you can modify the basic **QuickSort** to seek different records on the disk, instead of indexing an array. Unlike sorting a sequential disk file, sorting a random-access disk file in place means that a full disk does not have to have room for both the sorted and unsorted file—which can be important for systems based on floppy disks.

Each sorting situation differs in relation to the exact data structure that is sorted and the key that is used. However, you can understand the general idea of sorting random-access disk files by studying a program that will sort a mailing list that is comprised of records of type **address**, which was defined earlier. The following mailing-list sorting program assumes that the number of elements is fixed at 80. However, you would have to maintain a record count as part of the disk file to allow flexibility.

```
MODULE DiskSortDriver;  (* sort a file of addresses *)

  FROM InOut IMPORT Read, Write, WriteLn, WriteString;

  FROM Strings IMPORT CompareStr;

  FROM SYSTEM IMPORT TSIZE, ADR;

  FROM FileSystem IMPORT File, Response, Lookup, SetPos,
        SetModify, Close, ReadNBytes, WriteNBytes;

  CONST
    NUM = 80;   (* arbitrary number of addresses to sort -
                   should be changed to fit your application *)

  TYPE
    address = RECORD
            name : ARRAY [0..30] OF CHAR;
            street: ARRAY [0..40] OF CHAR;
            city: ARRAY [0..20] OF CHAR;
            state: ARRAY [0..2] OF CHAR;
            zip: ARRAY [0..9] OF CHAR;
    END;

    DataItem = address;
    DataArray = ARRAY [1..100] OF DataItem;

  VAR
    i,j: CARDINAL;
    data: DataArray;
    F1: File;

  PROCEDURE Find(VAR fp:File; i:CARDINAL; VAR u: DataItem);
  VAR
     t:DataItem;
     l,c:CARDINAL;
     read: CARDINAL;
  BEGIN
    DEC(i);   (* files start at zero *)
    l:=TSIZE(DataItem)*i;
    SetPos(fp,0,l);
    ReadNBytes(fp,ADR(t),TSIZE(DataItem), read);
    IF read<>TSIZE(DataItem) THEN WriteString("File error!"); END;
    u:=t;
  END Find;

  PROCEDURE SwapRecords(VAR fp: File; i,j: CARDINAL);

  VAR
    t,u: DataItem;
    read, written: CARDINAL;
  BEGIN
    DEC(i); DEC(j);
    SetPos(fp, 0, TSIZE(DataItem)*i);
    ReadNBytes(fp,ADR(t),TSIZE(DataItem), read);
    SetPos(fp, 0, TSIZE(DataItem)*j);
    ReadNBytes(fp,ADR(u),TSIZE(DataItem), read);
    SetPos(fp, 0, TSIZE(DataItem)*i);
```

```
         WriteNBytes(fp,ADR(u),TSIZE(DataItem), written);
         SetPos(fp, 0, TSIZE(DataItem)*j);
         WriteNBytes(fp,ADR(t),TSIZE(DataItem), written);
      END SwapRecords;

   PROCEDURE FileQuickSort(VAR fp: File; count:CARDINAL);
      PROCEDURE qs(l,r:CARDINAL; fp: File);
         VAR
            i,j: CARDINAL;
            x,y,u: DataItem;
         BEGIN
         i:=l; j:=r;
         Find(fp,l+r DIV 2, x);   (* find the middle element *)
         REPEAT
            Find(fp,i,u);
            WHILE CompareStr(u.zip,x.zip)=-1 DO
               i:= i+1;
               Find(fp,i,u);
            END;
            Find(fp,j,u);
            WHILE (CompareStr(x.zip,u.zip)=-1) AND (j>1) DO
               j:=j-1;
               Find(fp,j,u);

            END;
            IF (i<=j) AND (j>1) THEN
               SwapRecords(fp,i,j);
               INC(i); DEC(j);
            END;
         UNTIL i>j;
         IF l<j THEN qs(l,j,fp) END;
         IF l<r THEN qs(i,r,fp) END;
      END qs;

   BEGIN
        qs(1,count,fp);
   END FileQuickSort;


   BEGIN
      REPEAT     (* open mailing list file *)
         Lookup(F1,"mlist",FALSE); (* must be there *)
      UNTIL F1.res = done;

      SetModify(F1);

      FileQuickSort(F1,NUM);

      Close(F1);
   END DiskSortDriver.
```

The function **Find** was written in order to keep the **QuickSort** code essentially unchanged. The purpose of **Find** is to return the **name** string from a record on disk. You must constantly subtract one from the index argument **i** in **Find** because disk-file records are numbered starting at zero. Similarly, the procedure **SwapRecords** was written to keep the actual sorting code short.

Sorting Sequential Disk Files   Unlike random-access disk files, sequential disk files generally do not use fixed-record lengths and may be organized on a storage device that does not allow easy random access. Despite these limitations, sequential disk files are common because a specific application may be best suited to variable record lengths or because the storage device is sequential in nature. For example, most text files are sequential.

Although sorting a disk file as if it were an array has several advantages, you cannot use this method with sequential files because there is no way to achieve access quickly enough to any arbitrary element. For example, there is no quick way to reach arbitrary records of a sequential file that is located on tape. For this reason, it would be difficult to apply any of the array-sorting algorithms given earlier to sequential files.

There are two primary approaches to sorting sequential files. The first is to read the information into memory and then sort by using one of the standard array-sorting algorithms. This approach has the advantage of speed, but memory constraints limit the size of the file that you can sort.

The second method, called a *Merge sort*, divides the file to be sorted into two files of equal length. Then, using these files, the Merge sort reads an element from each file, orders that pair, and writes the elements to a third disk file. Then the new file is split again, and the ordered doubles are merged into ordered quadruples. The new file is split again, and the same procedure is followed until the list is sorted. This Merge sort is called a *three-tape merge* because it requires three files (tape drives) to be active at one time.

To understand how the Merge sort works, consider the following sequence:

1 4 3 8 6 7 2 5

The Merge sort splits the sequence to produce

1 4 3 8
6 7 2 5

It then merges the two parts to yield

$$1\ 6\ -\ 4\ 7\ -\ 2\ 3\ -\ 5\ 8$$

This is then split again to be

$$1\ 6\ -\ 4\ 7$$
$$2\ 3\ -\ 5\ 8$$

The next merge yields

$$1\ 2\ 3\ 6\ -\ 4\ 5\ 7\ 8$$

The final split is

$$1\ 2\ 3\ 6$$
$$4\ 5\ 7\ 8$$

with the outcome

$$1\ 2\ 3\ 4\ 5\ 6\ 7\ 8$$

As you may have guessed, the Merge sort requires passes equal to $\log_2 n$, where n is the number of total elements to sort.

A simple version of the Merge sort is shown here. For simplicity, this version assumes that the input file is twice as long as the information in it, so that only one file is actually needed; however, the Merge sort method is still the same.

```
FROM FileSystem IMPORT File, Response, Lookup, SetPos,
    SetModify, Close, ReadChar, WriteChar;

PROCEDURE Find(VAR fp:File; i:INTEGER; VAR u: DataItem);
VAR
    l:INTEGER;
    ch: CHAR;
BEGIN
    DEC(i);    (* files start at zero *)
    l:=INTEGER(TSIZE(DataItem))*i;
```

```
      SetPos(fp,0,l);
      ReadChar(fp,u);
   END Find;


PROCEDURE Mergesort(VAR fp: File; count:INTEGER);
VAR
   i,j,k,l,t,h,m,p,q,r: INTEGER;
   d,t1,t2:DataItem;
   up: BOOLEAN;

BEGIN
up:=TRUE;
p:=1;
REPEAT
   h:=1; m:=count;
   IF up THEN
      i:=1; j:=count; k:=count+1; l:=2*count;
   ELSE
      k:=1; l:=count; i:=count+1; j:=2*count;
   END;
   REPEAT
      IF m>=p THEN q:=p ELSE q:=m; END;
      m:=m-q;
      IF m>=p THEN r:=p ELSE r:=m; END;
      m:=m-r;
      WHILE (q<>0) AND (r<>0) DO
         Find(fp,i,t1); Find(fp,j,t2);
         IF t1<t2 THEN
            SetPos(fp,0,i-1); ReadChar(fp,d);
            SetPos(fp,0,k-1); WriteChar(fp,d);
            k:=k+h; i:=i+1; q:=q-1;
         ELSE
            SetPos(fp,0,j-1); ReadChar(fp,d);
            SetPos(fp,0,k-1); WriteChar(fp,d);
            k:=k+h; j:=j-1; r:=r-1;
         END ;
      END;
      WHILE r<>0 DO
         SetPos(fp,0,j-1); ReadChar(fp,d);
         SetPos(fp,0,k-1); WriteChar(fp,d);
         k:=k+h; j:=j-1; r:=r-1;
      END;
      WHILE q<>0 DO
         SetPos(fp,0,i-1); ReadChar(fp,d);
         SetPos(fp,0,k-1); WriteChar(fp,d);
         k:=k+h; i:=i+1; q:=q-1;
      END;
      h:=-1; t:=k;
      k:=l;
      l:=t;
   UNTIL m=0;
      up := NOT up;
      p:=p*2;
UNTIL p>=count;
```

```
    IF NOT up THEN
      FOR i:=1 TO count DO
        SetPos(fp,0,i-1+count); ReadChar(fp,d);
        SetPos(fp,0,i-1); WriteChar(fp,d);
      END;
    END;
END Mergesort;
```

As shown, when you use this routine, you must remember to import the necessary disk routines from **FileSystem**.

Searching

Databases of information exist so that, from time to time, a user can locate a record as long as the user knows its key. There is only one method of finding information in an unsorted file or array, and another for a sorted file or array.

Search Methods

Finding information in an unsorted array requires a sequential search, starting at the first element and stopping either when a match is found or at the end of the array. You must use this method on unsorted data, but you can apply it to sorted data as well. If the data has been sorted, then you can use a *binary search*, which will greatly speed up any search.

The Sequential Search   The sequential search is simple to code. The following function will search a character array of known length until it finds a match with the specified key.

```
PROCEDURE SeqSearch(item: DataArray; count:INTEGER;
                           key:DataItem):INTEGER;
VAR
    t:INTEGER;
BEGIN
    t:=1;
```

```
      WHILE (key<>item[t]) AND (t<=count) DO
        t:=t+1;
      END;
      IF t>count THEN RETURN 0;
      ELSE RETURN t;
      END;
   END SeqSearch;
```

This function will return the index number of the matching entry if there is one, or a 0 if not.

It is easy to see that a straight sequential search will, on the average, test $1/2n$ elements. In the best case, it will test only 1 element and, in the worst case, it will test n elements. If the information is stored on disk, the search time can be very long—but if the data is unsorted, this is the only way to search it.

The Binary Search   If the data that you want to search is sorted, then to find a match you can use a superior method called the *binary search*. It uses the "divide and conquer" approach. The method tests the middle element. If it is larger than the key, then the method tests the middle element of the first part; if it is not larger than the key, then the method tests the middle element of the second part. This method repeats until either it finds a match or there are no more elements to test.

For example, given the sequence

$$1\ 2\ 3\ 4\ 5\ 6\ 7\ 8\ 9$$

to find the number 4, the binary search would first test the middle number, which is 5. Since this is greater than 4, the search would continue with the first half.

$$1\ 2\ 3\ 4\ 5$$

Here, the middle element is 3. This is less than 4, so the first half is discarded and the search continues with

$$4\ 5$$

This time, the match is found.

In the binary search, the number of comparisons in the worst case is $\log_2 n$, with an average case being somewhat better and the best case being one.

A binary search function for character arrays is shown here. You can make this function search any arbitrary data structure by changing both the comparison portion of the routine and the type definition of **DataItem**.

```
PROCEDURE BinarySearch(a:ARRAY OF INTEGER;
                        key:INTEGER;
                        VAR pos: INTEGER): BOOLEAN;
                        (* return TRUE if found *)
   VAR
      n,i,j,middle:INTEGER;

BEGIN
   i:=0; j:=HIGH(a);
   REPEAT
      middle:=(i+j) DIV 2;   (* find middle element *)
      IF key<a[middle] THEN j:=middle-1;
      ELSIF key>a[middle] THEN i:=middle+1;
      ELSE
         pos:=middle;   (* location in array *)
         RETURN TRUE;
      END; (* if *)
   UNTIL i>j;
   RETURN FALSE;
END BinarySearch;
```

The next chapter explores different approaches to data storage and retrieval, which in some cases can make sorting and searching a much easier job.

Queues, Stacks, Linked Lists, and Binary Trees

CHAPTER 3

Programs consist of algorithms and data structures. A good program is a blend of both of these. Choosing and implementing a data structure are as important as the routines that manipulate it. The nature of the programming problem usually determines the way that information is organized and accessed. Therefore, as a programmer, you must have in your "bag of tricks" the right storage-and-retrieval methods for a variety of situations.

The actual representation of data in the computer is built "from the ground up," starting with the basic data types, such as **CHAR**, **INTEGER**, and **REAL**. At the next level are arrays, which are organized collections of the basic data types. Next, there are **RECORD**s, which are conglomerate data types accessed under one name. Transcending these physical aspects of the data, the final level concentrates on the sequence in which this data will be used—that is, *stored* and *retrieved*. In essence, the physical data is linked with "data machines," or methods, that control the way that your program can access information. There are basically four of these machines:

- A queue
- A stack
- A linked list
- A binary tree

Each machine provides a solution to a class of problems. Each is essentially a device that performs a specific storage-and-retrieval operation on the information that it is given and the requests that it receives. The methods share two operations: *store an item* and *retrieve an item*, in which the item is one informational unit. This chapter will show you how to build these methods for use in your own programs.

Queues

A *queue* is simply a linear list of information that is accessed in *first-in, first-out order*, sometimes called FIFO. The first item that is placed on the queue is the first item retrieved, the second item that is placed on the queue is the second item retrieved, and so on. This order is the only means of storage and retrieval; a queue does not allow random access of any specific item.

Queues are common in real life. For example, lines at a bank or a fast food restaurant are queues—except when patrons push their way to the front. To visualize how a queue works, consider the two routines **Qstore** and **Qretrieve**. **Qstore** places an item onto the end of the queue, and **Qretrieve** removes the first item from the queue and returns its value. Figure 3-1 shows the effect of a series of these operations.

Keep in mind that a retrieve operation removes an item from the queue and, if the item is not stored elsewhere, effectively destroys it—the item cannot be accessed again.

Many types of programming situations use queues, such as simulations, which are discussed later in their own chapter, event scheduling (as in a PERT or Gantt chart), and I/O buffering.

Action	Contents of Queue
Qstore(A)	A
Qstore(B)	A B
Qstore(C)	A B C
Qretrieve returns A	B C
Qstore(D)	B C D
Qretrieve returns B	C D
Qretrieve returns C	D

Figure 3-1. A queue in action

For example, consider a simple event-scheduling program. This program will allow you to enter a number of events. Then, as each event is performed, the program takes it off the list and displays the next event. You might use a program like this to organize such events as appointments during a day. To simplify the examples, the program will use an array of strings to hold the events, and will limit each event description to 80 characters and the number of events to 100. First, you need the procedures **Qstore** and **Qretrieve** for the scheduling program. They are shown here, with the necessary global variables and type definitions:

```
CONST
  MaxEvent = 100;

TYPE
  EvtType = ARRAY [0..79] OF CHAR;

VAR
  event: ARRAY[0..MaxEvent] OF EvtType;
  spos, rpos: INTEGER;

PROCEDURE Qstore(q:EvtType);
BEGIN
  IF spos=MaxEvent THEN
    WriteString('List full');
    WriteLn;
  ELSE
    event[spos]:=q;
    spos:=spos+1;
  END;
```

```
END Qstore;

PROCEDURE Qretrieve(VAR q:EvtType);
BEGIN
  IF rpos=spos THEN
    WriteString('No events in the Queue');
    WriteLn;
    q:='';
  ELSE
    rpos:=rpos+1;
    q:=event[rpos-1];
  END;
END Qretrieve;
```

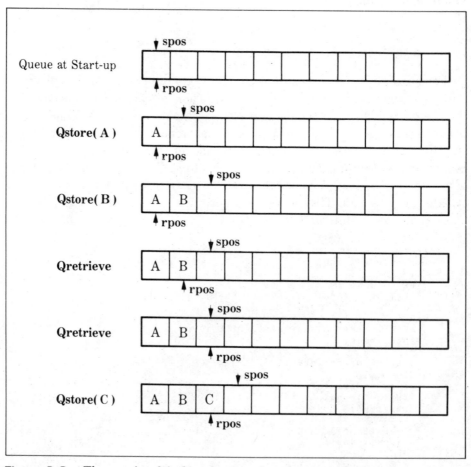

Figure 3-2. The retrieval index chasing the storage index

Notice that these functions require three global variables: **spos**, which holds the index of the next free storage location; **rpos**, which holds the index of the next item to retrieve; and **event**, which is a string array that holds the information. Before the program can call either **Qretrieve** or **Qstore**, you must initialize the variables **spos** and **rpos** to zero elsewhere.

In the program, the procedure **Qstore** places new events on the end of the list and checks if the list is full. The function **Qretrieve** takes events off the queue while there are events to perform. With each new event scheduled, the program increments **spos** and, with each event completed, it increments **rpos**. In essence, **rpos** chases **spos** through the queue. Figure 3-2 shows how this process may appear in memory as the program executes. If **rpos** and **spos** are equal, then there are no events left in the schedule. Keep in mind that even though the **Qretrieve** function does not actually destroy the information that is stored in the queue, it can never be accessed again and is, in effect, gone.

Here is the entire program for the simple event scheduler called Mini-Scheduler. You may find it fun to enhance this program for your own specific use.

```
MODULE MiniScheduler;

FROM InOut IMPORT Write, WriteString, WriteInt, Read, ReadString,
                  WriteLn, EOL;

FROM Strings IMPORT Length;

CONST
  MaxEvent = 100;

TYPE
  EvtType = ARRAY [0..79] OF CHAR;

VAR
  event: ARRAY[0..MaxEvent] OF EvtType;
  spos, rpos,t: INTEGER;
  ch:CHAR;
  done:BOOLEAN;

PROCEDURE Qstore(q:EvtType);
BEGIN
  IF spos=MaxEvent THEN
    WriteString('List full');
    WriteLn;
  ELSE
    event[spos]:=q;
    spos:=spos+1;
  END;
END Qstore;

PROCEDURE Qretrieve(VAR q:EvtType);
BEGIN
```

```
    IF rpos=spos THEN
      WriteString('No events in the Queue');
      WriteLn;
      q:='';
    ELSE
      rpos:=rpos+1;
      q:=event[rpos-1];
    END;
END Qretrieve;

PROCEDURE Gets(VAR a:ARRAY OF CHAR);
    (* This procedure reads a string until a CRLF
       is typed.  This differs from ReadString.
    *)
    CONST
      BS = 8;  (* backspace *)

    VAR
      ch: CHAR;
      i:CARDINAL;
BEGIN
  i:=0;
  REPEAT
    Read(ch);
    Write(ch);
    IF ORD(ch)=BS THEN i:=i-1;  (* is backspace *)
    ELSIF (ch<>EOL) AND (i<HIGH(a)) THEN
      a[i]:=ch;
      i:=i+1;
    END;
  UNTIL (ch=EOL) OR (i=HIGH(a));
  a[i]:=CHR(0);  (* all strings end in 0 *)
END Gets;

PROCEDURE Enter;
VAR
  s:EvtType;

BEGIN
  REPEAT
    WriteString('Enter event ');
    WriteInt(spos+1,2);
    Write(':');
    Gets(s);
    WriteLn;
    IF Length(s)<>0 THEN Qstore(s); END;
  UNTIL Length(s)=0;  (* no more entries *)
END Enter;

PROCEDURE Review;
VAR
  t:INTEGER;
BEGIN
  FOR t:=rpos TO spos-1 DO
    WriteInt(t,2);
    Write(':');
    WriteString(event[t]);
    WriteLn;
  END
END Review;
```

```
PROCEDURE Perform;
VAR
  s:EvtType;
BEGIN
  Qretrieve(s);  (* get next event *)
  IF Length(s)<>0 THEN
    WriteString(s);
    WriteLn;
  END;
END Perform ;

BEGIN  (* scheduler *)
  FOR t:=1 TO MaxEvent DO
    event[t]:='';  (* init events *)
  END;

  spos:=0; rpos:=0;  done:=FALSE;

  REPEAT
    WriteString('Enter, Review, Perform, Quit: ');
    Read(ch);
    WriteLn;
    ch:=CAP(ch);
    CASE ch OF
      'E': Enter |
      'R': Review |
      'P': Perform |
      'Q': done:=TRUE;
    ELSE
      WriteString('Try Again');
      WriteLn;
    END;
  UNTIL done=TRUE;
END MiniScheduler.
```

The Circular Queue

As you study the MiniScheduler program just given, you may see that it is possible to make an improvement. Instead of stopping the program when the array reaches the storage limit of the queue, you could have both the storage index, **spos**, and the retrieval index, **rpos**, loop back to the beginning of the array. In this way, you could place any number of items on the queue as long as you also took off items. This method of implementing a queue is called a *circular queue* because it uses its storage array as if the array were a circle instead of a linear list.

To create a circular queue for use in the MiniScheduler program, you must change the procedures **Qstore** and **Qretrieve** as shown next.

```
PROCEDURE Qstore(q:EvtType);  (* Circular version *)
BEGIN
  IF spos+1=rpos THEN
    WriteString('List full');
    WriteLn;
  ELSE
    event[spos]:=q;
    spos:=spos+1;
    IF spos=MaxEvent THEN spos:=1; END; (* loop back *)
  END;
END Qstore;

PROCEDURE Qretrieve(VAR q:EvtType);  (* Circular version *)
BEGIN
  IF rpos=MaxEvent THEN rpos:=1; END; (* loop back *)
  IF rpos=spos THEN
    WriteString('No events in the Queue');
    WriteLn;
    q:=';';
  ELSE
    rpos:=rpos+1;
    q:=event[rpos-1];
  END;
END Qretrieve;
```

In essence, the queue is only full when both the store index and the retrieve index are equal; otherwise, the queue has room for another event. However, when the program starts, the retrieval index, **rpos**, must not be set to zero, but rather to **MAX_EVENT** so that the first call to **Qstore** does not produce the message **queue full**. Notice that the queue will only contain **MAX_EVENT**−1 elements because **rpos** and **spos** must always be at least one element apart; otherwise, it would be impossible to know whether the queue was full or empty. Figure 3-3 shows what the array that is used for the circular version of the MiniScheduler program looks like.

Perhaps the most common use of a circular queue is in operating systems that buffer information read from and written to disk files or the console. Another common use is in real-time application programs in which, for example, the user may continue to input from the keyboard while the program performs another task. Many word processors do this when they reformat a paragraph or justify a line. There is a brief period during which what is being typed is not displayed until the other process is completed. To accomplish this, the application program needs to continue to check for keyboard entry during the other process's execution. If the user presses a key, the program places the data in the queue, and the process continues. After the process is complete, the program retrieves the characters from the queue.

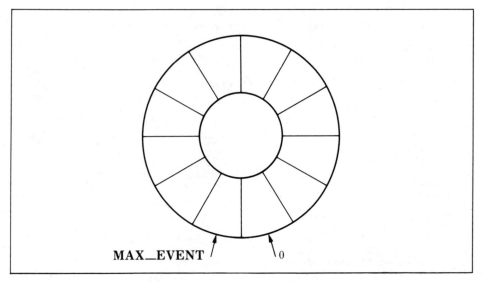

Figure 3-3. The circular array for the MiniScheduler program

To see how you can do this with a circular queue, study the following simple program, which contains two processes. For simplicity, the program simulates the two processes. (However, Chapter 11 covers concurrent processes in detail.) The first process in the program will count to 32,000. The second process will place characters into a circular queue as you type them, without echoing them to the screen, until you press a semicolon. The program will not display the characters that you type, because the first process is given priority until either you type a semicolon or the count is finished. Then the program retrieves and prints the characters in the queue.

```
MODULE KeyBuffer;

FROM InOut IMPORT Write, WriteString, Read, WriteLn;

FROM Terminal IMPORT KeyPressed;

CONST MaxEvent = 100;

TYPE EvtType = CHAR;

VAR
```

```
    event: ARRAY[0..MaxEvent] OF EvtType;
    spos, rpos,t: INTEGER;
    ch:CHAR;
    done:BOOLEAN;

PROCEDURE Qstore(q:EvtType);  (* Circular version *)
BEGIN
  IF spos+1=rpos THEN
    WriteString('List full');
    WriteLn;
  ELSE
    event[spos]:=q;
    spos:=spos+1;
    IF spos=MaxEvent THEN spos:=1; END; (* loop back *)
  END;
END Qstore;

PROCEDURE Qretrieve(VAR q:EvtType);  (* Circular version *)
BEGIN
  IF rpos=MaxEvent THEN rpos:=1; END; (* loop back *)
  IF rpos=spos THEN
    WriteString('No events in the Queue');
    WriteLn;
    q:=';';
  ELSE
    rpos:=rpos+1;
    q:=event[rpos-1];
  END;
END Qretrieve;

BEGIN  (* key buffer *)
  t:=1; rpos:=MaxEvent; spos:=0;
  REPEAT
    IF KeyPressed() THEN
      Read(ch); (* Read with no echo *)
      Qstore(ch);
    END;
    t:=t+1;
  UNTIL (t=32000) OR (ch=';');
  REPEAT
    Qretrieve(ch);
    IF ch<>';' THEN Write(ch); END;
  UNTIL ch=';';
END KeyBuffer.
```

Stacks

A *stack* is the opposite of a queue because it uses *last-in, first-out accessing*, which is sometimes called LIFO. To visualize a stack, imagine a stack of plates. The bottom plate in the stack is the last to be used, and the top plate (the last plate that is placed on the stack) is the first to be used. Stacks are used a great deal in system software, including compilers and interpreters.

For historical reasons, the two primary stack operations—*store* and *retrieve*—are usually called *push* and *pop*, respectively. Therefore, to implement a stack, you will need two functions: **Push**, which places a value on the stack; and **Pop**, which will retrieve a value from the stack. You will also need a region of memory to use as the stack: you could use an array for this purpose, or you could allocate a region of memory by using Modula-2's dynamic memory-allocation routines. Like the queue, the retrieval function takes a value off the list and, if it is not stored elsewhere, destroys it. The general forms of **Push** and **Pop** that use an integer array are shown here:

```
CONST
   MAX = 100;

VAR
   stack:ARRAY [1..MAX] OF INTEGER;
   tos:INTEGER;  (* points to top of stack *)

PROCEDURE Push(i:INTEGER);
BEGIN
  IF tos>=MAX THEN
    WriteString('Stack full');
    WriteLn;
  ELSE
    stack[tos]:=i;
    tos:=tos+1;
  END;
END Push;

PROCEDURE Pop():INTEGER;
BEGIN
  tos:=tos-1;
  IF tos<1 THEN
    WriteString('Stack underflow');
    WriteLn;
    tos:=tos+1;
    RETURN(0);
  ELSE RETURN(stack[tos]);
  END;
END Pop;
```

The variable **tos** is the index of the next open stack location. When implementing these functions, you must remember to prevent overflow and underflow. In these routines, if **tos** is 0, the stack is empty; if **tos** is greater than or equal to the last storage location, the stack is full. Figure 3-4 shows how a stack works.

An excellent example of stack usage is a four-function calculator. Most calculators today accept a standard form of expressions called *infix notation*, which takes the general form *operand-operator-operand*. For example, to add 100 to 200, you would enter **100**, then press +, then enter **200**, and press =.

Action	Contents of Stack
Push(A)	A
Push(B)	B A
Push(C)	C B A
Pop retrieve C	B A
Push(F)	F B A
Pop retrieve F	B A
Pop retrieve B	A
Pop retrieve A	*empty*

Figure 3-4. A stack in action

However, in an effort to save memory (which used to be expensive), many early calculators used a form of expression evaluation called *postfix notation*, in which you entered both operands first, and then entered the operator. For example, using postfix, to add 100 to 200, you would first enter **100**, then enter **200**, and then press **+**. As operands are entered, the calculator places them on a stack; each time that an operator is entered, it removes two operands from the stack and pushes the result back on the stack. The advantage of the postfix form is the calculator could easily evaluate complex expressions.

Here is the entire calculator program. It works just like a postfix calculator: first, you enter two numbers and then the operator. The program displays the result and pushes it back on the stack.

```
MODULE FourFunctionCalc;

FROM InOut IMPORT WriteString, WriteLn, WriteInt, ReadInt,
                  ReadString;

FROM NumberConversion IMPORT StringToInt;

FROM Strings IMPORT Length;

CONST
  MAX = 100;

TYPE
  str80 = ARRAY[0..79] OF CHAR;
```

```
VAR
  stack:ARRAY [1..MAX] OF INTEGER;
  tos:INTEGER;  (* points to top of stack *)
  a,b,num:INTEGER;
  s:str80;
  done: BOOLEAN;
PROCEDURE Push(i:INTEGER);
BEGIN
  IF tos>=MAX THEN
    WriteString('Stack full');
    WriteLn;
  ELSE
    stack[tos]:=i;
    tos:=tos+1;
  END;
END Push;

PROCEDURE Pop():INTEGER;
BEGIN
  tos:=tos-1;
  IF tos<1 THEN
    WriteString('Stack underflow');
    WriteLn;
    tos:=tos+1;
    RETURN(0);
  ELSE RETURN(stack[tos]);
  END;
END Pop;

BEGIN  (* calculator *)
  tos:=1;
  WriteString('Four Function Calculator');
  WriteLn;
  REPEAT
    WriteLn;
    WriteString(': ');
    ReadString(s);
    WriteLn;
    CASE s[0] OF
      '+':
          a:=Pop();
          b:=Pop();
          WriteInt(a+b,5);
          Push(a+b); |
      '-':
          IF Length(s)=1 THEN (* is subtraction *)
            a:=Pop();
            b:=Pop();
           .WriteInt(b-a,5);
            Push(b-a);
          ELSE  (* is a negative number *)
            StringToInt(s,num,done);
            IF done THEN Push(num); END;
          END  |
      '*':
        . a:=Pop();
```

```
        b:=Pop();
        WriteInt(a*b,5);
        Push(a*b); |
    '/':
        a:=Pop();
        b:=Pop();
        IF a=0 THEN WriteString('divide by zero')
        ELSE
           WriteInt((b DIV a),5);
           Push(b DIV a);
        END;
    ELSE
        StringToInt(s,num,done);
        IF done THEN Push(num); END;
    END;
  UNTIL CAP(s[0])='Q';
END FourFunctionCalc.
```

Although this version is capable of only integer arithmetic, you can easily switch it to full floating-point operation by simply changing the data type of the stack and converting the **DIV** operator to the floating-point operator /.

Linked Lists

Both queues and stacks share two common traits; first, they both have strict rules for referencing the data that is stored in them. Second, the retrieval operations are, by nature, consumptive: accessing an item in a stack or queue requires its removal and, unless it is stored elsewhere, its destruction. Both stacks and queues also use, at least in concept, a contiguous region of memory to operate. Unlike a stack or a queue, a *linked list* may access its storage randomly because each piece of information carries a *link* to the next data item in the chain. This means that a linked list requires a complex data structure instead of a stack or queue, which can operate on both simple and complex data items. A linked-list-retrieval operation does not remove and destroy an item from the list. In fact, you must add a specific *deletion* operation to do this.

Linked lists are used for two purposes. The first purpose is to create arrays of unknown size in memory. If you know the size of the list in advance, then you can use a simple array; but if you do not know the size of a list, then you must use a linked list. The second purpose is for disk-file storage of data-bases. The linked list allows you to insert and delete items quickly and easily without having to rearrange the entire disk file. For these reasons, linked lists are used extensively in database managers.

When a linked list is RAM-based, each element must be dynamically allocated and the information must be accessed through pointers. This is the only way that the list can grow or shrink as necessary, and that all free memory is automatically available for the list. Therefore, all of the following linked-list routines are designed to work with pointers.

Linked lists can be either singly linked or doubly linked. A *singly linked list* contains a link to the next data item. A *doubly linked list* contains links to both the next element and the previous element in the list. The type that you use will depend upon your application.

Singly Linked Lists

A singly linked list requires that each item of information contains a link to the next element in the list. Generally, each data item will consist of a **RECORD** that contains information fields and a link pointer. Figure 3-5 shows what a singly linked list looks like.

There are two ways to build a singly linked list. The first way is to put each new item on the end of the list. The other way is to add items into specific places in the list—for example, in ascending sorted order. How you build the list determines the way the storage function will be coded, as shown in the simple case of creating a linked list by adding items on the end. You will first need to define a **RECORD** to hold the information and the links.

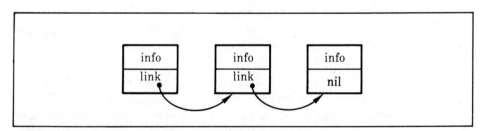

Figure 3-5. A singly linked list in memory

Because mailing lists are common, this example will use one. The **RECORD** type for each element in the mailing list is defined here. (It is similar to the one that was defined in Chapter 2.)

```
TYPE
   AddrPointer = POINTER TO address;

   address = RECORD
       name : ARRAY[0..29] OF CHAR;
       street: ARRAY[0..39] OF CHAR;
       city: ARRAY[0..19] OF CHAR;
       state: ARRAY[0..1] OF CHAR;
       zip: ARRAY[0..8] OF CHAR;
       next: AddrPointer;  (* pointer to next record *)
   END;

VAR
   start,last:AddrPointer;
```

The function **SLStore** builds a singly linked list by placing each new element on the end. A pointer to a record of type **address** must be passed to **SLStore**, as shown here:

```
PROCEDURE SLStore(i:AddrPointer);
BEGIN
  IF last=NIL THEN (* first item in list *)
    last:=i;
    start:=i;
    i^.next:=NIL;
  ELSE
    last^.next:=i;
    i^.next:=NIL;
    last:=i;
  END;
END SLStore;
```

Although you can sort the list created with **SLStore** as a separate operation, it would be easier to sort while building the list by inserting each new item in the proper sequence of the chain. In addition, if the list is already sorted, then it would be advantageous to keep the list sorted by inserting new items in their proper location. You can do this by sequentially scanning the list until the proper location is found, inserting the new address at that point, and rearranging the links as necessary.

There are three possible situations that can occur when you insert an item in a singly linked list. First, the first item may become the new first item; second, it could go in the middle between two other items; or third, it could become the last element. Figure 3-6 shows how the links are changed for each case.

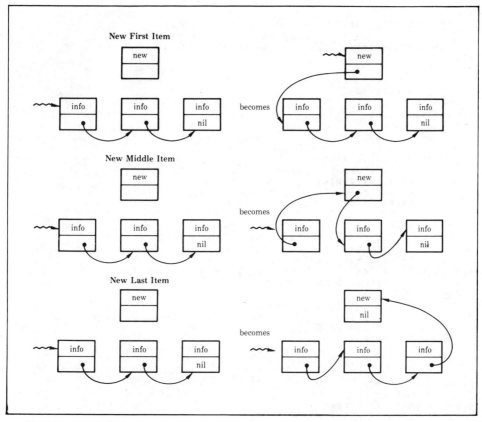

Figure 3-6. Inserting an item into a singly linked list

If you change the first item in the list, then you must update the entry point to the list elsewhere in your program. To avoid this, you can use a *sentinel* as a first item. A sentinel is a special value that always will be first in the list. In this way, the entry point to the list will not change. However, this method does have the disadvantage of using one extra storage location to hold the sentinel, so it is not used here.

The function **SLSortStore**, given here, will insert addresses into the mail list in ascending order based on the **name** field. In addition to a pointer to the new element, **SLSortStore** requires that pointers to both the beginning and the end of the list be passed to it. Upon exit, it returns a pointer to the first element in the list. The calling routine is responsible for saving the pointer.

```
PROCEDURE SLSortStore(info,start:AddrPointer;
              VAR last:AddrPointer):AddrPointer;
(* store entries in sorted order *)

VAR
  old, top: AddrPointer;
  done:BOOLEAN;
BEGIN
  top:=start;
  old:=NIL;
  done:=FALSE;

  IF start=NIL THEN
  (* first element in list *)
    info^.next:=NIL;
    last:=info;
    RETURN info ;
  ELSE
    WHILE (start<>NIL) AND (NOT done) DO
      IF CompareStr(start^.name,info^.name)=-1 THEN
        old:=start;
        start:=start^.next;
      ELSE (* goes in middle *)
        IF old<>NIL THEN
          old^.next:=info;
          info^.next:=start;
          RETURN top;  (* keep same starting point *)
          done:=TRUE;
        ELSE
          info^.next:=start;  (* new first element *)
          RETURN info;
          done:=TRUE;
        END;
      END;
    END;  (*WHILE*)
    IF NOT done THEN
      last^.next:=info;  (* goes on END *)
      info^.next:=NIL;
      last:=info;
      RETURN top;
    END;
  END;
END SLSortStore;
```

For a linked list, it is uncommon to find a specific function that is dedicated to the retrieval process, which returns item after item in list order. This code is usually so short that it is simply placed inside another routine such as a search, delete, or display function. Retrieving items from the list is as simple as following a chain. For example, this routine will display all names in a mailing list:

```
PROCEDURE Display(start:AddrPointer);
BEGIN
  WHILE start<>NIL DO
    WriteString(start^.name);
    WriteLn;
    start:=start^.next;
  END;
END Display ;
```

Here, **start** is a pointer to the first **RECORD** in the list.

You could write a search routine that is based on the **name** field like this:

```
PROCEDURE Search(start:AddrPointer;
                 name:ARRAY OF CHAR):AddrPointer;
BEGIN
  WHILE start<>NIL DO
    IF CompareStr(name,start^.name)=0 THEN
        RETURN start;
    ELSE
        start:=start^.next;
    END
  END;
  RETURN NIL;   (* not in list *)
END Search;
```

Because **Search** returns a pointer to the list item that matches the search name, **Search** must be declared to be returning a record pointer of type **address**. If there is no match, **Search** returns a **NIL** pointer; if there is a match, it returns a pointer to the desired entry.

The process of deleting an item from a singly linked list is straightforward. As with insertion, there are three cases: deleting the first item, deleting an item in the middle, and deleting the last item. Figure 3-7 shows each of these operations. The procedure shown here will delete a given item from a list of **RECORD**s of type **address**:

```
PROCEDURE SLDelete(start,item,PriorItem:AddrPointer)
                  :AddrPointer;
BEGIN
  IF PriorItem<>NIL THEN
    PriorItem^.next:=item^.next;
    DISPOSE(item)
  ELSE
    start:=item^.next;
    DISPOSE(item)
  END;
  RETURN start;
END SLDelete;
```

SLDelete must be sent pointers to the deleted item, the item before the deleted item in the chain, and the beginning of the list. If you want to remove the first item, then the previous pointer must be **NIL**. The function must return a pointer to the start of the list because, in the case where the first item is deleted, the calling routine must know where the new first element is located.

Singly linked lists have a major drawback that prevents their extensive use: the list cannot be followed in reverse order. For this reason, doubly linked lists are generally used.

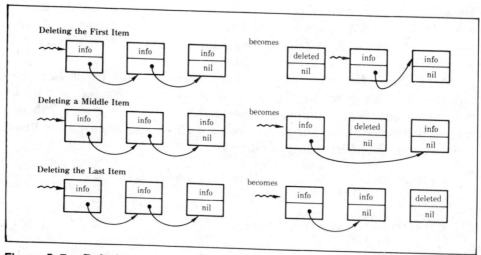

Figure 3-7. Deleting an item from a singly linked list

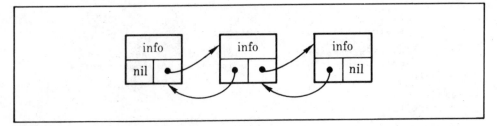

Figure 3-8. A doubly linked list

Doubly Linked Lists

Doubly linked lists consist of data and links to both the next item and the preceding item. Figure 3-8 shows how these links are arranged.

A list that uses two links instead of just one has two major advantages. First, you can read the list in either direction. This not only simplifies sorting the list but also, in the case of a database, allows a user to scan the list in either direction. Second, because either the forward links or the backward links can read the entire list, if one of the links becomes invalid, the list can be reconstructed by using the other link. (This is meaningful only in the case of equipment failure.)

Three basic insertion operations can be performed on a doubly linked list: insert a new first element, insert in the middle, and insert a new last element. Figure 3-9 shows these operations.

Building a doubly linked list is similar to building a singly linked list except that the **RECORD** must have room to maintain two links. Using the mailing-list example again, you can modify **address** to accommodate this, as shown here:

```
TYPE
   AddrPointer = POINTER TO address;
   address = RECORD
         name : ARRAY[0..29] OF CHAR;
```

```
            street: ARRAY[0..39] OF CHAR;
            city: ARRAY[0..19] OF CHAR;
            state: ARRAY[0..2] OF CHAR;
            zip: ARRAY[0..9] OF CHAR;
            next: AddrPointer;  (* pointer to next record *)
            prior: AddrPointer;  (* pointer to previous record*)
        END;

    VAR
        start,last: AddrPointer;
```

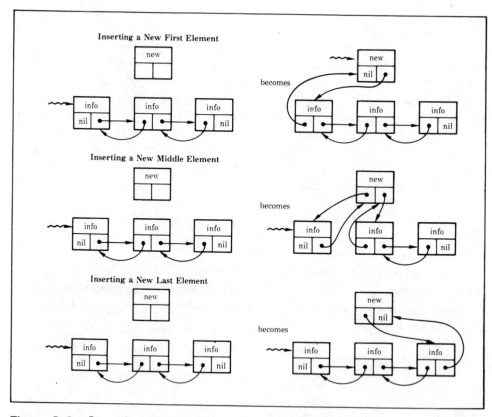

Figure 3-9. Inserting an item into a doubly linked list

Using **address** as the basic data item, the procedure **DLStore** will build a doubly linked list by placing new entries on the end of the list:

```
PROCEDURE DLStore(i:AddrPointer);
BEGIN
    IF last=NIL THEN (* first item in list *)
        last:=i;
        start:=i;
        i^.next:=NIL;
        i^.prior:=NIL;
    ELSE  (* put on end *)
        last^.next:=i;
        i^.next:=NIL;
        i^.prior:=last;
        last:=i;
    END;
END DLStore;
```

Like the singly linked list, a doubly linked list can have a function that stores each element in a specific location in the list as it is built, instead of always placing each new item on the end. The function called **DLSortStore**, shown here, will create a list that is sorted in ascending order based on the **name** field.

```
PROCEDURE DLSortStore(info,start:AddrPointer;
                VAR last:AddrPointer):AddrPointer;
(* store entries in sorted order *)

VAR
  old, top: AddrPointer;
BEGIN
  top:=start;
  old:=NIL;

  IF start=NIL THEN
  (* first element in list *)
    info^.next:=NIL;
    last:=info;
    info^.prior:=NIL;
    RETURN(info);
  ELSE
    WHILE start<>NIL DO
      IF CompareStr(start^.name,info^.name)=-1 THEN
          old:=start;
          start:=start^.next;
      ELSE
      (* goes in middle *)
        IF old<>NIL THEN
          old^.next:=info;
```

```
            info^.next:=start;
            start^.prior:=info;
            info^.prior:=old;
            RETURN top;  (* keep same starting point *)
          ELSE
            info^.next:=start;  (* new first element *)
            info^.prior:=NIL;
            RETURN info;
          END;
        END;
      END;  (*WHILE*)

      last^.next:=info;  (* goes on END *)
      info^.next:=NIL;
      info^.prior:=last;
      last:=info;
      RETURN top;
    END;
END DLSortStore;
```

Because an item may be inserted at the top of the list, this function must return a pointer to the first item in the list so that the calling routine will know where the list begins. As with the singly linked list, to retrieve a specific data item, the program simply follows the links until it finds the proper element. However, remember that you can read the list in either direction.

You should consider three cases when deleting an element from a doubly linked list: deleting the first item, deleting an item from the middle, and deleting the last item. Figure 3-10 shows how the links are rearranged.

The following function will delete an item of type **address** from a doubly linked list.

```
PROCEDURE DLDelete(start:AddrPointer;
              key:ARRAY OF CHAR):AddrPointer;
VAR
  temp,temp2:AddrPointer;
  done:BOOLEAN;
BEGIN
  temp:=start;
  IF CompareStr(start^.name,key)=0 THEN
    (* is first in list *)
    IF temp^.next <> NIL THEN
      temp:=start^.next;
      temp^.prior:=NIL;
    END;
    DISPOSE(start);
    RETURN temp;
ELSE
  done:=FALSE;
  temp:=start^.next;
  temp2:=start;
  WHILE temp<>NIL DO
    IF CompareStr(temp^.name,key)=0 THEN
```

```
            temp2^.next:=temp^.next;
            IF temp^.next<>NIL THEN
                temp^.next^.prior:=temp2;
            END;
            done:=TRUE;
            DISPOSE(temp);
          ELSE
            temp2:=temp;
            temp:=temp^.next;
          END;
      END;
      IF NOT done THEN
        WriteString('not found');
        WriteLn;
      END;
      RETURN start;  (* still same starting point *)
    END;
  END DLDelete;
```

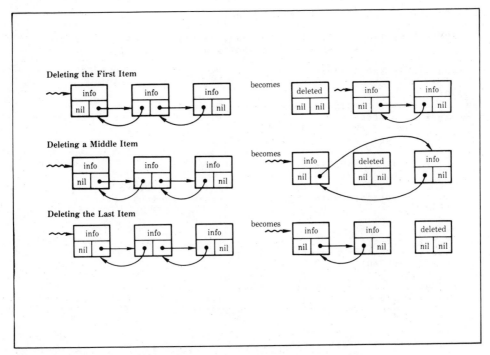

Figure 3-10.   Deleting an item from a doubly linked list

As you can see, this function requires one less pointer to be passed to it than the singly linked list version required. The reason for this is the data item that is being deleted already carries a link to the previous element and the next element. Because the first element in the list could change, the procedure passes the pointer to the top element back to the calling routine.

A Mailing List

Here is a simple but complete mailing-list program. It keeps the entire list in memory while in use; however, it may be saved in a disk file for later use.

```
MODULE Mlist;
        (* A simple mailing list program that uses
           doubly linked lists. *)

FROM InOut IMPORT WriteString, ReadString, WriteLn,
                 EOL, Read, Write;

FROM Storage IMPORT ALLOCATE, DEALLOCATE;

FROM Strings IMPORT CompareStr, Length;

FROM FileSystem IMPORT File, SetRead, SetWrite, Close, ReadNBytes,
                 WriteNBytes, Response, Reset, Lookup;

FROM SYSTEM IMPORT TSIZE;

TYPE
  AddrPointer = POINTER TO address;
  address = RECORD
        name : ARRAY[0..29] OF CHAR;
        street: ARRAY[0..39] OF CHAR;
        city: ARRAY[0..19] OF CHAR;
        state: ARRAY[0..2] OF CHAR;
        zip: ARRAY[0..9] OF CHAR;
        next: AddrPointer;  (* pointer to next record *)
        prior: AddrPointer;  (* pointer to previous record*)
    END;

VAR
  t,t2: INTEGER;
  start,last: AddrPointer;
  quit: BOOLEAN;

PROCEDURE Gets(VAR a:ARRAY OF CHAR);
  (* This procedure reads a string until a CRLF
     is typed.  This differs from ReadString.
  *)
  CONST
    BS = 8;  (* backspace *)

  VAR
```

```
    ch: CHAR;
    i:CARDINAL;
BEGIN
  i:=0;
  REPEAT
    Read(ch);
    Write(ch);
    IF (ORD(ch)=BS) AND (i>0) THEN i:=i-1;  (* is backspace *)
    ELSIF (ch<>EOL) AND (i<HIGH(a)) THEN
      a[i]:=ch;
      i:=i+1;
    END;
  UNTIL (ch=EOL) OR (i=HIGH(a));
  a[i]:=CHR(0);  (* all strings end in 0 *)
END Gets;


PROCEDURE MenuSelect():CHAR;  (* returns the users selection *)

VAR
  ch:CHAR;

BEGIN
  WriteString('1. Enter names'); WriteLn;
  WriteString('2. Delete a name'); WriteLn;
  WriteString('3. Display the list'); WriteLn;
  WriteString('4. Search FOR a name'); WriteLn;
  WriteString('5. Save the list'); WriteLn;
  WriteString('6. Load the list'); WriteLn;
  WriteString('7. Quit'); WriteLn;
  REPEAT
    WriteLn;
    WriteString('Enter your choice: ');
    Read(ch);  WriteLn;
  UNTIL (ch>='1') AND (ch<='7');
  RETURN ch;
END MenuSelect ;


PROCEDURE DLSortStore(info,start:AddrPointer;
              VAR last:AddrPointer):AddrPointer;
(* store entries in sorted order *)

VAR
  old, top: AddrPointer;
BEGIN
  top:=start;
  old:=NIL;

  IF start=NIL THEN
  (* first element in list *)
    info^.next:=NIL;
    last:=info;
    info^.prior:=NIL;
    RETURN(info);
  ELSE
    WHILE start<>NIL DO
      IF CompareStr(start^.name,info^.name)=-1 THEN
        old:=start;
        start:=start^.next;
```

```
          ELSE
          (* goes in middle *)
            IF old<>NIL THEN
              old^.next:=info;
              info^.next:=start;
              start^.prior:=info;
              info^.prior:=old;
              RETURN top;  (* keep same starting point *)
            ELSE
              info^.next:=start;  (* new first element *)
              info^.prior:=NIL;
              RETURN info;
            END;
          END;
        END;  (*WHILE*)

        last^.next:=info;  (* goes on END *)
        info^.next:=NIL;
        info^.prior:=last;
        last:=info;
        RETURN top;
      END;
    END DLSortStore;

    PROCEDURE DLDelete(start:AddrPointer;
                  key:ARRAY OF CHAR):AddrPointer;
    VAR
      temp,temp2:AddrPointer;
      done:BOOLEAN;
    BEGIN
      IF CompareStr(start^.name,key)=0 THEN
        (* is first in list *)
        IF temp^.next <> NIL THEN
          temp:=start^.next;
          temp^.prior:=NIL;
        END;
        DISPOSE(start);
        RETURN temp;
      ELSE
        done:=FALSE;
        temp:=start^.next;
        temp2:=start;
        WHILE temp<>NIL DO
          IF CompareStr(temp^.name,key)=0 THEN
            temp2^.next:=temp^.next;
            IF temp^.next<>NIL THEN
              temp^.next^.prior:=temp2;
            END;
            done:=TRUE;
            DISPOSE(temp);
          ELSE
            temp2:=temp;
            temp:=temp^.next;
          END;
        END;
        IF NOT done THEN
          WriteString('not found');
          WriteLn;
        END;
        RETURN start;  (* still same starting point *)
```

```
      END;
END DLDelete;

PROCEDURE Remove;
VAR
   name:ARRAY [0..79] OF CHAR;
BEGIN
   WriteString('Enter name to delete: ');
   Gets(name); WriteLn;
   start:=DLDelete(start,name);
END Remove;

PROCEDURE Enter;
VAR
   info: AddrPointer;
   done: BOOLEAN;
BEGIN
   done:=FALSE;
   REPEAT
     NEW(info);  (* get a new record *)
     WriteString('Enter name: ');
     Gets(info^.name);  WriteLn;
     IF Length(info^.name)=0 THEN done:=TRUE
     ELSE
       WriteString('Enter street: ');
       Gets(info^.street);
       WriteString('Enter city: ');
       Gets(info^.city);
       WriteString('Enter state: ');
       Gets(info^.state);
       WriteString('Enter zip: ');
       Gets(info^.zip);
       start:=DLSortStore(info,start,last);  (* store it *)
     END;
   UNTIL done;
END Enter;

PROCEDURE Display(start:AddrPointer);
BEGIN
   WHILE start<>NIL DO
     WriteString(start^.name); WriteLn;
     WriteString(start^.street); WriteLn;
     WriteString(start^.city); WriteLn;
     WriteString(start^.state); WriteLn;
     WriteString(start^.zip); WriteLn;
     start:=start^.next;
   END;
END Display;

PROCEDURE Search(start:AddrPointer;
                 name:ARRAY OF CHAR):AddrPointer;
BEGIN
   WHILE start<>NIL DO
     IF CompareStr(name,start^.name)=0 THEN
       RETURN start;
     ELSE
       start:=start^.next;
     END
   END;
   RETURN NIL;  (* not in list *)
```

```
  END Search;

  PROCEDURE Find;
  VAR
    loc:AddrPointer;
    name:ARRAY[0..79] OF CHAR;
  BEGIN
    WriteString('Enter name to find: ');
    Gets(name); WriteLn;
    loc:=Search(start,name);
    IF loc<>NIL THEN
      WriteString(loc^.name); WriteLn;
      WriteString(loc^.street); WriteLn;
      WriteString(loc^.city); WriteLn;
      WriteString(loc^.state); WriteLn;
      WriteString(loc^.zip); WriteLn;
      WriteLn;
    ELSE
      WriteString('not in list');
      WriteLn;
    END;
  END Find;

  PROCEDURE Save(start: AddrPointer);  (* save the mailing list *)
    VAR
      i,w:CARDINAL;
      f: File;
      fname: ARRAY[0..30] OF CHAR;
  BEGIN
    REPEAT
      WriteString('Enter Filename: ');
      ReadString(fname);  WriteLn;
      Lookup(f,fname ,TRUE); (* create if not there *)
    UNTIL f.res = done;

    Reset(f);  (* re-write from the beginning *)
    SetWrite(f);  (* enable write *)

    WHILE start<>NIL DO
      (* Write the record *)
      WriteNBytes(f,start, TSIZE(address), w);
      IF w<>TSIZE(address) THEN WriteString('write error'); END;
      start:=start^.next;
    END;
    Close(f);
  END Save;

  PROCEDURE Load(start:AddrPointer):AddrPointer;
  (* returns a pointer TO the start OF the list *)
  VAR
    begin,temp,temp2:AddrPointer;
    first:BOOLEAN;
    r,i:CARDINAL;
    f: File;
    fname: ARRAY[0..30] OF CHAR;
  BEGIN
```

```
REPEAT
  WriteString('Enter Filename: ');
  ReadString(fname);  WriteLn;
  Lookup(f,fname ,FALSE); (* do not create if not there *)
UNTIL f.res = done;

Reset(f);  (* read from the beginning *)
SetRead(f);  (* enable read *)

WHILE start<>NIL DO
  (* free memory, IF any *)
  temp:=start^.next;
  DISPOSE(start);
  start:=temp;
END;

last:=NIL;

(* read the first record *)
NEW(begin);
ReadNBytes(f,begin, TSIZE(address), r);
IF r<>TSIZE(address) THEN WriteString('read error'); END;
temp:=begin;   (* save begining of list *)
temp^.next:=NIL;  temp^.prior:=NIL;

WHILE NOT f.eof DO (* until end-of-file *)
  (* read the records *)
  NEW(temp2);
  ReadNBytes(f,temp2, TSIZE(address), r);
  IF r=TSIZE(address) THEN
    temp^.next:=temp2;   (* link together *)
    temp2^.next:=NIL;
    temp^.prior:=temp;
    temp:=temp2;
  END;
END;
Close(f);
RETURN(begin);  (* return the start of the list *)
END Load;


BEGIN
  start:=NIL;  (* initially empty list *)
  last:=NIL;
  quit:=FALSE;

  REPEAT
    CASE MenuSelect() OF
      '1': Enter;  |
      '2': Remove;  |
      '3': Display(start);  |
      '4': Find;  |
      '5': Save(start);  |
      '6': start:=Load(start);  |
      '7': quit:=TRUE;
    END ;
  UNTIL quit=TRUE;

END Mlist.
```

Binary Trees

The fourth data structure is the *binary tree*. Although there can be many different types of trees, binary trees are special because, when sorted, they lend themselves to rapid searches, insertions, and deletions. Each item in a tree consists of information with a link to the left member and a link to the right member. Figure 3-11 shows a small tree.

The special terminology needed to discuss trees is a classic case of mixed metaphors. The *root* is the first item in the tree. Each data item is called a *node* (sometimes called a *leaf*) of the tree, and any piece of the tree is called a *subtree*. A node that has no subtrees attached to it is called a *terminal node*.

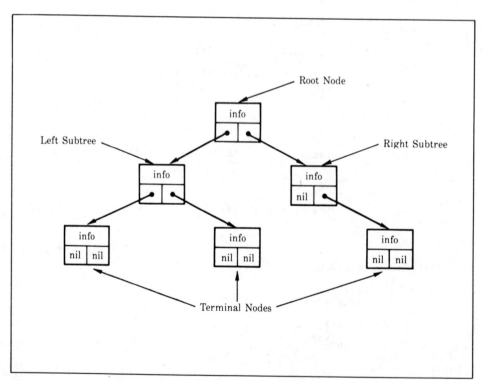

Figure 3-11. A sample binary tree

The *height* of the tree is equal to the number of layers deep that its roots grow. Throughout this discussion, think of binary trees as appearing in memory the way that they do on paper. However, remember that a tree is only a way to structure data in memory, and memory is linear in form.

In a sense, the binary tree is a special form of linked list. You can insert, delete, and access items in any order. The retrieval operation is also nondestructive. Although trees are visually easy to understand, they present some difficult programming problems that this section can only introduce.

Most functions that use trees are recursive because the tree itself is a recursive data structure; that is, each subtree is a tree. Therefore, the routines that are developed here will be recursive as well. However, remember that nonrecursive versions of these functions exist, but their code is much harder to understand.

The order of a tree depends on how the tree is going to be referenced. The process of accessing each node in a tree is called a *tree traversal*. Consider the following tree:

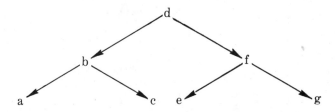

There are three ways to traverse a tree: *inorder*, *preorder*, and *postorder*. Using inorder, you visit the left subtree, then the root, and then the right subtree. With preorder, you visit the root, then the left subtree, and then the right subtree. With postorder, you visit the left subtree, then the right subtree, and then the root. The order of traversing the tree just shown using each method is as follows:

Inorder	a	b	c	d	e	f	g
Preorder	d	b	a	c	f	e	g
Postorder	a	c	b	e	g	f	d

Although a tree does not need to be sorted, most uses require it. What constitutes a sorted tree depends on how you will be traversing the tree. The rest of this chapter will access the tree inorder. Therefore, a sorted binary tree is one in which the subtree on the left contains nodes that are less than or equal to the root, while the subtree on the right contains nodes that are greater than the root. The following function, **STree**, will build a sorted binary tree. The function uses character data to keep the code simple, but you could use any data type.

```
TYPE
  TreePointer = POINTER TO tree;
  tree = RECORD
      data: CHAR;
      left: TreePointer;
      right: TreePointer;
  END;
VAR
  root,dummy: TreePointer;

PROCEDURE STree(root,r:TreePointer;data:CHAR):TreePointer;
BEGIN
  IF r=NIL THEN
    NEW(r);   (* get a new node *)
    r^.left:=NIL;
    r^.right:=NIL;
    r^.data:=data;
    IF root<>NIL THEN
      IF data<root^.data THEN root^.left:=r
      ELSE root^.right:=r;
      END;
    END;
    RETURN r;
  ELSIF data<r^.data THEN RETURN STree(r,r^.left,data)
  ELSE RETURN STree(r,r^.right,data);
  END;
END STree;
```

This algorithm simply follows the links through the tree, going left or right based on the **data** field. To use this function, you will need a global variable that holds the root of the tree. This global variable initially must be set to **NIL**, and a pointer to the root will be assigned on the first call to **STree**. Subsequent calls will not need to reassign the root so the function uses the variable **dummy**. If you assume that the name of this global was **rt**, then to call the **STree** function, you would use

```
(* call STree  *)
IF root=NIL THEN root:=STree(root,root,ch)
ELSE dummy:=STree(root,root,ch);
END;
```

Using this call allows you to insert both the first and subsequent elements correctly.

STree is a recursive algorithm, as are most tree routines. The same routine would be several times longer if you used straight iterative methods. You must call the function with a pointer to the root and a pointer to the subtree, and with the information that must be stored.

To traverse the tree that was built by using **STree** inorder and to print the **data** field of each node, you could use the function **inorder**, shown here:

```
PROCEDURE InOrder(root:TreePointer);
BEGIN
  IF root<>NIL THEN
    InOrder(root^.left);
    Write(root^.data);
    InOrder(root^.right);
  END;
END InOrder;
```

This recursive function returns when it encounters a terminal node (a **NIL** pointer). The functions to traverse the tree in preorder and in postorder are shown here:

```
PROCEDURE PreOrder(root:TreePointer);
BEGIN
  IF root<>NIL THEN
    Write(root^.data);
    PreOrder(root^.left);
    PreOrder(root^.right);
  END;
END PreOrder;

PROCEDURE PostOrder(root:TreePointer);
BEGIN
  IF root<>NIL THEN
    PostOrder(root^.left);
    PostOrder(root^.right);
    Write(root^.data);
  END;
END PostOrder;
```

You can write a short but interesting program that will build a sorted binary tree and print that tree sideways on the screen of your computer. We need only a small modification to the **inorder** procedure. Here is the new function called **PrintTree**, which prints a tree in inorder fashion. To use it, simply enter some letters of alphabet. After you type **Q**, the program will display the tree.

```
MODULE PrintTree;

FROM Storage IMPORT ALLOCATE, DEALLOCATE;

FROM InOut IMPORT Read, Write, WriteLn, WriteString;

TYPE
  TreePointer = POINTER TO tree;
  tree = RECORD
      data: CHAR;
      left: TreePointer;
      right: TreePointer;
  END;

VAR
  root,dummy: TreePointer;
  ch: CHAR;

PROCEDURE STree(root,r:TreePointer;data:CHAR):TreePointer;
BEGIN
  IF r=NIL THEN
    NEW(r);  (* get a new node *)
    r^.left:=NIL;
    r^.right:=NIL;
    r^.data:=data;
    IF root<>NIL THEN
      IF data<root^.data THEN root^.left:=r
      ELSE root^.right:=r;
      END;
    END;
    RETURN r;
  ELSIF data<r^.data THEN RETURN STree(r,r^.left,data)
  ELSE RETURN STree(r,r^.right,data);
  END;
END STree;

PROCEDURE PrintTree(r:TreePointer;n:INTEGER);
VAR
  i:INTEGER;

BEGIN
  IF r<>NIL THEN
    PrintTree(r^.left,n+1);
    FOR i:=1 TO n DO WriteString('   '); END;
    Write(r^.data); WriteLn;
    PrintTree(r^.right,n+1);
  END;
END PrintTree;

BEGIN
  root:=NIL;
  REPEAT
```

```
    WriteString('enter a letter (Q to quit): ');
    Read(ch); Write(ch); WriteLn;
    IF root=NIL THEN root:=STree(root,root,ch)
    ELSE dummy:=STree(root,root,ch);
    END;
    ch:=CAP(ch);
  UNTIL ch='Q';

  PrintTree(root,0);

END PrintTree.
```

The **STree** procedure actually sorts the information that you give it. This process is essentially a variation on the Insertion sort that Chapter 2 presented. For the average case, its performance can be quite good, but the QuickSort is still a better general-purpose sorting method because it uses less memory and has less processing overhead. However, if you have to build a tree from scratch or if you have to maintain an already sorted tree, then you should always insert new entries in sorted order by using the **STree** routine.

If you have run the **PrintTree** program, you have probably noticed that some trees are *balanced*—each subtree is the same or nearly the same height as any other—and that other trees are far out of balance. In fact, if you entered the tree "abcd," it would have been built to look like this:

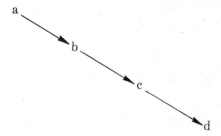

There would be no left subtrees. This tree is called a *degenerate tree* because it has degenerated into a linear list. In general, if the data that you use to build a binary tree is fairly random, the tree produced will approximate a balanced tree. However, if the information is already sorted, a degenerate tree will result. (You can readjust the tree with each insertion to keep the tree in balance. The algorithms to do this are fairly complex, and you should refer to books on advanced tree-handling algorithms.)

Search procedures are easy to implement for binary trees. This function returns a pointer to the node in the tree that matches the key; otherwise, it will return **NIL**:

```
PROCEDURE Search(root:TreePointer;
                 key:CHAR):TreePointer;
BEGIN
  IF root<>NIL THEN
    WHILE (root^.data<>key) AND (root<>NIL) DO
      IF key < root^.data THEN root:=root^.left
      ELSE root:=root^.right;
      END;
    END;
  END;
  RETURN root;
END Search;
```

Unfortunately, deleting a node from a tree is not as simple as searching the tree. The deleted node may be either the root, a left node, or a right node. Also, the node may have from zero to two subtrees attached to it. Rearranging the pointers lends itself to the recursive algorithm shown here:

```
PROCEDURE DTree(root:TreePointer; key:CHAR):TreePointer;
(* Delete a node from a tree *)
VAR
  temp,temp2:TreePointer;

BEGIN
  IF root^.data=key THEN
    (*delete root*)
    IF root^.left=root^.right THEN
      (*empty tree*)
      DISPOSE(root);
      RETURN NIL;
    ELSIF root^.left=NIL THEN
      temp:=root^.right;
      DISPOSE(root);
      RETURN temp;
    ELSIF root^.right=NIL THEN
      temp:=root^.left;
      DISPOSE(root);
      RETURN temp;
    ELSE   (*both leaves present*)
      temp2:=root^.right;
      temp:=root^.right;
      WHILE temp^.left<>NIL DO
        temp:=temp^.left;
      END;
      temp^.left:=root^.left;
      DISPOSE(root);
      RETURN temp2;
    END;
```

```
   ELSE
      IF root^.data<key THEN root^.right:=DTree(root^.right,key)
      ELSE root^.left:=DTree(root^.left,key);
      END;
      RETURN root;
   END;

   END DTree;
```

DTree returns a pointer to the root. The calling routine must save this pointer because the deleted node could be the root of the tree, which means that a new root will have been formed.

When used with database management programs, binary trees offer tremendous power, flexibility, and efficiency because the information for these databases must reside on disk and access times are important. Since a balanced binary tree has, as a worst case, $\log_2 n$ comparisons in searching, it is far better than a linked list, which must rely on a sequential search.

Dynamic Allocation
CHAPTER 4

Designing a computer program can be similar to designing a building that has numerous functional and aesthetic considerations that contribute to the final outcome. For example, some programs are functionally rigid like a house, in which there are a certain number of bedrooms, a kitchen, two baths, and so on. Other programs must be open-ended like convention centers, with movable walls and modular flooring—which enable them to adapt to various needs and sizes. In this chapter, you will study the storage mechanisms that allow you to write flexible programs that you can adapt to the needs and capabilities of the user and the computer.

There are two primary ways in which a Modula-2 program can store information in the main memory of the computer. The first way uses *global* and *local* variables—including arrays and records—that the Modula-2 language defines. With global variables, the storage is fixed throughout the run time of your program. With local variables, storage is allocated from the stack space of the computer. Although these variables are efficiently implemented in Modula-2, they require that the programmer know in advance the amount of storage that every situtation needs.

The second way that you can store information is by using Modula-2's dynamic allocation functions **NEW** and **DISPOSE**. In this approach, storage for information is allocated from the free memory area that lies between your program with its permanent storage area and the stack. This area is called the *heap*.

Figure 4-1 shows how a Modula-2 program would appear in memory. The stack grows downward as it is used; how your program is designed determines the amount of memory that it needs. For example, a program with many recursive functions makes greater demands on stack memory than a program that does not have recursive functions. The reason for this is that each recursive call allocates stack memory. The memory that the program and global data require is fixed during the execution of the program.

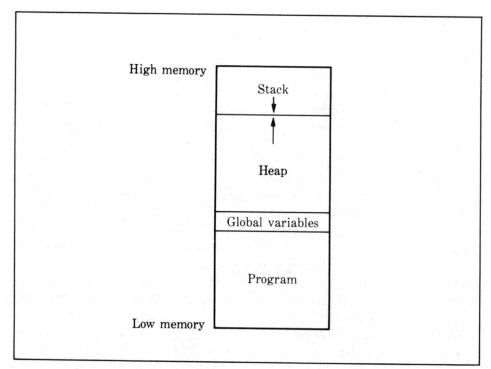

Figure 4-1. A Modula-2 program's memory usage

Memory to satisfy a **NEW** request is taken from the free memory area, starting just above the global variables and growing towards the stack. In fairly extreme cases, it is possible for the stack to run into the heap, which creates a run-time error or a system crash.

Before you examine dynamic allocation in detail, a short review of **NEW** and **DISPOSE** is in order.

ALLOCATE and DEALLOCATE

Although both **NEW** and **DISPOSE** are standard identifiers that are built into the Modula-2 language, they depend upon the two library procedures, **ALLOCATE** and **DEALLOCATE**, which you can find in the module **Storage**. Therefore, you must include the following import line with each program that uses dynamic allocation:

```
FROM Storage IMPORT ALLOCATE, DEALLOCATE;
```

NEW

Using **NEW** allocates memory from the heap. This built-in procedure accepts a pointer argument and allocates enough memory from the heap to hold the type of variable that the pointer is declared as pointing to. After the call, the pointer argument will contain the address of the allocated memory. For example, to allocate room for a **REAL**, you could use the code shown here:

```
FROM Storage IMPORT ALLOCATE, DEALLOCATE;

TYPE
    rpntr = POINTER TO REAL;

VAR
    p:rpntr;

BEGIN
    NEW(p);
  .
  .
  .
```

If there is no free memory left on the heap, a run-time error will occur, which indicates a *heap/stack collision*. To avoid this run-time error, you should precede all calls to **NEW** with a call to **AVAILABLE**, which is also found in **Storage**. **AVAILABLE** is defined as

AVAILABLE(*NumBytes*: CARDINAL): BOOLEAN;

To see if there is sufficient room left on the heap to allocate the number of bytes that you need, you call **AVAILABLE** with that number of bytes and **AVAILABLE** will return **TRUE** or **FALSE**. Therefore, if written more properly, the preceding allocation example becomes

```
FROM Storage IMPORT ALLOCATE, DEALLOCATE,
        AVAILABLE;
FROM SYSTEM IMPORT TSIZE;

TYPE
    rpntr = POINTER TO REAL;

VAR
  p:rpntr;

BEGIN
  IF AVAILABLE(TSIZE(REAL)) THEN
    NEW(p);
  END;
 .
 .
 .
```

Notice that **TSIZE** was imported from **SYSTEM** to determine the size of a **REAL**. Although you might know the number of actual bytes that are needed for a **REAL** for the specific compiler that you are using, generally you should use **TSIZE** because it adds to the portability of your code.

The examples in this chapter do not check for heap/stack collisions, but you may need to in your applications.

DISPOSE

Generally, applications that use dynamic memory allocation do so, in part, so that memory can be reused. One way to return memory to the heap is to use **DISPOSE**. You call **DISPOSE** by using a pointer that you previously used in a call to **NEW** — it contains a pointer to a validly allocated region of memory from the heap. After a call to **DISPOSE**, the memory that had been allocated to that pointer will be freed and available for allocation. For example, the short program shown here will allocate a pointer to a 40-element array of integers and return them to the system before termination.

```
MODULE Sample;  (* Example of New and Dispose working
                   together *)

  FROM InOut IMPORT Write, WriteLn, WriteInt;
  FROM Storage IMPORT ALLOCATE, DEALLOCATE;

TYPE
  pntr = POINTER TO RecType;
  RecType = ARRAY[1..40] OF INTEGER;

VAR
  p:pntr;
  t:INTEGER;

BEGIN
  NEW(p);
  FOR t:=1 TO 40 DO p^[t]:=t*2; END;
  FOR t:=1 TO 40 DO
    WriteInt(p^[t],3);
    Write(' ');
  END;
  WriteLn;
  DISPOSE(p);
END Sample.
```

You should never attempt to **DISPOSE** a pointer that has never been allocated. If you do, you will most likely crash your program. Also, never attempt to **DISPOSE** of a **NIL** pointer, because it will generally cause a system crash.

Sparse-Array Processing

One of the two major uses of dynamic allocation is for *sparse-array processing*. In a sparse array, not all of the elements are actually present. You may want or need to create an array like this if the array dimensions that you need are larger than will fit in the memory of the machine, and if you will not be using all array locations. Arrays — especially multidimensional arrays — can consume vast quantities of memory because their storage needs are exponentially related to their size. For example, a character array of 10×10 needs only 100 bytes of memory, a 100×100 character array needs 10,000, but a 1000×1000 character array needs 1,000,000 bytes of memory—which is clearly too big for most microcomputers!

A spreadsheet program is a good example of a sparse array. Even though the matrix is large—say 999×999—only a portion of it may actually be in use at any one time. Spreadsheets use the matrix to hold formulas, values, and strings that are associated with each location. In a sparse array, storage for each element generally is allocated from the pool of free memory as needed. Although only a small portion of the elements is actually in use, the array may appear to be large—larger than would normally fit in the memory of the computer.

There are three distinct techniques for creating a sparse array: the linked list, the binary tree, and a pointer array. All of these examples assume that the spreadsheet matrix is organized like this:

```
     ----A----   ----B----   ----C----   ----D----   . . .
1
2                    X
3
4
5
6
7
.
.
.
```

In this example, the X is located in cell B2.

The Linked-List Approach to Sparse Arrays

When you implement a sparse array by using a linked list, a **RECORD** holds the information, including its logical position in the array, and links to the previous element and the next element. Each **RECORD** is placed in the list with the elements inserted in sorted order, which is based on the array index. The array is accessed by following the links.

For example, you could use the following **RECORD** to create a sparse array to use in a spreadsheet program:

```
TYPE
  str128 = ARRAY[0..128] OF CHAR;
  str9 = ARRAY[0..9] OF CHAR;

  CellPointer = POINTER TO cell;

  cell = RECORD
      CellName: str9;       (* holds name of cell *)
      formula: str128;      (* information *)
      next: CellPointer;    (* pointer to next RECORD *)
      prior: CellPointer;   (* pointer to previous RECORD*)
  END;
```

Here, the field **CellName** holds a string that contains the cell name, such as A1, B34, or Z19. The **formula** string holds the formula that is assigned to each spreadsheet location. While an entire spreadsheet program would be too large to use as an example, here are a few sample functions that the spreadsheet that used a linked-list sparse array would utilize. (Remember that there are many ways to implement a spreadsheet program, and the data structure and routines that are used here serve only as examples of sparse-array techniques.) The following global variables point to the beginning and the end of the linked array list:

```
VAR
    start,last:CellPointer;
```

In most spreadsheets, when you enter a formula into a cell, in effect you are creating a new element in the sparse array. If the spreadsheet uses a linked list, then that new cell would be inserted by using the function **DLSortStore**, which was developed in Chapter 3. (Because of Modula-2's ability to create stand-alone, reusable functions, you can utilize it with virtually no changes.) Here, the list is sorted by using the cell name—A12 precedes A13, and so on:

```
PROCEDURE DLSortStore(info,start:CellPointer;
              VAR last:CellPointer):CellPointer;
(* store entries in sorted order *)

VAR
  old, top: CellPointer;
```

```
BEGIN
  top:=start;
  old:=NIL;

  IF start=NIL THEN
  (* first element in list *)
    info^.next:=NIL;
    last:=info;
    info^.prior:=NIL;
    RETURN(info);
  ELSE
    WHILE start<>NIL DO
      IF CompareStr(start^.CellName,info^.CellName)=-1 THEN
        old:=start;
        start:=start^.next;
      ELSE
      (* goes in middle *)
        IF old<>NIL THEN
          old^.next:=info;
          info^.next:=start;
          start^.prior:=info;
          info^.prior:=old;
          RETURN top;  (* keep same starting point *)
        ELSE
          info^.next:=start;  (* new first element *)
          info^.prior:=NIL;
          RETURN info;
        END;
      END;
    END;  (*WHILE*)

    last^.next:=info;  (* goes on END *)
    info^.next:=NIL;
    info^.prior:=last;
    last:=info;
    RETURN top;
  END;
END DLSortStore;
```

To remove a cell from the spreadsheet, you remove the proper **RECORD** from the list and return the memory to the system by using **DISPOSE**. The **DLDelete** function shown here will remove a cell from the list when given the cell name:

```
PROCEDURE DLDelete(start:CellPointer;
                   key:ARRAY OF CHAR):CellPointer;
VAR
  temp,temp2:CellPointer;
  done:BOOLEAN;
BEGIN
  IF CompareStr(start^.CellName,key)=0 THEN
    (* is first in list *)
    IF temp^.next <> NIL THEN
      temp:=start^.next;
      temp^.prior:=NIL;
    END;
```

```
        DISPOSE(start);
        RETURN temp;
      ELSE
        done:=FALSE;
        temp:=start^.next;
        temp2:=start;
        WHILE temp<>NIL DO
          IF CompareStr(temp^.CellName,key)=0 THEN
            temp2^.next:=temp^.next;
            IF temp^.next<>NIL THEN
                temp^.next^.prior:=temp2;
            END;
            done:=TRUE;
            DISPOSE(temp);
          ELSE
            temp2:=temp;
            temp:=temp^.next;
          END;
        END;
        IF NOT done THEN
          WriteString('not found');
          WriteLn;
        END;
        RETURN start;   (* still same starting point *)
      END;
    END DLDelete;
```

Find locates any specific cell. It is important because many spreadsheet formulas have references to other cells; you have to find them to update their values. Hence, the performance of **Find** is critical to the performance of the spreadsheet in general. **Find** requires the use of a linear search to locate each item and, as you saw in Chapter 3, the average number of comparisons in a linear search is $n/2$, where n is the number of elements in the list. A significant loss of performance can occur if a cell's formula contains references to other cells and you must search for the other cells. Here is an example of **Find**:

```
PROCEDURE Find(cell:CellPointer):CellPointer;
VAR
  c:CellPointer;
BEGIN
  c:=start;
  WHILE c<>NIL DO
    IF CompareStr(c^.CellName,cell^.CellName)=0 THEN RETURN c;
    ELSE c:=c^.next; END;
  END;
  WriteString('cell NOT found');
  RETURN NIL;
END Find;
```

The linked-list approach to creating, maintaining, and processing a sparse array has one major drawback—it must use a linear search to access each cell in the list. Without using additional information, which requires more memory overhead, you cannot perform a binary search to locate a cell. Even the store routine uses a linear search to find the proper location in order to insert a new cell into the list. You can solve these problems by using a binary tree to support the sparse array.

The Binary Tree Approach to Sparse Arrays

As discussed in Chapter 3, the binary tree is simply a modified doubly linked list. Its major advantage over a linked list is that it can be searched quickly so that insertions and lookups can be very fast. In applications in which you want a linked-list **RECORD** but need rapid search times, the binary tree is perfect.

To use a binary tree to support the spreadsheet example, you must change the **RECORD** cell, as shown here:

```
str128 = ARRAY[C..128] OF CHAR;
str9 = ARRAY[0..9] OF CHAR;

CellPointer = POINTER TO tree;
tree = RECORD
    CellName: str9;  (* name of cell *)
    formula: str128;  (* information *)
    left: CellPointer; (* pointer to left subtree *)
    right: CellPointer; (* pointer to right subtree *)
END;
```

You can modify the **STree** function from Chapter 3 so that it builds a tree that is based on the cell name. Notice that it assumes that the parameter **NewCell** is a pointer to a new entry in the tree.

```
PROCEDURE STree(root,r:CellPointer;NewCell:str9):CellPointer;
BEGIN
  IF r=NIL THEN
    NEW(r);  (* get a new node *)
    r^.left:=NIL;
    r^.right:=NIL;
    r^.CellName:=NewCell;
    IF root<>NIL THEN
      IF CompareStr(NewCell,root^.CellName)<0 THEN root^.left:=r
      ELSE root^.right:=r;
      END;
```

```
      END;
      RETURN r;
    ELSIF CompareStr(NewCell,r^.CellName)<0 THEN
      RETURN STree(r,r^.left,NewCell)
    ELSE RETURN STree(r,r^.right,NewCell);
    END;
  END STree;
```

You must call **STree** with a pointer to the root node for the first two parameters and a pointer to the new cell for the third parameter. **STree** will return a pointer to the root.

To delete a cell from the spreadsheet, you must modify the **DTree** function as shown here to accept the name of the cell as a key:

```
PROCEDURE DTree(root:CellPointer; key:str9):CellPointer;
(* Delete a node from a tree *)
VAR
   temp,temp2:CellPointer;

BEGIN
  IF CompareStr(root^.CellName,key)=0 THEN
    (*delete root*)
    IF root^.left=root^.right THEN
      (*empty tree*)
      DISPOSE(root);
      RETURN NIL;
    ELSIF root^.left=NIL THEN
      temp:=root^.right;
      DISPOSE(root);
      RETURN temp;
    ELSIF root^.right=NIL THEN
      temp:=root^.left;
      DISPOSE(root);
      RETURN temp;
    ELSE    (*both leaves present*)
      temp2:=root^.right;
      temp:=root^.right;
      WHILE temp^.left<>NIL DO
        temp:=temp^.left;
      END;
      temp^.left:=root^.left;
      DISPOSE(root);
      RETURN temp2;
    END;
  ELSE
    IF CompareStr(root^.CellName,key)<0 THEN
      root^.right:=DTree(root^.right,key)
    ELSE root^.left:=DTree(root^.left,key);
    END;
    RETURN root;
  END;

END DTree;
```

Finally, you can use a modified **Search** function to locate any cell in the spreadsheet quickly when given its cell name:

```
PROCEDURE Search(root:CellPointer;key:str9):CellPointer;
BEGIN
   IF root<>NIL THEN
      WHILE (CompareStr(root^.CellName,key)<>0) AND (root<>NIL) DO
        IF CompareStr(key,root^.CellName)<0 THEN root:=root^.left
        ELSE root:=root^.right;
        END;
      END;
   END;
   RETURN root;
END Search;
```

The most important aspect of using a binary tree over a linked list is that a binary tree produces much faster search times. Remember that a sequential search requires an average of $n/2$ comparisions, where n is the number of elements in the list; a binary search requires only $\log_2 n$ comparisons.

The Pointer-Array Approach to Sparse Arrays

Suppose that your spreadsheet's dimensions were 26×100 (A1 through Z100), a total of 2,600 elements. In theory, then you could use the following array of **RECORD**s to hold the spreadsheet entries:

```
        str9 = ARRAY[0..9] OF CHAR;
        str128 = ARRAY[0..127] OF CHAR;

        cell = RECORD
              CellName:str9;
              formula:str128;
        end;
  var
        sheet:ARRAY[1..2600] OF cell;
```

However, 2,600 cells multiplied by 128 (the **formula** field alone) requires 332,800 bytes of memory. This approach is obviously not practical. However, you can create an array of pointers to **RECORD**s. This method requires significantly less permanent storage, and yet offers superior performance over the linked-list and binary tree methods. The declaration for this array is shown here:

```
TYPE
    str128 = ARRAY[0..128] OF CHAR;
    str9 = ARRAY[0..9] OF CHAR;

    CellPointer = POINTER TO cell;
    cell = RECORD
        CellName:str9;
        formula:str128;
    END;

VAR
    sheet:ARRAY[1..2600] OF CellPointer;
```

You can use this smaller array to hold pointers to the information that the spreadsheet user actually enters. As each entry is made, a pointer to the information about the cell is stored in the proper location in the array. Figure 4-2 shows how this process might appear in memory, with the pointer array providing support for the sparse array.

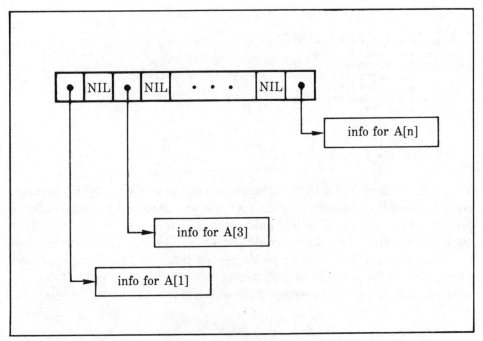

Figure 4-2. A pointer array as support for a sparse array

Before you can use the pointer array, you must first initialize each element to **NIL**, which indicates that there is no entry in that location. The procedure to do this is shown here:

```
PROCEDURE InitSheet;
VAR
   t:INTEGER;
BEGIN
   FOR t:=1 TO 2600 DO sheet[t]:=NIL; END;
END InitSheet;
```

Before you can write the **Store** procedure, you need a function called **FindIndex**. **FindIndex** will return the proper pointer-array index when given the cell name. When computing the index, **FindIndex** assumes that all cell names start with a capital letter and are followed by an integer—B34, C19, and so on. **FindIndex** is shown here:

```
PROCEDURE FindIndex(i:CellPointer):INTEGER;
VAR
   loc,temp:INTEGER;
   code:BOOLEAN;
   t:str9;
BEGIN
   loc:=ORD(i^.CellName[0]); (* get letter *)
   loc:=loc-ORD('A')+1;
   Copy(i^.CellName,1,8,t);
   StringToInt(t,temp,code);  (* get number part *)
   IF code<>TRUE THEN
     WriteString("error");
     RETURN -1;
   END;
   loc:=loc*26+temp;
   RETURN loc;
END FindIndex;
```

You need this function so that the **Store** procedure will know which pointer-array location to use for each cell. As you can see, finding the proper index is easy and fast because it is a simple computation—no search or lookup is needed. This type of scheme is sometimes referred to as a *direct hash* because the name of item to be stored produces the index of the storage location directly. When the user of the spreadsheet enters a formula for a cell, the cell location (defined by its name) produces an index for the pointer array **sheet**.

The index is derived from the cell name by converting the name into a number with **FindIndex**, and is stored by using **Store**, as shown here:

```
PROCEDURE Store(New:CellPointer);
VAR
  loc:INTEGER;

BEGIN
  loc:=FindIndex(New);
  IF loc>2600 THEN WriteString('location out of bounds')
  ELSE sheet[loc]:=New;
  END;
END Store;
```

Because each cell name is unique, each index is also unique; because the ASCII collating sequence is used, the pointer to each entry is stored into the proper array element. If you compare this procedure to the linked-list version, you will see how much shorter and simpler it is.

The **Delete** function also becomes short. When called with the index of the cell to remove, **Delete** simply places a **NIL** pointer in the proper location and returns the deallocated memory to the system.

```
PROCEDURE Delete(cell:CellPointer);
VAR
  loc:INTEGER;
BEGIN
  loc:=FindIndex(cell);

  IF (loc>2600) OR (loc=-1) THEN WriteString('Cell out of bounds')
  ELSE
    DISPOSE(cell);
    sheet[loc]:=NIL;
  END;
END Delete;
```

Again, when you compare this to the linked-list or binary tree version, this code is much faster and simpler.

Remember that the pointer array itself uses some memory for every location—whether an element points to information or not. This can be a serious limitation for some situations.

Deciding on an Approach to Sparse Arrays

When deciding whether to use a linked-list approach, a binary tree approach, or a pointer-array approach to implement a sparse array, you should consider memory efficiency and speed.

When the array is very sparse, the most memory-efficient approaches are the linked-list and binary tree implementations because only array elements that are actually in use have memory allocated to them. The links themselves require little additional memory and generally have a negligible effect. The pointer-array approach requires a permanently allocated array. This means that each array element exists whether it points to its associated information or is **NIL**; not only must the entire pointer array fit in memory, but enough memory must be left over for the application to use. This could be a serious problem for certain applications, whereas it may not be a problem for others. You can usually decide this issue by calculating the approximate amount of free memory and determining whether that amount is sufficient for your program.

However, when the array is fairly full, the pointer-array approach makes better use of memory. Both the linked-list and binary tree implementations need two pointers, whereas the pointer-array implementation only has one pointer. For example, if a 1000-element array is full, and if pointers are 2 bytes long, then both the linked-list and binary tree approaches would use 4000 bytes for pointers—but the pointer-array approach would only need 2000 bytes, a savings of 2000 bytes.

The fastest executing approach is the pointer array. Often, as in the spreadsheet example, an easy method exists to index the pointer array and link it with the sparse-array elements. This makes accessing the elements of the sparse array nearly as fast as accessing the elements of a normal array. The linked-list version is very slow by comparison because it must use a linear search to locate each element. Even if you added extra information to the linked list to allow faster accessing of elements, the linked list would still be slower than the pointer-array approach's direct accessing capability. The binary tree method certainly speeds up the search time, but when you compare it with the pointer-array's direct indexing capability, it still seems sluggish.

Whenever possible, it is best to use a pointer-array implementation because it is much faster. But if memory usage is critical or if you cannot compute an easy direct hash, then you have no choice but to use the linked-list or binary tree approach.

Reusable Buffers

When memory is scarce, you can use dynamic allocation in place of normal variables. For example, imagine that two procedures, **A** and **B**, exist inside one program. Assume that **A** requires 60% of free memory while executing, and that **B** needs 55% of free memory while executing. If both **A** and **B** derive their storage needs from local variables, then **A** cannot call **B** and **B** cannot call **A** because more than 100% of memory would be required. If **A** never calls **B**, then there is no trouble—until you want **A** to be able to call **B**. The only way that you can do this is for both **A** and **B** to use dynamic storage and to free that allocated memory before one procedure calls the other. In other words, if both **A** and **B** require more than one half of available free memory while executing, and if **A** must call **B**, then they must use dynamic allocation. In this way, both **A** and **B** will have the memory that they need when they need it.

For example, imagine that there are 100,000 bytes of free memory left in a computer that runs a program with the following two functions in it:

```
PROCEDURE A;
VAR
     a: ARRAY[1..60000] OF CHAR;
                 .
BEGIN
              .
              .
           B;
              .
              .
              .
END;


PROCEDURE B;
VAR
      b:ARRAY[1..55000] OF CHAR;
BEGIN
              .
              .
              .
END;
```

Here, both **A** and **B** have local variables that require more than one half of free memory. In this case, **B** cannot execute because there is not enough memory available to allocate the 55,000 bytes that the local array **b** needs.

Often, a situation like this is insurmountable but, in certain instances, you can work around it. If **A** did not need to preserve the contents of the array **A** while **B** was executing, then **A** and **B** could share the same memory. The way to do this is to allocate **A** and **B**'s array dynamically. Then **A** could free the memory before the call to **B** and reallocate it later. The code to do this would look like this:

```
PROCEDURE A;
VAR
        a: POINTER TO ARRAY[1..60000] OF CHAR;
BEGIN
        NEW(a);
        .
        .
        .
        DISPOSE(a); (*Release memory for B*)
        B;
        NEW(a);    (*get it back*)
        .
        .
        DISPOSE(a);
END;


PROCEDURE B;
VAR
    b:POINTER TO ARRAY[1..55000] OF CHAR;
BEGIN
        NEW(b);
        .
        .
        DISPOSE(b);
END;
```

Only the pointer **A** exists while **B** is executing. Although there are few times when you will need to use this technique, you should master it anyway because it is often the only way around this type of problem.

The "Unknown Memory" Dilemma

If you are a professional programmer, you almost certainly have faced the "unknown memory" dilemma. This problem occurs when you write a program that has some of its performance based on the amount of memory inside any and all computers that can run it. Examples of programs that exhibit this problem are spreadsheets, in-RAM mailing-list programs, and sorts. For example, an in-memory sort that can handle 10,000 addresses in a 256K machine may only be able to sort 5000 addresses in a 128K computer. If you are going to use this program on computers of unknown memory sizes, then you could not use a fixed-size array to hold the sort information: either the program would not work on machines with small memory capacity because the array would not fit, or you would have to create an array for the worst case and not allow users with more memory to use it. The solution is to use dynamic allocation to hold the information.

A text editor can illustrate the memory dilemma problem and its solution well. Many text editors do not have a fixed number of characters that they can hold, but rather use all available memory to store the text that you type in. As each line is entered, storage is allocated and a linked list is maintained. When a line is deleted, memory is returned to the system. One way to implement such a text editor would be to use the following **RECORD** for each line:

```
TYPE
   str80 = ARRAY[0..79] OF CHAR;
   LinePointer = POINTER TO line;
   line = RECORD
           text: str80;    (* holds each line *)
           num: INTEGER;   (* number of each line *)
           next: LinePointer;   (* pointer to next RECORD *)
           prior: LinePointer;  (* pointer to previous RECORD*)
   END;
   DataItem = line;
```

For simplicity, the **RECORD** always allocates enough memory for each line to be 80 characters long. In reality, only the exact length of the line would be allocated and additional overhead would be incurred when you change the line. The element **num** holds the line number for each line of text. This allows you to use the standard sorted doubly linked-list-storage function **DLSortStore** to create and maintain the text file as a linked list.

The entire program for a simple text editor is presented next. It supports only the insertion of lines (at any point based on the line number that you specify) and the deletion of any line. You may also list the text and store it in a disk file.

The general method of operation for the editor is based on a sorted linked list that consists of lines of text. The sort key is the line number of each line. With this method, not only can you insert text easily at any point by specifying the starting line number, but you can also make deletions easily. The only function that may not be intuitive is **patchup**. It will renumber the element **num** for each line of text as needed when insertions or deletions cause a change in the line number.

In this example, the amount of text that the editor can hold is based directly on the amount of free memory in the user's system. The editor automatically uses additional memory without having to be reprogrammed. This is probably the most important reason to use dynamic allocation when you are faced with the unknown memory dilemma.

As shown, the program is very limited, but the basic text editing support is solid. You may enhance it to create a customized text editor.

```
MODULE TextEd;

FROM InOut IMPORT WriteString, WriteLn, Read, ReadInt,
        EOL, Write, WriteInt, ReadString;
FROM FileSystem IMPORT File, Response, Lookup, SetWrite,
        Close, ReadNBytes, WriteNBytes, WriteChar,
        SetRead;
FROM SYSTEM IMPORT ADR, TSIZE;
FROM Strings IMPORT Length, CompareStr;
FROM Storage IMPORT ALLOCATE, DEALLOCATE;

TYPE
  str80 = ARRAY[0..79] OF CHAR;
  LinePointer = POINTER TO line;
  line = RECORD
        text: str80;    (* holds each line *)
        num: INTEGER;    (* number of each line *)
        next: LinePointer;   (* pointer to next RECORD *)
        prior: LinePointer;  (* pointer to previous RECORD*)
  END;
  DataItem = line;
```

```
VAR
  start,last:LinePointer;
  alldone: BOOLEAN;

PROCEDURE MenuSelect():CHAR;  (* returns the user's selection *)
VAR
  ch:CHAR;

BEGIN
  WriteString('1. Enter text'); WriteLn;
  WriteString('2. Delete a line'); WriteLn;
  WriteString('3. Display the file'); WriteLn;
  WriteString('4. Save the file'); WriteLn;
  WriteString('5. Load the file'); WriteLn;
  WriteString('6. Quit'); WriteLn;
  REPEAT
    WriteLn;
    WriteString('Enter your choice: ');
    Read(ch);  ch:=CAP(ch); WriteLn;
  UNTIL (ch>='1') AND (ch<='6');
  RETURN ch;
END MenuSelect;

PROCEDURE Find(lnum:INTEGER):LinePointer;
VAR
  i:LinePointer;
BEGIN
  i:=start;
  WHILE(i<>NIL) DO
    IF lnum=i^.num THEN RETURN i; END;
    i:=i^.next;
  END;
  RETURN NIL;
END Find;

PROCEDURE PatchUp(lnum,incr:INTEGER);
VAR
  i:LinePointer;

BEGIN
  i:=Find(lnum);
  WHILE(i<>NIL) DO
    i^.num:=i^.num+incr;
    i:=i^.next
  END;
END PatchUp;


PROCEDURE DLSortStore(info,start:LinePointer;
             VAR last:LinePointer):LinePointer;
(* store entries in sorted order *)

VAR
  old, top: LinePointer;
BEGIN
  top:=start;
  old:=NIL;

  IF start=NIL THEN
```

```
      (* first element in list *)
      info^.next:=NIL;
      last:=info;
      info^.prior:=NIL;
      RETURN(info);
   ELSE
      WHILE start<>NIL DO
        IF start^.num<info^.num THEN
          old:=start;
          start:=start^.next;
        ELSE
        (* goes in middle *)
          IF old<>NIL THEN
            old^.next:=info;
            info^.next:=start;
            start^.prior:=info;
            info^.prior:=old;
            RETURN top;  (* keep same starting point *)
          ELSE
            info^.next:=start;  (* new first element *)
            info^.prior:=NIL;
            RETURN info;
          END;
        END;
      END;  (*WHILE*)

      last^.next:=info;  (* goes on END *)
      info^.next:=NIL;
      info^.prior:=last;
      last:=info;
      RETURN top;
END;
END DLSortStore;

PROCEDURE DLDelete(start:LinePointer;
            key:INTEGER):LinePointer;
VAR
   temp,temp2:LinePointer;
   done:BOOLEAN;
BEGIN
   IF start^.num=key THEN
      (* is first in list *)
      IF temp^.next <> NIL THEN
        temp:=start^.next;
        temp^.prior:=NIL;
      END;
      DISPOSE(start);
      RETURN temp;
   ELSE
      done:=FALSE;
      temp:=start^.next;
      temp2:=start;
      WHILE temp<>NIL DO
        IF temp^.num=key THEN
          temp2^.next:=temp^.next;
          IF temp^.next<>NIL THEN
            temp^.next^.prior:=temp2;
          END;
          done:=TRUE;
          DISPOSE(temp);
```

```
      ELSE
        temp2:=temp;
        temp:=temp^.next;
      END;
    END;
    IF NOT done THEN
      WriteString('not found');
      WriteLn;
    END;
    RETURN start;   (* still same starting point *)
  END;
END DLDelete;

PROCEDURE Remove;
VAR
  num:INTEGER;
BEGIN
  WriteString('Enter line to delete: ');
  ReadInt(num); WriteLn;
  start:=DLDelete(start,num);
END Remove;

PROCEDURE Gets(VAR str: ARRAY OF CHAR);
(* read a string until a CR is received *)
  CONST
    BS = 8;  (* backspace *)
  VAR
    ch: CHAR;
    i: CARDINAL;
BEGIN
  i:=0;
  REPEAT
    Read(ch);
    Write(ch);
    IF (ORD(ch)=BS) AND (i>0) THEN i:=i-1;  (* is backspace *)
    ELSIF (ch<>EOL) AND (i<HIGH(str)) THEN
      str[i]:=ch;
      i:=i+1;
    END;
  UNTIL (ch=EOL) OR (i=HIGH(str));
  str[i]:=CHR(0);  (* all strings end in 0 *)
END Gets;


PROCEDURE Enter;
VAR
  info: LinePointer;
  num: INTEGER;
  done: BOOLEAN;
BEGIN
  done:=FALSE;
  WriteString('Enter starting line number: ');
  ReadInt(num); WriteLn;
  REPEAT
  NEW(info);  (* get a New RECORD *)
  info^.num:=num;
  WriteInt(info^.num,3); WriteString(': ');
  Gets(info^.text);
  IF Length(info^.text)=0 THEN done:=TRUE;
  ELSE
```

```
        IF Find(num)<>NIL THEN PatchUp(num,1); END;
        start:=DLSortStore(info,start,last);
      END;
      num:=num+1;
    UNTIL done;
END Enter;

PROCEDURE Display(start:LinePointer);
BEGIN
  WHILE start<>NIL DO
    WriteInt(start^.num,3); WriteString(': ');
    WriteString(start^.text); WriteLn;
    start:=start^.next;
  END;
  WriteLn;
END Display;


PROCEDURE Save(start:LinePointer);
  VAR
    w: CARDINAL;
    fname: ARRAY[0..40] OF CHAR;
    f: File;

BEGIN
  REPEAT
    WriteString('Enter Filename: ');
    ReadString(fname); WriteLn;
    Lookup(f,fname,TRUE);
  UNTIL f.res=done;
  SetWrite(f);
  WriteString('saving file'); WriteLn;

  WHILE start<>NIL DO
    WriteNBytes(f,start, TSIZE(line),w);
    IF w<>TSIZE(line) THEN WriteString("file error"); END;
    start:=start^.next;
  END;
  WriteChar(f,CHR(26)); (* eof marker *)
  Close(f);
END Save;

PROCEDURE Load():LinePointer;
(* returns a pointer to the start of the list *)
VAR
  temp:LinePointer;
  r:CARDINAL;
  fname: ARRAY[0..40] OF CHAR;
  f: File;

BEGIN
  REPEAT
    WriteString('Enter Filename: ');
    ReadString(fname); WriteLn;
    Lookup(f,fname,FALSE);
  UNTIL f.res=done;
  SetRead(f);

  WriteString('load file'); WriteLn;
  WHILE start<>NIL DO
```

```
    (* free memory, IF any *)
    temp:=start^.next;
    DISPOSE(start);
    start:=temp;
  END;
  last:=NIL; start:=NIL;
  REPEAT
    NEW(temp);
    ReadNBytes(f,temp,TSIZE(line),r);
    IF (r<>TSIZE(line)) AND (NOT f.eof) THEN
      WriteString("file error"); WriteLn;
    ELSE
      IF NOT f.eof THEN
        start:=DLSortStore(temp,start,last);
      END;
    END;
  UNTIL f.eof OR (f.res<>done);
  Close(f);
  RETURN start;
END Load;

BEGIN

  start:=NIL;  (* initially empty list *)
  last:=NIL;
  alldone:=FALSE;

  REPEAT
    CASE MenuSelect() OF
        '1': Enter;       |
        '2': Remove;      |
        '3': Display(start);  |
        '4': Save(start); |
        '5': start:=Load();|
        '6': alldone:=TRUE;
    END ;
  UNTIL alldone=TRUE;
END TextEd.
```

Fragmentation

Fragmentation is essentially a situation in which free memory lies between blocks of allocated memory. A problem develops when each block is too little by itself to fill a request, even though, if all blocks were added together, there would be sufficient memory. Figure 4-3 shows how a sequence of calls to **NEW** and **DISPOSE** can produce this situation.

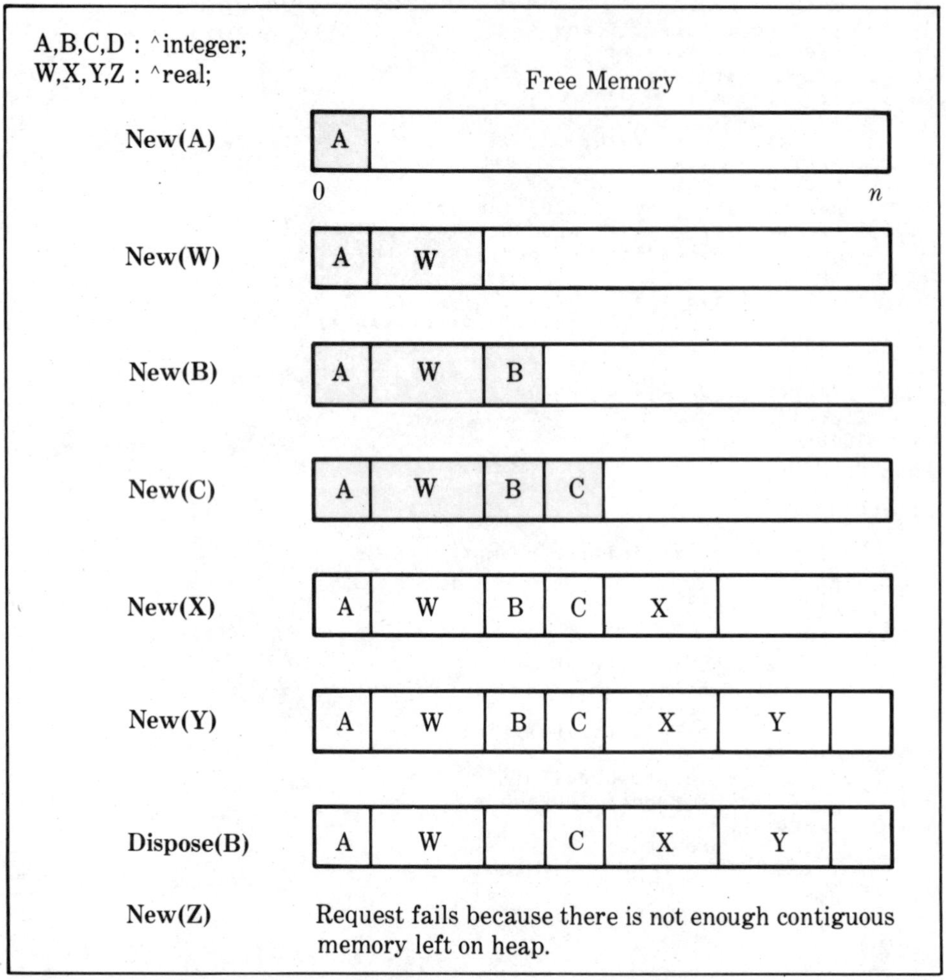

A,B,C,D : ^integer;
W,X,Y,Z : ^real;

Free Memory

New(A)

| A | | |

0   n

New(W)

| A | W | |

New(B)

| A | W | B | |

New(C)

| A | W | B | C | |

New(X)

| A | W | B | C | X | |

New(Y)

| A | W | B | C | X | Y | |

Dispose(B)

| A | W | | C | X | Y | |

New(Z)   Request fails because there is not enough contiguous
          memory left on heap.

Figure 4-3. Fragmentation in dynamic allocation

You can avoid some types of fragmentation because often the dynamic allocation functions combine adjacent regions of memory. For example, if memory regions A, B, C, and D (shown here) were allocated, and then regions B and C were freed, in theory B and C could be combined because they are next to each other. However, if B and D were freed, there is no way to combine them because Modula-2 lies between them and is still in use.

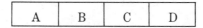

A	B	C	D

Since B and D were free while C was allocated, you might wonder why you could not move C's contents to D, and then combine B and C. The trouble is that your program would have no way of knowing that what was in C had been moved to D!

One way to avoid excess fragmentation is always to allocate equal amounts of memory. In this way, you can reallocate all deallocated regions to subsequent requests, and use all free memory. If this method is not possible, then try to limit the different sizes to just a few. You can sometimes do this by compacting several small requests into a large request. You should never allocate more memory than you need just to avoid fragmentation, because the amount of wasted memory will far outweigh any gains that you may receive. Here is another solution: as the program runs, write all information out to a temporary disk file, free all memory, and then read the information back in. In this way, you eliminate gaps when the information is read back in.

Dynamic Allocation and Artificial Intelligence

Although Modula-2 is not a mainstream artificial intelligence (AI) language, you can use it to experiment. A trait common to many artificial intelligence programs is the existence of a list of information items that the program can extend automatically as it learns new things. In a language like Prolog, which many people consider to be the premier artificial intelligence language, the language itself performs list maintenance. In Modula-2, you must program such procedures by using linked lists and dynamic allocation. Although the example developed here is simple, you can apply many of the concepts to more sophisticated intelligent programs.

One interesting area of AI covers programs that act like people. For example, the famous Eliza program appeared to be a psychiatrist. It would be wonderful to have a computer program that could carry on a conversation about anything—a great program to run when you were tired of programming and feeling lonely! The example here will create an extremely simple version of this program by using words and their definitions to carry on a simple conversation with the user. One device common to many AI programs is the linking of an informational item with its meaning; this example links words with their meanings. The following **RECORD** holds each word, its definition, its part of speech, and its connotation:

```
str8C = ARRAY[0..79] OF CHAR;
str30 = ARRAY[0..30] OF CHAR;
VocabPointer = POINTER TO vocab;
vocab = RECORD
        typ:CHAR;          (* type of word *)
        connotate:CHAR;(* connotation *)
        word:str30;        (* word itself *)
        def:str8C;         (* definition *)
        next: VocabPointer;    (* pointer to next RECORD *)
        prior: VocabPointer;   (* pointer to previous RECORD*)
END;

DataItem = vocab;
DataArray = ARRAY [1..100] OF VocabPointer;
(* hold pointers to vocab RECORDs *)
```

In the program that follows, you enter words, their definitions, what type of word each is, and each word's connotation of good, bad, or indifferent. By using dynamic allocation, the program builds a linked list to hold these dictionary entries. The program uses **DLSortStore** to create and maintain a sorted doubly linked list of the dictionary. After you have entered a few words into the dictionary, you can begin to converse with the computer. For example, you type in a sentence, such as "It is a nice day." The program scans the sentence to find words that it knows. If it finds one, it makes a comment about it based on its meaning. If it encounters a word that it does not know, the program prompts you to enter the word with its definition. You should type quit to exit conversation mode.

The part of the program that carries on the conversation is in the function **Talk**. **Talk** uses a support function called **Dissect** to look at one word at a time from your input sentence. The variable **sentence** holds your input sentence. **Dissect** removes one word at a time from **sentence** and returns it in **word**. Here are the functions **Talk** and **Dissect**:

```
PROCEDURE Dissect(VAR s:str80;VAR w:str30);
VAR
  t,x:CARDINAL;
  temp:str80;
```

```
BEGIN
  t:=0;
  WHILE(s[t]=' ') DO t:=t+1; END;
  x:=t;
  WHILE(s[t]<>' ') AND (t<=Length(s)) DO t:=t+1; END;
  IF t<=Length(s) THEN t:=t-1; END;
  Copy(s,x,t-x+1,w);
  temp:=s;
  Copy(temp,t+1,Length(s),s);
END Dissect;

PROCEDURE Talk;
VAR
  sentence:str80;
  word:str30;
  w:VocabPointer;
BEGIN
  WriteString('Conversation mode (quit to exit)');
  REPEAT
    WriteString(': ');
    Gets(sentence); WriteLn;
    REPEAT
      Dissect(sentence,word);
      w:=Search(start,word);
      IF w<>NIL THEN
        IF w^.typ='n' THEN
          CASE w^.connotate OF
            'g': WriteString('I like ');|
            'b': WriteString('I DO NOT like ');
          END;
          WriteString(w^.def);
        ELSE WriteString(w^.def);
        END
      ELSIF CompareStr(word,"quit")<>0 THEN
        WriteString(word);
        WriteString(' is unknown.');
        WriteLn;
        Enter(TRUE);
      END;
    UNTIL Length(sentence)=0;
  UNTIL CompareStr(word,"quit")=0;
END Talk;
```

This program is easy to write and you should be able to make it appear smarter. One suggestion is to have the program also scan your sentence for verbs, and then have it substitute an alternate verb in its comment. You might also make it ask questions. Here is the entire program:

```
MODULE Smart;

FROM InOut IMPORT WriteString, WriteLn, Read, ReadInt,
        EOL, Write, WriteInt, ReadString;
FROM FileSystem IMPORT File, Response, Lookup, SetWrite,
```

```
          Close, ReadNBytes, WriteNBytes, WriteChar,
          SetRead;
FROM SYSTEM IMPORT ADR, TSIZE;
FROM Strings IMPORT Length, CompareStr, Copy;
FROM Storage IMPORT ALLOCATE, DEALLOCATE;

TYPE
   str80 = ARRAY[0..79] OF CHAR;
   str30 = ARRAY[0..30] OF CHAR;
   VocabPointer = POINTER TO vocab;
   vocab = RECORD
         typ:CHAR;          (* type of word *)
         connotate:CHAR;(* connotation *)
         word:str30;        (* word itself *)
         def:str80;         (* definition *)
         next: VocabPointer;    (* pointer to next RECORD *)
         prior: VocabPointer;   (* pointer to previous RECORD*)
   END;

   DataItem = vocab;
   DataArray = ARRAY [1..100] OF VocabPointer; (* hold pointers to *)
                                           (* vocab RECORDs *)
VAR
   test: DataArray;
   start,last:VocabPointer;
   alldone: BOOLEAN;

PROCEDURE MenuSelect():CHAR;  (* returns the user's selection *)

VAR
   ch:CHAR;

BEGIN
   WriteString('1. Enter words'); WriteLn;
   WriteString('2. Delete a word'); WriteLn;
   WriteString('3. Display the list'); WriteLn;
   WriteString('4. Search for a word'); WriteLn;
   WriteString('5. Save the list'); WriteLn;
   WriteString('6. Load the list'); WriteLn;
   WriteString('7. Converse'); WriteLn;
   WriteString('8. Quit'); WriteLn;
   REPEAT
     WriteLn;
     WriteString('Enter your choice: ');
     Read(ch);  ch:=CAP(ch); WriteLn;
   UNTIL (ch>='1') AND (ch<='8');
   RETURN ch;
END MenuSelect;

PROCEDURE DLSortStore(info,start:VocabPointer;
            VAR last:VocabPointer):VocabPointer;
(* store entries in sorted order *)

VAR
   old, top: VocabPointer;
BEGIN
```

```
     top:=start;
     old:=NIL;

   IF start=NIL THEN
     (* first element in list *)
     info^.next:=NIL;
   · last:=info;
     info^.prior:=NIL;
     RETURN(info);
   ELSE
     WHILE start<>NIL DO
       IF CompareStr(start^.word,info^.word)<0 THEN
         old:=start;
         start:=start^.next;
       ELSE
       (* goes in middle *)
         IF old<>NIL THEN
           old^.next:=info;
           info^.next:=start;
           start^.prior:=info;
           info^.prior:=old;
           RETURN top;  (* keep same starting point *)
         ELSE
            info^.next:=start;  (* new first element *)
           info^.prior:=NIL;
           RETURN info;
         END;
       END;
     END;  (*WHILE*)

     last^.next:=info;  (* goes on END *)
     info^.next:=NIL;
     info^.prior:=last;
     last:=info;
     RETURN top;
   END;
END DLSortStore;

PROCEDURE DLDelete(start:VocabPointer;
           key:str30):VocabPointer;
VAR
   temp,temp2:VocabPointer;
   done:BOOLEAN;
BEGIN
   IF CompareStr(start^.word,key)=0 THEN
     (* is first in list *)
     IF temp^.next <> NIL THEN
       temp:=start^.next;
       temp^.prior:=NIL;
     END;
     DISPOSE(start);
     RETURN temp;
   ELSE
     done:=FALSE;
     temp:=start^.next;
```

```
      temp2:=start;
      WHILE temp<>NIL DO
        IF CompareStr(temp^.word,key)=0 THEN
          temp2^.next:=temp^.next;
          IF temp^.next<>NIL THEN
            temp^.next^.prior:=temp2;
          END;
          done:=TRUE;
          DISPOSE(temp);
        ELSE
          temp2:=temp;
          temp:=temp^.next;
        END;
      END;
      IF NOT done THEN
        WriteString('not found');
        WriteLn;
      END;
      RETURN start;  (* still same starting point *)
   END;
END DLDelete;

PROCEDURE Remove;
VAR
  name:str30;
BEGIN
  WriteString('Enter word to delete: ');
  ReadString(name); WriteLn;
  start:=DLDelete(start,name);
END Remove;

PROCEDURE Gets(VAR str: ARRAY OF CHAR);
(* read a string until a CR is read *)
  CONST
    BS = 8;  (* backspace *)
  VAR
    ch: CHAR;
    i: CARDINAL;
BEGIN
  i:=0;
  REPEAT
    Read(ch);
    Write(ch);
    IF (ORD(ch)=BS) AND (i>0) THEN i:=i-1;  (* is backspace *)
    ELSIF (ch<>EOL) AND (i<HIGH(str)) THEN
      str[i]:=ch;
      i:=i+1;
    END;
  UNTIL (ch=EOL) OR (i=HIGH(str));
  str[i]:=CHR(0);  (* all strings end in 0 *)
END Gets;

PROCEDURE Enter(one:BOOLEAN);
VAR
  info: VocabPointer;
```

```
    done: BOOLEAN;
BEGIN
  done:=FALSE;
  REPEAT
    NEW(info);   (* get a NEW RECORD *)
    WriteString('Enter word: ');
    Gets(info^.word);   WriteLn;
    IF Length(info^.word)=0 THEN done:=TRUE
    ELSE
      WriteString('Enter TYPE (n,v,a): ');
      Read(info^.typ);   WriteLn;
      WriteString('Enter connotation (g,b,n): ');
      Read(info^.connotate);   WriteLn;
      WriteString('Enter definition: ');
      Gets(info^.def);   WriteLn;
      start:=DLSortStore(info,start,last);   (* store it *)
    END;
  UNTIL done OR one;
END Enter;

PROCEDURE Display(start:VocabPointer);
BEGIN
  WHILE start<>NIL DO
    WriteString('word: ');
    WriteString(start^.word); WriteLn;
    WriteString('type: ');
    WriteString(start^.typ); WriteLn;
    WriteString('connotation: ');
    WriteString(start^.connotate); WriteLn;
    WriteString('definition'); WriteLn;
    WriteString(start^.def); WriteLn;
    WriteLn;
    start:=start^.next;
  END;
END Display;

PROCEDURE Search(start:VocabPointer;word:str30):VocabPointer;
BEGIN
  WHILE (start<>NIL) DO
    IF CompareStr(word,start^.word)=0 THEN
      RETURN start;
    ELSE
        start:=start^.next;
    END;
  END;
  IF start=NIL THEN RETURN NIL; END; (* NOT in list *)
END Search;


PROCEDURE Find;
VAR
  loc:VocabPointer;
  word:str30;
BEGIN
  WriteString('Enter word to Find: ');
```

```
      ReadString(word); WriteLn;
      loc:=Search(start,word);
      IF loc<>NIL THEN
        WriteString('word: ');
        WriteString(loc^.word); WriteLn;
        WriteString('type: ');
        WriteString(loc^.typ); WriteLn;
        WriteString('connotation: ');
        WriteString(loc^.connotate); WriteLn;
        WriteString('definition'); WriteLn;
        WriteString(loc^.def); WriteLn;
        WriteLn;
      ELSE
        WriteString('not in list');
        WriteLn;
      END;
    END Find;

    PROCEDURE Save(start:VocabPointer);
      VAR
        w: CARDINAL;
        fname: ARRAY[0..40] OF CHAR;
        f: File;

    BEGIN
      REPEAT
        WriteString('Enter Filename: ');
        ReadString(fname); WriteLn;
        Lookup(f,fname,TRUE);
      UNTIL f.res=done;
      SetWrite(f);
      WriteString('saving file'); WriteLn;

      WHILE start<>NIL DO
        WriteNBytes(f,start, TSIZE(vocab),w);
        IF w<>TSIZE(vocab) THEN WriteString("file error"); END;
        start:=start^.next;
      END;
      WriteChar(f,CHR(26)); (* eof marker *)
      Close(f);
    END Save;

    PROCEDURE Load():VocabPointer;
    (* returns a pointer to the start of the list *)
    VAR
      temp:VocabPointer;
      r:CARDINAL;
      fname: ARRAY[0..40] OF CHAR;
      f: File;

    BEGIN
      REPEAT
        WriteString('Enter Filename: ');
        ReadString(fname); WriteLn;
        Lookup(f,fname,FALSE);
```

```
    UNTIL f.res=done;
    SetRead(f);

    WriteString('load file'); WriteLn;
    WHILE start<>NIL DO
      (* free memory, IF any *)
      temp:=start^.next;
      DISPOSE(start);
      start:=temp;
    END;
    last:=NIL; start:=NIL;
    REPEAT
      NEW(temp);
      ReadNBytes(f,temp,TSIZE(vocab),r);
      IF (r<>TSIZE(vocab)) AND (NOT f.eof) THEN
        WriteString("file error"); WriteLn;
      ELSE
        IF NOT f.eof THEN
          start:=DLSortStore(temp,start,last);
        END;
      END;
    UNTIL f.eof OR (f.res<>done);
    Close(f);
    RETURN start;
END Load;

PROCEDURE Dissect(VAR s:str80;VAR w:str30);
VAR
    t,x:CARDINAL;
    temp:str80;
BEGIN
    t:=0;
    WHILE(s[t]=' ') DO t:=t+1; END;
    x:=t;
    WHILE(s[t]<>' ') AND (t<=Length(s)) DO t:=t+1; END
    IF t<=Length(s) THEN t:=t-1; END;
    Copy(s,x,t-x+1,w);
    temp:=s;
    Copy(temp,t+1,Length(s),s);
END Dissect;

PROCEDURE Talk;
VAR
    sentence:str80;
    word:str30;
    w:VocabPointer;
BEGIN
    WriteString('Conversation mode (quit to exit)');
    REPEAT
      WriteString(': ');
      Gets(sentence); WriteLn;
      REPEAT
        Dissect(sentence,word);
        w:=Search(start,word);
      IF w<>NIL THEN
```

```
        IF w^.typ='n' THEN
          CASE w^.connotate OF
            'g': WriteString('I like ');|
            'b': WriteString('I DO NOT like ');
          END;
          WriteString(w^.def);
        ELSE WriteString(w^.def);
        END
      ELSIF CompareStr(word,"quit")<>0 THEN
        WriteString(word);
        WriteString(' is unknown.');
        WriteLn;
        Enter(TRUE);
      END;
    UNTIL Length(sentence)=0;
  UNTIL CompareStr(word,"quit")=0;
END Talk;

BEGIN
  start:=NIL;  (* initially empty list *)
  last:=NIL;
  alldone:=FALSE;

  REPEAT
    CASE MenuSelect() OF
      '1': Enter(FALSE); |
      '2': Remove; |
      '3': Display(start); |
      '4': Find; |
      '5': Save(start); |
      '6': start:=Load(); |
      '7': Talk; |
      '8': alldone:=TRUE;
    END ;
  UNTIL alldone=TRUE;
END Smart.
```

Interfacing to Assembly Language Routines and the Operating System

CHAPTER 5

As powerful as Modula-2 is, sometimes you must either write a routine by using assembler, or use a system call into the operating system. You may have to do this to achieve faster run-time execution or to interface to some special hardware device that Modula-2 does not directly support. Whatever the reason, most Modula-2 compilers are designed with the flexibility to support such language additions.

Each processor has a different assembly language and each operating system has a different interface structure. Also, the calling convention, which defines how information is passed to and from a subroutine, varies between Modula-2 compilers. Even the same compiler will have slight variances between the CP/M, CP/M-86, and MS-DOS versions. This chapter will use the IBM PC-DOS operating system and the 8086/8088 assembly language because they are the most popular. Most of the examples in the chapter are designed for use with the Logitech Modula-2 compiler. However, even if you have different equipment, use the following discussions and the general principles presented as your guide.

Assembly Language Interfacing

There are several reasons to use a routine that is written in assembler:

- To enhance speed and efficiency
- To perform some machine-specific function that is unavailable in Modula-2
- To use third-party library routines

Although all Modula-2 compilers tend to produce fast, compact object code, no compiler consistently creates code that is as fast or compact as that written by a competent programmer who uses assembler. The small difference usually does not matter and does not warrant the extra time needed to write a program in assembler. However, there are special cases in which you must code a specific routine in assembler so that it runs quickly. This is necessary for a procedure that is used frequently and therefore has a great effect on the execution speed of a program. A good example is a floating-point math package. In addition, special hardware devices need exact timing, so that you must have complete control over the specific machine instructions that you use.

Many computers, including 8086/8088-based machines, have certain instructions that Modula-2 cannot execute directly. For example, you cannot change data segments with any standard Modula-2 instruction, or control the contents of specific registers by using the Modula-2 language. (Some compilers will supply library routines to perform these types of processes, but they still do not have the flexibility of using assembly language directly.)

In professional programming environments, it is common to purchase subroutine libraries for graphics, floating-point math, and so on. Sometimes, you must take these in object format because the developer will not sell the source code. Occasionally, you can simply link these routines with your Modula-2 program; at other times, you must write an interface module to correct any differences in the interface that your Modula-2 compiler and the routines that you purchased use.

There are basically two ways to integrate assembly code modules into your Modula-2 programs. The first is to code the routine separately and link it with the rest of your program by using an **IMPORT** statement; the second is to use the inline assembly code capabilities that many Modula-2 compilers have. This section explores both methods.

It is not within the scope of this book to teach assembly language programming. This section assumes that you are familiar with the assembly language that your computer uses. The examples presented only serve as a guide.

Table 5-1.   Memory Requirements of the Built-in Data Types

Type	Length	Comments
BYTE	8 bits	
CHAR	8 bits	
INTEGER	16 bits	
CARDINAL	16 bits	
REAL	8 bytes	IEEE floating-point standard
SET BITSET	16 bits	
POINTER ADDRESS PROCESS	4 bytes	The two least significant bytes hold the offset address, while the most significant bytes hold the segment.
ARRAY	varies	The lowest index values are at the lowest address in memory; the highest index value is at the highest address of the array in memory.
RECORD	varies	The first field is at the lowest address; the last field is in the highest address.
Enumeration Types	8 bits	

Internal Data Formats and Calling Conventions

Before you can link assembly code to a Modula-2 program, you must know how data is stored in a program and how it is passed between subroutines. Most 8086/8088-based Modula-2 compilers store all global variables in the data segment. These compilers also store all local variables on the stack, and access them by using the BP register to index into the stack. The way that each built-in data type is stored will vary slightly from compiler to compiler. Table 5-1 shows the storage necessary for the built-in data types that the Logitech compiler uses.

A *calling convention* is the method a Modula-2 compiler uses to pass information into subroutines and to return values. Modula-2 uses the stack both to pass parameters into a subroutine and to return certain function results. (For example, Logitech uses the BX register to return byte-sized and word-sized function results and the stack for other types.) Exactly what is on the stack when a subroutine is called depends both on the type of the variable passed, and whether it is declared as a *variable* parameter or a *value* parameter.

Value Parameters

Value parameters are *unidirectional:* information is passed into a subroutine by using a value parameter, but any changes to that parameter will not affect the actual variable that is used to call the subroutine. Instead of operating on the actual variable used to call the subroutine, using a value parameter causes a copy of the value of the variable to be made and passed, thereby leaving the calling variable unchanged. In essence, only a *value* is passed to the procedure or function, which is the reason that this type of parameter passing is referred to as *call by value*.

INTEGER, CHAR, BYTE, and **BOOLEAN** value parameters are passed on the stack in single words. Also, any user-declared scalars other than **REAL** are passed by using single words on the stack. As in the case of **BOOLEAN** value variables, if only one byte is needed, the high-order half of the word is zero. **REAL**s use eight bytes.

Pointers consist of two words: the segment and the offset. If the pointer is **NIL**, then both words are zero. (Occasionally, both words are FFh.)

Generally, all **ARRAY**s and **RECORD**s are passed as a two-word address — consisting of the segment and the offset — of the actual variable. If these variables will not be modified, then copies are made. (Note: this is an exception to the general rule — unless your routine makes a copy of these types of variables, it will be operating directly on the calling variables and any changes will be reflected in the calling routine.)

Variable Parameters

Unlike the value parameters, variable parameters have their *addresses* passed on the stack. This means that a subroutine can operate on them directly. Variable parameters are *bidirectional:* they pass information into a subroutine and can return information back to the calling routine, because the value of the parameters can be modified. Two words are used on the stack to pass both the segment and the offset of the variable parameter, no matter what type it is. This parameter-passing convention is referred to as *call by reference.*

Return Values

When a Modula-2 function procedure terminates, it passes a return value back to the calling routine. This can be accomplished by using one of two possible ways. First, you return byte or word values in a register. Second, you return arrays, records, and reals through the stack. However, check your Modula-2 user manual to determine exactly how values are returned from procedures. With the Logitech compiler, return values use the BX register for byte and word values, and the stack for all other values.

Preserving Registers

Among Modula-2 compilers, each type differs with respect to what registers you may use freely, and which registers you must preserve and restore prior to a return from your assembly code routine. Generally, you must always save the stack pointer (SP), and sometimes you must save the contents of the segment registers. Check your compiler's user manual for explicit advice. (Some compilers require you to save the direction flag.)

When you write an assembly language module that must interface with code that was compiled by Modula-2, you must follow all of the conventions that were defined earlier. Only by doing this can you hope to have your assembly language routines correctly interfaced with your Modula-2 code.

The Activation Record

Each time that you make a call to a procedure (standard or an assembly routine), you must save the current state of the program, and place the parameters, if any, and the return address on the stack. This combination of events creates an *activation record* on the stack. Although the exact form of the activation record will vary between compilers, Figure 5-1 presents a general form.

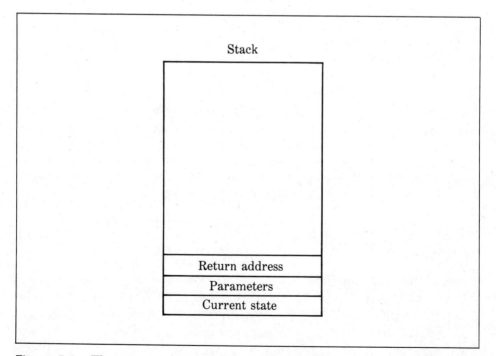

Figure 5-1. The general form of an activation record

The Duties of the Called Procedure

A called routine must follow a strict entry-and-exit method in order to access correctly parameters that are on the stack, to return values, and to prevent a program crash.

After control is passed to the called procedure, it must first place the contents of the stack pointer (SP) into the BP register so that it can use the stack pointer to index any parameters on the stack. (Remember, some implementations may require that you first save the current value of BP before you use it.)

Prior to exit, the called procedure should restore any registers that need to be saved. Many compilers also make the called routine responsible for removing the parameters from the stack. If your compiler requires you to do this, the easiest method to use is the **RET N** assembly language statement, where **N** is the number of bytes to remove from the stack. You calculate **N** by adding the lengths, which are in bytes, of the parameters.

Creating an External Assembly Code Routine

Now that you have seen the basics, you are ready to look at an actual external subroutine. For example, assume that, for some reason, you must code the following function in assembler:

```
PROCEDURE mul(a,b:INTEGER):INTEGER;
BEGIN
        a:=a*b;
        mul:=a;
END mul;
```

Since this function will be called from a Modula-2 program, you know that the two integer arguments will be passed on the stack as two words. This means that if **mul** is called with

```
mul(10,20);
```

then the value 10 is pushed first, and the value 20 is pushed second. Remember that if the calling arguments are scalar variables, then their value is passed on the stack. The return value of **mul** is placed in the BX register, as required by the Logitech calling conventions.

In assembly language, the function **mul** is

```
code      segment 'code'
          assume cs:code
xmul      proc near   ; check your compiler manual
                      ; to determine whether this should
                      ; be near or far.
          push bp
          mov bp,sp

; get first parm
          mov ax,[bp]+4
; multiply by second
          mul [bp]+6
; restore bp and clear the stack
; return result is already in BX
          mov bx,ax
          pop bp
          ret 4    ; remove parameters from stack
xmul      endp
code      ends
          end
```

Notice that the **push** and **pop** instructions save all appropriate registers, and that the arguments are accessed on the stack. The code

```
mov bp,sp

mov ax,[bp]+4

mul [bp]+6
```

puts the address of the top of the stack into register BP and then moves the fourth word down on the stack, which is parameter **a**, into the AX register. The parameters are the fourth and sixth bytes down on the stack because the return address plus the **push bp** uses four bytes. Therefore, you can find the parameters by starting at byte four down from the top of the stack. (This distance from the top of the stack may increase as local variables are added to a routine.)

External procedures may need to be either *near* or *far*, depending upon what compiler you are using. Make sure to check your user manual because choosing the wrong method causes a program to crash.

Before you can use the assembly routine **mul**, you must assemble it into a relocatable object file. Then, you can find in your user manual what method to use to link the file to the code that your compiler produces. However, you can safely assume that you will need to import the routine into any module that uses it.

Now your Modula-2 programs can use the external function **mul**. For example, if you assume that **mul** is stored in the library called **MyLib**, then this program uses it to multiply two numbers together:

```
MODULE test;
  FROM MyLib IMPORT mul;
  FROM InOut IMPORT WriteLn, WriteInt;

VAR
    a,b,c:INTEGER;

BEGIN
  a := 10;
  b := 20;
  c := mul(a, b);
  WriteInt(c,3);
  WriteLn;
END test.
```

Inline Assembly Code

Although not defined by Professor Wirth, many Modula-2 compilers provide a method that allows you to make inline assembly code part of a Modula-2 program, instead of making you use a completely separate external subroutine. There are two advantages to this. First, you are not required to write all interface code; second, all the code is in "one place," making support a little easier. Unfortunately, the only drawback is that often the inline assembly code is in a rather awkward format.

However, the exact way that your compiler supports this concept will vary. The examples here use Logitech's **CODE** procedure, which is in the **SYSTEM** library. The **CODE** statement allows assembly code to become part of a Modula-2 program. The general form of the statement is

CODE(*value/value/.../value*);

where *value* is the proper code for any valid assembly instruction or data. (If you know Turbo Pascal, keep in mind that the **CODE** statement is similar to Turbo Pascal's **inline** procedure.)

The actual values must be of type **CARDINAL**, which means that you cannot use assembly code pseudo-ops. There are two ways to find the proper values: you can compute them by hand, which is not recommended; or you can first code the routine as an assembly language file, assemble it with an assembler such as MASM, and use the listing file to find the codes for each instruction. Regardless of which way you choose, both are still tedious operations, which is a major drawback to using inline assembly code.

The following short program will multiply two integers together by using the inline code version of the assembly procedure **mul** to perform the actual multiplication. Compare this program to the external subroutine version given in the preceding section.

```
MODULE AsmInline;

   FROM SYSTEM IMPORT CODE,AX, BX, GETREG;
   FROM InOut IMPORT WriteInt, WriteLn;

(* this program shows an example of
   inline assembly code *)

   VAR

     a, b, c: INTEGER;

   PROCEDURE mul(x, y: INTEGER): INTEGER;
     VAR mulResult: INTEGER;
   BEGIN
     CODE (8BH, 46H,  04H, (* mov ax,[bp]+4 *)
           0F6H, 66H,  06H, (* mul [bp]+6    *)
           8BH, 0D8H);  (* mov bx,ax *)
     GETREG(BX,mulResult);
     RETURN mulResult
   END mul; (*mul*)


BEGIN
   a := 10;
   b := 20;
   c := mul(a,b);
   WriteInt(c,6);
   WriteLn;
END AsmInline.
```

Here, the Modula-2 compiler automatically provides the code to set up the BP register and to return from the function. This process also includes removing the parameters from the stack. When the compiler compiles the inline code, it places the actual instructions into the function at the point where the inline statement occurs.

A common use of inline assembly code is to communicate with special hardware devices that Modula-2 does not support directly. For example, you could use the following subroutine to turn on a fan when a temperature sensor reaches a target value. This example assumes that sending a 1 out to port 200 will turn on the fan.

```
PROCEDURE fan(temp:INTEGER);
(* If temp >=100 degrees C, then turn on fan *)
BEGIN
        IF temp>=100 THEN
                CODE(0B8H,00,01,   (* mov AX,1 *)
                     0E7H,0C8H);   (* out 200,AX *)
END;
```

Remember that the Modula-2 compiler provides all customary support for setting up and returning from a procedure call. Thus, you only have to provide the body of the routine and follow the calling conventions to access the arguments.

Keep in mind that, whatever method you use, you are creating machine dependencies that will make your program difficult to port to a new machine or another operating system. However, for the demanding situations that require assembly code, using assembler will usually be worth the effort.

When to Code
in Assembler

Because of the difficulty of coding in assembler, most programmers only do it when absolutely necessary. As a general rule, you should not use it—it creates too many problems! However, there are two situations when coding in assembler makes sense. The first situation is when there is absolutely no other way to do it—for example, when you have to interface directly to a hardware device that Modula-2 cannot handle. The second situation is when you must reduce a program's execution time.

When you need to speed up a program, you should choose carefully which procedures to code in assembler. If you code the wrong ones, then you will see little increase in speed. If you choose the right one, your program will fly! To determine which subroutines need recoding, you must review the way that your program runs. Generally, the routines that are used inside loops are the ones to program in assembler because they are executed repeatedly. Coding a procedure or function that is used only once or twice in assembler will not speed up your program much, but a routine that is used several times will. For example, consider the following procedure:

```
PROCEDURE ABC;
VAR
    t:INTEGER;

BEGIN
    init;
    FOR t:=0 TO 1000 DO
        phase1;
        phase2;
        IF t=10 THEN phase3; END;
    END;
    byebye;
END ABC;
```

Recoding **init** and **byebye** may not measurably affect the speed of this program because they are executed only once. However, **phase1** and **phase2** are executed 1000 times and recoding them will have a major effect on the run time of this program; **phase3** is only executed once, even though it is inside the loop, so you should not recode this subroutine into assembler.

With careful thought, you can improve the speed of your program by recoding only a few subroutines in assembler.

Operating-System Interfacing

Because many Modula-2 programs fall into the category of system programs, you often need to interface directly to the operating system—bypassing Modula-2's normal interface—to perform certain operations. Also, you may want to make use of operating-system functions that you cannot access through the library routines that are supplied by your Modula-2 compiler.

For these reasons, using the low-level resources of the operating system is a common occurrence in Modula-2 programming.

There are several operating systems that are currently supported by Modula-2:

- PC-DOS or MS-DOS
- CP/M
- CP/M-86

All operating systems have a set of functions that a program uses to perform various tasks, such as open disk files, read and write characters to and from the console, and allocate memory for the program to run in. The way

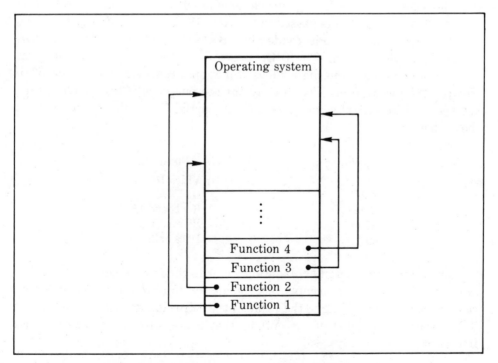

Figure 5-2. An operating system and its jump table in memory

that these functions are accessed varies from system to system, but all systems use the concept of a *jump table.* In an operating system like CP/M, the system calls are executed by using a CALL instruction to a specific region of memory with the desired function code in a register. In PC-DOS, a software interrupt is used. In either system, the jump table routes the proper function to your program. Figure 5-2 shows how an operating system and its jump table might appear in memory.

Since it is impossible to discuss all operating systems here, this discussion is limited to PC-DOS, which is in the widest use. However, the general techniques that are applied here are applicable to all operating systems.

Accessing System Resources in PC-DOS

In PC-DOS, the operating system functions are accessed by using software interrupts. Each interrupt has its own category of functions that it accesses, and the value of the AH register determines the functions. If additional information is needed, it is passed in the AL, BX, CX, and DX registers. The PC-DOS operating system is divided into BIOS (Basic I/O System) and DOS (Disk Operating System). The BIOS provides the lowest-level routines that DOS uses to provide the higher-level functions. However, there is overlap between the two systems. Fortunately, for the purposes of this chapter, they are accessed in basically the same way. A partial list of these interrupts is shown here:

Interrupt	Function
10h	Video I/O
13h	Disk I/O
16h	Keyboard I/O
17h	Printer I/O
21h	DOS calls

For a complete list and explanation, refer to the *IBM Technical Reference Manual.* Each of the interrupts is associated with a number of options that can be accessed according to the value of the AH register when called. Table 5-2 shows a partial list of the options that are available for each of these interrupts.

There are basically two ways to access the functions that are given in Table 5-2. The first is by using a built-in system call library procedure, sometimes called **DOSCALL** or **MsDos**, which is supplied by the Modula-2 compiler. The second is by using assembly language interfacing.

Table 5-2.   A Partial List of System Routines that are Accessed Through Interrupts

Video I/O Functions—Interrupt 10h

AH Register	Function
0	Set video mode if AL=0: 40×25 BW 1: 40×25 color 2: 80×25 BW 3: 80×25 color 4: 320×200 color graphics 5: 320×200 BW graphics 6: 340×200 BW graphics
1	Set cursor lines CH bits 0-4 contain start of line bits 5-7 are 0 CL bits 0-4 contain end of line bits 5-7 are 0
2	Set cursor position DH: row DL: column BH: video page number
3	Read cursor position BH: video page number Returns DH: row DL: column CX: mode

Table 5-2. A Partial List of System Routines that are Accessed Through Interrupts (*continued*)

Video I/O Functions — Interrupt 10h

AH Register	Function

4	Read light pen position
	Returns
	    if AH=0 pen not triggered
	    if AH=1 pen triggered
	    DH: row
	    DL: column
	    CH: raster line (0-199)
	    BX: pixel column (0-319 or 0-639)

5	Set active video page AL may be 0-7

6	Scroll page up
	    AL: number of lines to scroll, 0 for all
	    H: row of upper-left corner of scroll
	    CL: column of upper-left corner of scroll
	    DH: row of lower-right corner of scroll
	    DL: column of lower-right corner of scroll
	    BH: attribute to be used on blank line

7	Scroll page down same as 6

8	Read character at cursor position
	    BH: video page
	Returns
	    AL: character read
	    AH: attribute

9	Write character and attribute at cursor position
	    BH: video page
	    BL: attribute
	    CX: number of characters to write
	    AL: character

10	Write character at current cursor position
	    BH: video page
	    CX: number of characters to write
	    AL: character

11	Set color palette
	    BH: palette number
	    BL: color

Table 5-2. A Partial List of System Routines that are Accessed Through Interrupts (*continued*)

Video I/O Functions—Interrupt 10h

AH Register	Function
12	Write a dot DX: row number CX: column number AL: color
13	Read a dot DX: row number CX: column number Returns AL: dot read
14	Write character to screen and advance cursor AL: character BL: foreground color BH: video page

15	Read video state
	Returns
	    AL: current mode
	    AH: number of columns on screen
	    BH: current active video page

BIOS Disk IO Functions—Interrupt 13h

AH Register	Function
0	Reset disk system
1	Read disk status Returns AL: status (see *IBM Technical Reference Manual*)
2	Read sectors into memory DL: drive number DH: head number CH: track number CL: sector number AL: number of sectors to read ES:BX: address of buffer

---

Table 5-2. A Partial List of System Routines that are Accessed Through Interrupts (*continued*)

BIOS Disk IO Functions — Interrupt 13h

AH Register	Function
	Returns
	AL: number of sectors read
	AH: 0 if successful, status if unsuccessful
3	Write sectors to disk
	(same as Read given earlier)
4	Verify
	(same as Read given earlier)
5	Format a track
	DL: drive number
	DH: head number
	CH: track number
	ES:BX: sector information

BIOS Keyboard I/O Functions — Interrupt 16h

AH Register	Function
0	Read scan code
	Returns
	AH: scan code
	AL: character code
1	Get status of buffer
	Returns
	ZF: 1 then buffer empty
	0 then characters waiting
	with next char in AX as
	described earlier
2	Get status of keyboard
	(see *IBM Technical Reference Manual*)

BIOS Printer I/O Functions — Interrupt 17h

AH Register	Function
0	Print a character
	AL: character

Table 5-2. A Partial List of System Routines that are Accessed Through Interrupts (*continued*)

BIOS Printer I/O Functions—Interrupt 17h

AH Register	Function
	DX: printer number
	Returns
	AH: status
1	Initialize printer
	DX: printer number
	Returns
	AH: status
2	Read status
	DX: printer number
	Returns
	AH: status

High-level DOS Functions Calls—Interrupt 21h (partial list)

AH Register	Function
1	Read character from the keyboard
	Returns
	AL: character
2	Display a character on the screen
	DL: character
3	Read a character from async port
	Returns
	AL: character
4	Write a character to async port
	DL: character
5	Print a character to list device
	DL: character
7	Read character from keyboard but do not display it
	Returns
	AL: character
B	Check keyboard status
	Returns
	AL: 0FFH if key struck; 0 if not

Table 5-2.   A Partial List of System Routines that are Accessed Through Interrupts (*continued*)

High-level DOS Functions Calls — Interrupt 21h (partial list)

AH Register	Function
D	Reset disk
E	Set default drive DL: drive number (0=A, 1=B,...)

11
(4E under 2.x)
	Search for filename
	    DX: Address of FCB
	Returns
	    AL: 0 if found, FFh if not
	        with name in disk transfer address

12 (4F under 2.x)	Find next occurrence of filename same as 11
1A	Set disk transfer address DX: disk transfer address

2A	Get system date
	Returns
	    CX: year (1980-2099)
	    DH: month (1-12)
	    DL: day (1-31)

2B	Set system date
	    CX: year (1980-2099)
	    DH: month (1-12)
	    DL: day (1-31)

2C	Get system time
	Returns
	    CH: hours (0-23)
	    CL: minutes (0-59)
	    DH: seconds (0-59)
	    DL: hundredths of seconds (0-99)

2D	Set system time
	    CH: hours (0-23)
	    CL: minutes (0-59)
	    DH: seconds (0-59)
	    DL: hundredths of seconds (0-99)

Using the DOSCALL Procedure

The **DOSCALL** procedure performs an interrupt 21h call to access one of the higher-level functions in the operating system. **DOSCALL** takes the general form

DOSCALL(*function number, registers*);

where *function number* is the number of the DOS function requested and *registers* is a list of values to be placed in the proper register. For the Logitech compiler, **DOSCALL** is in the **SYSTEM** library.

Here is a simple example. The following procedure determines whether the user has pressed a key. This procedure, called **KbHit**, returns **TRUE** if a key has been pressed and **FALSE** if not. It uses interrupt 21h, function number 0BH, as shown here. The program prints periods on the screen until a key is struck. The **DOSCALL** routine automatically places in **Status** the value that is returned by DOS interrupt 21h call.

```
MODULE kb;

   FROM SYSTEM IMPORT DOSCALL, ADR;
   FROM InOut IMPORT Write;
   (*wait for keypress - PCDOSCALL specific *)

PROCEDURE KbHit(): BOOLEAN;
   VAR
     Status: BOOLEAN;
BEGIN
   DOSCALL(0BH,Status);
   RETURN Status;
END KbHit;

BEGIN
   REPEAT
     Write('.');
   UNTIL KbHit();
END kb.
```

Using Assembly Interfacing to BIOS Functions

Although most Modula-2 compilers support a **DOSCALL** type procedure, not all compilers give you direct access to BIOS. Therefore, you will now study the inline assembly code that you can use to access BIOS functions.

Suppose that you wish to change the screen mode during the execution of a program. For the IBM PC using the standard graphics adapter there are seven modes that the screen can have:

0	40×25 BW
1	40×25 color
2	80×25 BW
3	80×25 color
4	320×200 color graphics
5	320×200 BW graphics
6	640×200 BW graphics

The procedure **Mode**, shown here, executes a BIOS call number 1—set mode—first to switch the screen to 640×200 graphics, print **hi** on the screen, and wait for the user to press RETURN on the keyboard. This code only works for IBM PC and requires a color graphics adapter.

```
MODULE ModeExample;

   FROM InOut IMPORT WriteString, Read;
   FROM SYSTEM IMPORT CODE;

   VAR
      ch: CHAR;

PROCEDURE Mode;
BEGIN
   CODE(55H,        (* push bp *)
      0B8H,00,06,   (* mov ax, 6 *)
      0B4H, 00,     (* mov ah, 0 *)
      0CDH,10H,     (* int 10 *)
      5DH);         (* pop bp *)
END Mode;

BEGIN
   Mode;
   WriteString('hi'); Read(ch);
END ModeExample.
```

This program clears the screen by using the BIOS interrupt 10h, function 6:

```
MODULE ClrScreen;

   FROM InOut IMPORT WriteString, Read;
   FROM SYSTEM IMPORT CODE;

   VAR
      ch: CHAR;
```

```
PROCEDURE clr;
BEGIN
  CODE(
    0B9H,0,0,     (* mov cx,0 *)
    0B6H,18H,     (* mov dh,24 *)
    0B2H,4FH,     (* mov dl,79 *)
    0B4H,06,      (* mov ah,6 *)
    0B0H,00,      (* mov al,0 *)
    0B7H,07,      (* mov bh,7 *)
    0CDH,10H);    (* int 10 - do it *)
END clr;


BEGIN
  WriteString('strike any key to clear the screen');
  Read(ch);
  clr;
  WriteString('screen clear complete');
END ClrScreen.
```

Using the Scan Codes
from the PC keyboard

One of the most frustrating experiences that you can encounter while working with the IBM PC or its clones is trying to use the arrow keys (as well as
INS, DEL, PGUP, PGDN, END, and HOME) and the function keys. These special
keys do not return the normal 8-bit (1-byte) character in the way that the rest
of the keyboard does. When you press a key on the IBM PC, the computer
actually generates a 16-bit (2-byte) value called a *scan code*. The scan code
consists of the low-order byte, which, if a normal key, contains the ASCII
character code for the key, and a high order that contains the key's position
(the position code) on the keyboard. For most keys on the keyboard, the operating system converts these scan codes into 8-bit ASCII values and discards
the position code. But for the Function keys and arrow keys, this is not the
case, because the character code for a special key is 0. This means that you
must use the position code to determine which key was pressed. The routines
to read a character from the keyboard, which use the standard DOS routines, do not allow you to read the special keys. To use these special keys in a
program requires your program to have access to the position codes that are
associated with each key.

One easy way to access these keys is to write a small assembly language routine that calls interrupt 16h, function 0, to read the scan code. This routine is called **Scan** and is shown here by using inline code:

```
PROCEDURE Scan():INTEGER;
  VAR
    value:INTEGER;
BEGIN
  CODE(0B4h,0,   (* mov ah,0 *)
    0CDH,16H,    (* int 16 *)
    8BH,0D8H);   (* mov bx,ax *)
  GETREG(BX,value);
  RETURN value;
END Scan;
```

This routine uses a built-in procedure called **GETREG**, which is supplied with the Logitech compiler, to read the value that BIOS returns. This procedure is in the **SYSTEM** library and is not defined by Professor Wirth; different versions may call it by a different name. You could manually return the value, but this method lets the compiler do most of the work. After the call, the scan code and the character code are in AX and must be placed into another register prior to the call to **GETREG** because the contents of AX must be assumed to be volatile. Upon return, the position code is in **value**.

The trick to using **scan** is deciding when to use the position code instead of the character code. If you press a special key, the character code is 0; in this case, you then decode the position code to determine which key was actually typed. In other situations, you simply know that a standard character has been typed and you use the character code. Using **Scan** to do all keyboard input requires the calling routine to make decisions based on the contents of AH and AL. Because the **Scan** procedure returns an integer quantity that contains the character code in its lower byte and the scan code in its upper byte, you must perform a type transfer to allow each component to be referenced separately. You can do this most easily by creating a new user-defined type that is a two-character **CHAR** array, and by using the type name to make the type transfer. After you do this, you can reference the scan codes and the character codes individually. The following program illustrates both the **Scan** routine and the type transfer method of accessing each code:

```
MODULE arrow;
  FROM InOut IMPORT WriteString, Write, WriteCard;
  FROM SYSTEM IMPORT CODE, GETREG, BX;

TYPE
  STR = ARRAY[0..1] OF CHAR;

VAR
   t:INTEGER;
   s:STR;
PROCEDURE Scan():INTEGER;
  VAR
    value:INTEGER;
BEGIN
  CODE(0B4h,0,   (* mov ah,0 *)
    0CDH,16H,    (* int 16 *)
    8BH,0D8H);   (* mov bx,ax *)
  GETREG(BX,value);
  RETURN value;
END Scan;

BEGIN
  t:=Scan();
  s:=STR(t);
  IF ORD(s[0])=0 THEN    (* must be special key *)
    WriteString('scan code is ');
    WriteCard(ORD(s[1]),6);
  ELSE
    Write(s[0]);  (* write the character *)
  END;
END arrow.
```

There are essentially two ways to determine which key is associated with each position code. The first is to look in the *IBM Technical Reference Manual;* the other is to use the short program just given to determine the values experimentally. (The latter method is more fun!) To help you get started, here are the scan codes for the arrow keys:

Left arrow	75
Right arrow	77
Up arrow	72
Down arrow	80

To integrate the special keys with the normal keys completely requires you to write special input functions, and to bypass the normal **Read** and **ReadString** procedures. This is unfortunate, but it is often the only way to access the special keys. However, the reward is that your program will appear professional and will be much easier to use.

Final Thoughts on Operating-System Interfacing

This chapter has only scratched the surface of what you can do by creatively using system resources. To integrate your program completely with the operating system, you need to have access to information that describes all of the functions in detail.

There are several advantages to using operating-system functions. They can make your program look and feel professional. Bypassing some of Modula-2's built-in functions in favor of the operating-system functions sometimes can create programs that run faster and use less memory. You also have access to functions that are not available through Modula-2's standard functions.

However, you create more trouble for yourself when you use the operating-system functions instead of the standard procedures that are supplied with your compiler, because your code is no longer portable. You may also depend on specific versions of a given operating system and a Modula-2 compiler, which creates compatibility problems for distributing your program. Only you can decide when and if you should introduce machine and operating-system dependencies into your programs.

Statistics

CHAPTER 6

At some point, everyone who owns or has frequent access to a computer uses it to perform some sort of *statistical analysis*. This analysis could take the form of monitoring or trying to predict the movement of stock prices in a portfolio, performing clinical testing to establish safe limits for a new drug, or providing batting averages for the Little League team. The branch of mathematics that deals with the condensation, manipulation, and extrapolation of data is called *statistics*.

As a discipline, statistical analysis is quite young. It developed in the 1700s as an outgrowth of the study of games of chance. Indeed, probability and statistics are closely related. Modern statistical analysis began around the turn of this century when it became possible to sample and work with large sets of data. The computer made it possible to correlate and manipulate even larger amounts of data rapidly and to convert this data into a readily usable form. Today, because of the ever-increasing amount of information created and used by the government and media, every aspect of life is adorned with reams of statistical information. It is almost impossible to listen to the radio, watch the TV news, or read a newspaper article without being told of a statistic.

Although Modula-2 was not designed specifically for statistical programming, it adapts to the task quite well, and even offers some flexibility that is not found in the more common business languages, such as COBOL or BASIC. Two of Modula-2's advantages are the speed and the ease with which Modula-2 can interface with the graphics functions of the system to produce charts and graphs of data. Also, Modula-2's math routines are much faster than those commonly found in interpretive BASIC.

This chapter studies various statistics and procedures including

- The mean
- The median
- The standard deviation
- The regression equation (line of best fit)
- The coefficient of correlation

It also explores some simple graphing techniques.

Samples, Populations, Distributions, and Variables

Before you use statistics, you must understand a few key concepts. Generally, statistical information is derived by first taking a *sample* of specific data points and then drawing generalizations about them. Each sample comes from the *population*, which consists of all possible outcomes for the situation under study. For example, if you wished to measure the output of a box factory over a year by using only the Wednesday production figures and generalizing from them, then your sample would consist of a year's worth of Wednesday figures taken from the population of each day's output in the year.

A sample is *exhaustive* if it equals the population. In the case of the box factory, an exhaustive sample would equal the population if it consisted of the actual production figures—five days a week for the entire year. When the sample is less than the population, there is always room for error; in many cases, you can determine the probability for this error. This chapter assumes that the sample is the same as the population; hence, it does not cover the problem of sample error.

In election projections and opinion polls, a sample is used to project information about the population as a whole. For example, you might use statistical information about the Dow Jones stocks to make an inference about the stock market in general. Of course, the validity of these conclusions varies widely. In other uses of statistics, a sample that equals, or nearly equals, the population is used to summarize a large set of numbers for easier handling. For example, a board of education usually reports the *grade average* for a class, rather than reporting on each student's grade individually.

Statistics are affected by the way that events are distributed in the population. Of the several common distributions in nature, the most important (and the only one that this chapter uses) is the *normal distribution curve*, or the familiar "bell shaped curve," as shown in Figure 6-1.

As the graph suggests, the elements in a normal distribution curve are found mostly in the middle. In fact, the curve is completely symmetrical around its peak—which is also the average for all of the elements. The further from the middle in either direction on the curve, the fewer elements there are. Many situations in real life have a normal distribution.

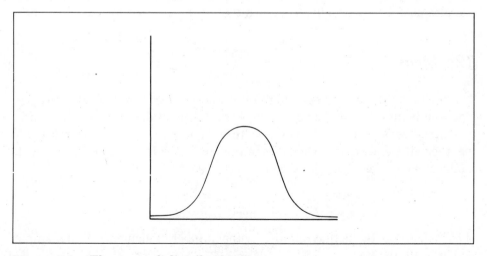

Figure 6-1.   The normal distribution curve

In any statistical process, there is always an *independent variable*, which is the number under study, and a *dependent variable*, which is the factor that determines the independent variable. This chapter uses *time*—the stepwise incremental passage of events—for the dependent variable. For example, when watching a stock portfolio, you may wish to see the movement of the stock on a daily basis. Therefore, you would be concerned with the movement of stock prices over a given period, and not with the actual calendar date of each price. (Of course, some advanced analysts might want to work with calendar dates if they were exploring a specific correlation between calendar dates and stock prices.)

Throughout this chapter, individual statistical functions are developed and assembled into a menu-driven program. You can use this program to perform a wide variety of statistical analyses, as well as to plot information on the screen.

Whenever the chapter discusses the elements of a sample, the elements are called D and indexed from 1 to N, where N is the number of the last element.

The Basic Statistics

Three important numbers form the basis of many statistical analyses, and are also useful individually. They are the *mean*, the *median*, and the *mode*.

The Mean

The mean, or the arithmetic average, is the most common of all statistics. This single number can be used to represent a set of data—the mean can be called the set's "center of gravity." To compute the mean, you must add together all elements and then divide that result by the number of elements in the sample. For example, the sum of the set

$$1 \quad 2 \quad 3 \quad 4 \quad 5 \quad 6 \quad 7 \quad 8 \quad 9 \quad 10$$

is 55. When you divide that number by the number of elements in the sample, which is 10, the mean is 5.5.

The general formula for finding the mean is

$$M = \frac{D_1 + D_2 + D_3 + \ldots + D_N}{N}$$

or

$$M = \frac{1}{N} \sum_{i=1}^{N} D_i$$

the symbol Σ indicates the summation of all elements between 1 and N.

As this chapter develops the statistical functions, you should assume that all data is stored in an array of floating-point numbers of user-defined **TYPE** called **DataArray**, and that the number of sample elements is known. All of the functions and procedures use the array **data** to hold the sample, and the variable **num** to contain the number of elements. The following function computes the mean of an array of **num** floating-point numbers and returns the floating-point average:

```
PROCEDURE Mean(data: DataArray;
               num: INTEGER): REAL;
  VAR
    t: INTEGER;
    avg: REAL;
BEGIN
  avg := 0.0;
  FOR t := 1 TO num DO
    avg := avg+data[t]
  END;
  RETURN avg/FLOAT(num);
END Mean; (*Mean*)
```

For example, if you called **Mean** with a 10-element array that contained the numbers 1 through 10, then **Mean** would return the result 5.5.

The Median

The median of a sample is the middle value, based on order of magnitude. For example, in the sample set

1 2 3 4 5 6 7 8 9

5 is the median because it is in the middle. In the set

$$1\ 2\ 3\ 4\ 5\ 6\ 7\ 8\ 9\ 10$$

you could use either 5 or 6 as the median. In a well-ordered sample that has a normal distribution, the median and the mean are similar. However, as the sample moves further from the standard normal distribution curve, the difference between the median and the mean increases. Calculating the mean of a sample is as simple as sorting the sample and then selecting the middle element, which is indexed as $N/2$.

The function **Median**, shown here, returns the value of the middle element in a sample. Because the data must be sorted to compute the median, a modified version of QuickSort, developed in Chapter 2, is used to sort the data array.

```
PROCEDURE QuickSort(VAR item: DataArray;
                    count: INTEGER);

  PROCEDURE qs(l, r: INTEGER;
               VAR it: DataArray);
    VAR
      i, j: INTEGER;
      x, y: DataItem;
    BEGIN
      i := l;
      j := r;
      x := it[(l+r) DIV 2];
      REPEAT
        WHILE it[i] < x DO
          INC(i, 1)
        END;
        WHILE x < it[j] DO
          DEC(j, 1)
        END;
        IF i <= j THEN
          y := it[i];
          it[i] := it[j];
          it[j] := y;
          INC(i, 1);
          DEC(j, 1);
        END;
      UNTIL i > j;
      IF l < j THEN
        qs(l, j, it)
      END;
      IF l < r THEN
        qs(i, r, it)
      END
    END qs;
```

```
BEGIN
  qs(1, count, item);
END QuickSort; (* quick sort *)

PROCEDURE Median(data: DataArray;
                 num: INTEGER): REAL;
  VAR
    dtemp: DataArray;
    t: INTEGER;
    MedianResult: REAL;
BEGIN
  FOR t := 1 TO num DO
    dtemp[t] := data[t]
  END; (*copy data for sort*)
  QuickSort(dtemp, num);
  MedianResult := dtemp[num DIV 2]; (*middle element*)
  RETURN MedianResult
END Median; (*Median*)
```

The Mode

The mode of a sample is the value of the most frequently occurring element. For example, in the set

$$1\ 2\ 3\ 3\ 4\ 5\ 6\ 6\ 6\ 7\ 8\ 9$$

the mode would be 6 because it occurs three times. There may be more than one mode: For example, the sample

$$10\ 20\ 30\ 30\ 40\ 50\ 60\ 60\ 70$$

has 2 modes — 30 and 60 — because they both occur twice.

The function **FindMode**, shown here, returns the mode of a sample. If there is more than one mode, then **FindMode** returns the last one found.

```
PROCEDURE FindMode(data: DataArray;
                   num: INTEGER): REAL;
  VAR
    t, w, count, oldcount: INTEGER;
    md, oldmd: REAL;
BEGIN
  oldmd := Float(0);
  oldcount := 0;
  FOR t := 1 TO num DO
    md := data[t];
    count := 1;
```

```
FOR w := t+1 TO num DO
  IF md = data[w] THEN
    INC(count, 1)
  END
END;
IF count > oldcount THEN
  oldmd := md;
  oldcount := count;
END;
END;
RETURN oldmd;
END FindMode; (*FindMode*)
```

Using the Mean, the Median, and the Mode

The mean, the median, and the mode share the same purpose—to provide a single number that is the condensation of all numbers in the sample. However, each represents the sample in a different way. The most useful number generally is the mean—the arithmetic average—of the sample. Because the mean uses all values in its computation, it reflects all elements in the sample. The main disadvantage to the mean is its sensitivity to one extreme value. For example, in a hypothetical company called Widget, Inc., the owner's salary is $100,000 per year, and the salary of each of the nine employees is $10,000. The average wage at Widget is $19,500, but this figure does not fairly represent the actual situation.

In cases like the salary dispersion at Widget, the mode is sometimes used instead of the mean. The mode of the salaries at Widget is $10,000—a figure that reflects more accurately the actual situation. However, the mode can also be misleading. Consider a car company that makes cars of five different colors. In a given week, the company made

> 100 green cars
> 100 orange cars
> 150 blue cars
> 200 black cars
> 190 white cars

Here, the mode of the sample is black because the company made 200 black cars—more than any other color. However, it would be misleading to suggest that the car company primarily makes black cars.

The median is an interesting number because its validity is based on the *hope* that the sample will reflect a normal distribution. For example, if the sample is

1 2 3 4 5 6 7 8 9 10

then the median is 5 or 6, and the mean is 5.5. Hence, in this case, the median and mean are similar. However, in the sample

1 1 1 1 5 100 100 100 100

the median is still 5, but the mean is about 46!

In certain circumstances, you can can count on neither the mean, the mode, nor the median to give meaningful numbers. This situation leads to two of the most important numbers in statistics — the *variance* and the *standard deviation*.

The Variance and the Standard Deviation

Although the one-number summary (such as the mean or median) is convenient, it suffers from the fact that it can be easily misleading. Thinking a bit about this problem, you can see that the cause of the difficulty is not in the number itself, but due to the fact that it does not convey any information about the variations of the data. For example, in the sample

1 1 1 1 9 9 9 9

the mean is 5. However, there is no element in the sample that is close to 5. What you probably want to know is how close each element in the sample is to the average; in other words, how *variable* the data is. Knowing the variability of the data can help you interpret the mean, the median, and the mode better. You can find the variability of a sample by computing its variance and its standard deviation.

The variance and its square root, the standard deviation, are numbers that tell you the average deviation from the sample mean. Of the two numbers, the standard deviation is the most important because you can think of it as the average of the distances that the elements are from the mean of the sample. The variance is computed as

$$V = \frac{1}{N} \sum_{i=1}^{N} (D_i - M)^2$$

where N is the number of elements in the sample, and M is the sample's mean. You must square the difference of the mean and each element in order to produce only positive numbers. If the numbers were not squared, they would by default always sum to 0.

The variance, V, produced by the formula just given is of limited value because it is difficult to understand. However, its square root, the standard deviation, is the number that you are really looking for. You derive the standard deviation by finding the variance and then taking its square root:

$$std = \sqrt{\frac{1}{N} \sum_{i=1}^{N} (D_i - M)^2}$$

where, again, N is the number of elements in the sample, and M is the sample's mean.

For example, consider this sample:

11 20 40 30 99 30 50

You compute the variance as follows:

	D	$D-M$	$(D-M)^2$
	11	-29	841
	20	-20	400
	40	0	0
	30	-10	100
	99	59	3481
	30	-10	100
	50	10	100
Sum	280	0	5022
Mean	40	0	717.42

Here, the average of the squared differences is 717.42. To derive the standard deviation, you take the square root of that number; the result is approximately 26.78. To interpret the standard deviation, remember that it is the *average distance the elements in the sample are from the mean of the sample.*

The standard deviation tells you how representative the mean is of the entire sample. For example, if you owned a candy-bar factory and your plant supervisor reported that the daily output averaged 2500 bars last month but that the standard deviation was 2000, you would know that your production line needed better supervision!

If your sample follows a standard normal distribution, then about 68% of the sample will be within 1 standard deviation from the mean, and about 95% will be within 2 standard deviations!

The following function computes and returns the standard deviation of a given sample:

```
PROCEDURE StdDev(data: DataArray;
                 num: INTEGER): REAL;
   VAR
     t: INTEGER;
     std, avg: REAL;
BEGIN
   avg := Mean(data, num);
   std := 0.0;
   FOR t := 1 TO num DO
     std := std+((data[t]-avg)*(data[t]-avg))
   END;
   std := std/FLOAT(num);
   RETURN sqrt(std);
END StdDev; (*StdDev*)
```

Plotting on the Screen

The advantage of using graphs with statistics is that graphs convey the meaning clearly and accurately. A graph shows at a glance how the sample is actually distributed and how the data varies. This discussion is limited to two-dimensional graphs, which use the X-Y coordinate system. (Creating three-dimensional graphs is a discipline unto itself and beyond the scope of this book.)

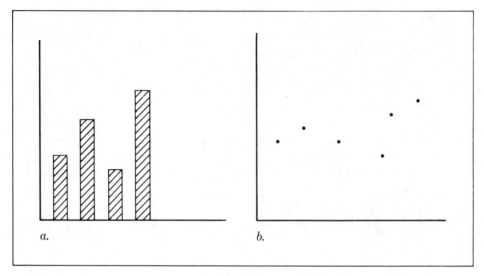

Figure 6-2. Examples of (*a*) a bar graph and (*b*) a scatter graph

There are two basic forms of two-dimensional graphs: the *bar graph* and the *scatter graph*. The bar graph uses solid bars to represent the magnitude of each element, while the scatter graph uses for each element one point that is located at its X-Y coordinates. Figure 6-2 shows an example of each.

The bar chart is usually used with a relatively small set of information, such as the gross national product for the last ten years, or the percentage output of a factory on a monthly basis. The scatter graph is generally used to display a large number of data points, such as the daily stock price of a company over a year. Also, you can plot projections by modifying the scatter graph to produce a solid line that connects the data points.

Although many Modula-2 compilers supply complete screen handling and graphics libraries, not all compilers do. For this reason, this section develops three routines that let you plot data on the screen. The first is a routine that clears the screen, the second is a routine that positions the cursor at a specified location, and the third is a routine that draws a vertical line when it is given the beginning and ending coordinates. To make certain that these routines can run on the widest variety of hardware, they are developed as text-mode procedures that use asterisks to indicate data points and that do not use any graphics. (However, if your Modula-2 compiler has a complete graphics library, feel free to enhance the examples.) If your compiler already supplies these routines, skip to the next section.

Using inline assembly code, the following routine uses a BIOS call to clear the screen:

```
PROCEDURE CLR; (* clear the screen *)
BEGIN
  CODE(55H,        (* push bp *)
    0B9H,0,0,       (* mov cx,0 *)
    0B6H,18H,       (* mov dh,24 *)
    0B2H,4FH,       (* mov dl,79 *)
    0B4H,6,         (* mov ah,6 *)
    0B0H,0,         (* mov al,0 *)
    0B7H,7,         (* mov bh,7 *)
    0CDH,10H,       (* int 10h *)
    5DH);           (* pop bp *)
END CLR;
```

The next routine positions the cursor at a specified X,Y location. The upper-left corner of the screen is location 0,0, while the lower-right corner is location 24,79.

```
PROCEDURE GotoXY(x,y:INTEGER);
(* go to specified XY position *)
BEGIN
  CODE(8AH,76H,4H,        (* get x *)
    8AH,56H,6,            (* get y *)
    0B4H,2,              (* xy function call *)
    0B7H,0,              (* video page is 0 *)
    0CDH,10H);           (* int 10h *)
END GotoXY;
```

This routine draws a vertical line of asterisks, when given the starting and ending coordinates:

```
PROCEDURE Line(startx,starty,endx,endy:INTEGER);
(* draw a line *)
BEGIN
  REPEAT
    GotoXY(startx,starty);
    Write('*');
    INC(starty);
  UNTIL starty>=endy;
END Line;
```

A Simple Plotting Procedure

Here is a simple plotting function that creates a bar graph on the IBM PC. Each bar is composed of asterisks. The variables **min** and **max** are globals that contain, respectively, the minimum and maximum values of the sample to be plotted. The procedure **GotoXY** sets the cursor to the desired X,Y position.

```
PROCEDURE SimplePlot(data:DataArray;num:INTEGER);
VAR
   t,incr:INTEGER;
   a:REAL;
   ch:CHAR;

BEGIN
  GotoXY(0,24); WriteInt(min,5);
  GotoXY(0,0); WriteInt(max,5);
  GotoXY(24,74); WriteInt(num,5);
  FOR t:=1 TO num DO
    a:=data[t];
    y:=Trunc(a);
    incr:=10;
    x:=((t-1)*incr)+10;
    Line(x,24-y,x,24);
  END;
END SimplePlot;
```

This simple plotting routine has a serious limitation—it assumes that all data is between 0 and 24. The reason for this is that the only valid numbers that can be used to call the **Line** procedure are within the range of 0 to 24, which is the resolution of the Y-axis of the IBM PC text mode. This range is fine as long as the data elements consistently fit in that range, which is an unlikely event. However, to make the plotting routine handle arbitrarily sized units, the routine must *normalize* the data before plotting it, and then alter the scale used, if necessary. Normalization involves first finding a ratio between the actual range of the data and the physical range of the screen, and then multiplying each data element by this ratio to produce a number that is within the range of the screen. The formula to do this for the Y-axis on the PC is

$$Y' = Y * \frac{24}{(max - min)}$$

where Y' is the value used to call the plotting function. It is also common to spread the scale to make the screen appear full when the data is located in only a small portion of the screen's range.

The function **BarPlot** will scale the X- and Y-axes and plot a bar graph of up to 70 elements. The X-axis is assumed to be time and is in one-unit increments. The general procedure for normalizing is to find the greatest value and the smallest value in the sample and find their difference. This number, which represents the spread between the minimum and maximum, is then used to divide the resolution of the screen. For the IBM PC, this number is 24 for the Y-axis and 78 for the X-axis (because you need a little room for the borders). You then use this ratio to convert the sample data into the proper scale.

```
(* Plots a bar graph of data on IBM PC display.*)
PROCEDURE BarPlot(data: DataArray;
                       num: INTEGER);
    VAR
        x, y, max, min, incr, t: INTEGER;
        a, norm, spread: REAL;
        ch: CHAR;

BEGIN
    (* first, find min and max value to enable normalization*)
    CLR;
    max := GetMax(data, num);
    min := GetMin(data, num);
    IF min > 0 THEN
        min := 0
    END;
    spread := FLOAT(max-min);
    norm := FLOAT(24)/spread;
    GotoXY(0, 24);
    WriteInt(min,5);
    GotoXY(0, 0);
    WriteInt(max,5);
    GotoXY(74,24);
    WriteInt(num,5);
    incr := 78 DIV num;
    FOR t := 1 TO num DO
        a := data[t]-FLOAT(min);
        a := a*norm;
        y := TRUNC(a);
        x := ((t-1)*incr)+10;
        IF y<>0 THEN Line(x,24-y,x,24); END;
    END;
    Read(ch);
    CLR;
END BarPlot; (*BarPlot*)
```

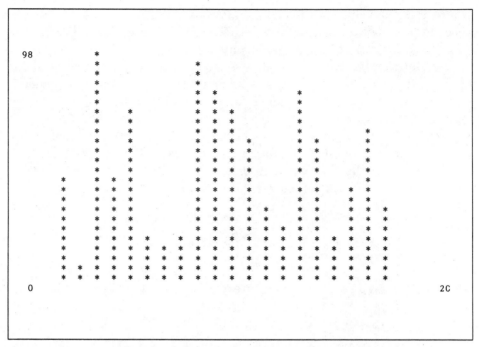

Figure 6-3. A sample bar graph that was produced by **BarPlot**

Figure 6-3 gives a sample of the output of **BarPlot** with 20 elements. By no means does **BarPlot** provide all the features that you may desire, but it does display a single sample accurately. You may also find it easy to expand **BarPlot** to fit your needs.

Only a slight modification to **BarPlot** is required to make a procedure that plots a scatter graph. The primary alteration is to exchange the **Line** function for one that plots only one point. You can do this by using **GotoXY** and then writing an asterisk. Here is the **ScatterPlot** procedure:

```
PROCEDURE ScatterPlot(data: DataArray;
                      num, ymin, ymax, xmax: INTEGER);
    VAR
      x, y, t, incr: INTEGER;
      a, spread, norm: REAL;

BEGIN
(* first, find min and max value to enable normalization*)
```

```
IF ymin > 0 THEN
  ymin := 0
END;
spread := FLOAT(ymax-ymin);
norm := FLOAT(24)/spread;
GotoXY(0,24);
WriteInt(ymin,5);
GotoXY(0,0);
  WriteInt(ymax,5);
  GotoXY(74,24);
  WriteInt(xmax,5);
  incr := 78 DIV xmax;
  FOR t := 1 TO num DO
    a := data[t]-FLOAT(ymin);
    a := a*norm;
    y := TRUNC(a);
    x := ((t-1)*incr)+10;
    IF y<>0 THEN
      GotoXY(x,24-y);
      Write('*');
    END;
  END;
END ScatterPlot; (*ScatterPlot*)
```

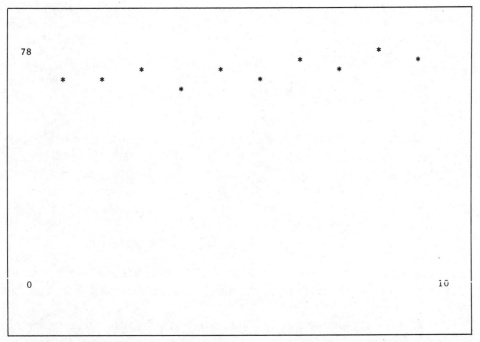

Figure 6-4. A sample scatter graph that was produced by **ScatterPlot**

In **ScatterPlot**, notice that the minimum and maximum values of the data are passed into the procedure instead of being computed by the procedure, as is the case in **BarPlot**. The reason for this is to allow the plotting of multiple data sets on the screen without changing the scale. Thus, you can call **Scatter-Plot** repeatedly with different sets of data to achieve an overlay effect. Figure 6-4 shows a sample scatter graph of 30 data elements that was produced by **ScatterPlot**.

Projections and the Regression Equation

Statistical information is commonly used to make "informed guesses" about the future. Even though everyone knows that the past does not necessarily predict the future and that there are exceptions to every rule, historical data is still used in this way. Often past and present trends do continue into the future. When they do, you can try to determine specific values at future points in time. This process is called making a *projection*, or *trend analysis*.

For example, consider a fictitious ten-year study of life spans that collected the following data:

Year	Life Span
1970	69
1971	70
1972	72
1973	68
1974	73
1975	71
1976	75
1977	74
1978	78
1979	77

You might wonder whether there is a trend here at all. If there is a trend, you may try to determine which way the trend is going, and then what the life expectancy is in, say, 1985.

First, study the bar graph and the scatter graph of this data, which are shown in Figure 6-5. By examining these graphs, you can see that generally

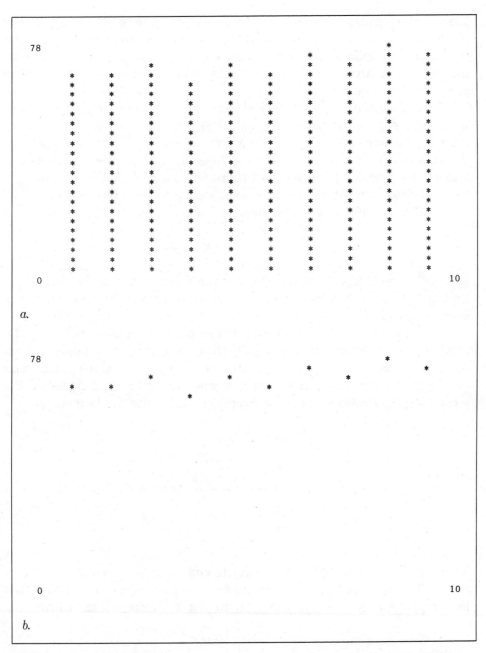

Figure 6-5. Examples of (a) a bar graph and (b) a scatter graph of life expectancy

life spans are getting longer. Also, if you placed a ruler on the graphs to try to fit the data and drew a line that extended into 1985, you could project that that year's life span would be about 82. While you may feel confident about this intuitive analysis, you probably would rather use a more formal method to project life span trends.

If you are given a set of historical data, the best way to make projections is to find the *line of best fit* in relation to the data. (This is what you did with the ruler.) A line of best fit is one that most closely represents each point of the data and its trend. Although some, or even all, of the actual data points may not be on the line, this line best represents them. The validity of the line is based upon how closely the sample data points come to being on the line.

Recall that a line in two-dimensional space has the basic equation

$$Y = a + bX$$

where Y is the independent variable, a is the Y-intercept, b is the slope of the line, and x is the dependent variable. Therefore, to find a line that best fits a sample, you must determine a and b.

Although you can use any number of methods to determine the values of a and b, the most common (and generally the best) is called the *method of least squares*. It tries to minimize the distance between the actual data points and the line through two steps. The first step computes b, the slope of the line; the second step computes a, the Y-intercept. To find b, use the formula

$$b = \frac{\sum\limits_{i=1}^{N} (X_i - M_x)(Y_i - M_y)}{\sum\limits_{i=1}^{N} (X_i - M_x)^2}$$

where M_x is the mean of the X coordinate and M_y is the mean of the Y coordinate. The derivation of this formula is beyond the scope of this book, but having found b, you can use it to compute the Y-intercept a as shown:

$$a = M_y - bM_x$$

With this equation, you can plug in any number for X and find the value of Y. For example, if you use the life-expectancy data, you find that the regression equation looks like

$$Y = 67.46 + 0.95 * X$$

Therefore, to find the life expectancy in 1985, which is 15 years from 1970, you find that

$$\text{Life Expectancy} = 67.46 + 0.95 * 15$$
$$\cong 82$$

However, even with a line of best fit for the data, you may still want to know how well that line actually correlates with the data. If the line and data have only a slight correlation, then the regression line is of little use. However, if the line fits the data well, then it is a more valid indicator. The most common way to determine and represent the correlation of the data to the regression line is to compute the *correlation coefficient*, which is a number between 0 and 1. The correlation coefficient is essentially a percentage that is related to the distance that each data point is from the line. If the correlation coefficient is 1, then the data corresponds perfectly to the line—that is, each element of the sample is also on the regression line. A coefficient of 0 means that there is no correlation between the line and the points—no points in the sample are actually on the line—and in fact, any line would be as good (or bad) as the one used. The formula to find the correlation coefficient Cor is

$$Cor = \frac{\dfrac{1}{N} \displaystyle\sum_{i=1}^{N} (X_i - M_x)(Y_i - M_y)}{\sqrt{\dfrac{1}{N} \displaystyle\sum_{i=1}^{N} (X_i - M_x)^2} \ \sqrt{\dfrac{1}{N} \displaystyle\sum_{i=1}^{N} (Y_i - M_y)^2}}$$

Here, M_x is the mean of X, and M_y is the mean of Y. Generally, a value of 0.81 is considered a strong correlation. It indicates that about 66% of the data fits the regression line. To convert any correlation coefficient into a percentage, you simply square it.

Here is the function **Regress**, which uses the methods just described to find the regression equation and the coefficient of correlation, and optionally to scatter plot both the sample data and the line. Plotting the regression line implies that several points on the line need to be computed. These values are held in the **data2** array.

```
(* Compute the regression equation and the coefficient of
  correlation - then plot the data and regress line.*)
PROCEDURE Regress(data: DataArray;
                       num: INTEGER);
    VAR
      a, b, xAvg, yAvg, temp, temp2, cor: REAL;
      data2: DataArray;
      t, min, max: INTEGER;
      ch: CHAR;

BEGIN
(*find Mean of x and y*)
  yAvg := FLOAT(0);
  xAvg := FLOAT(0);
  FOR t := 1 TO num DO
    yAvg := yAvg+data[t];
    xAvg := xAvg+FLOAT(t); (* because x is time*)
  END;
  xAvg := xAvg/FLOAT(num);
  yAvg := yAvg/FLOAT(num);
  (*find b fact in regress equation*)
  temp := FLOAT(0);
  temp2 := FLOAT(0);
  FOR t := 1 TO num DO
    temp := temp+(data[t]-yAvg)*(FLOAT(t)-xAvg);
    temp2 := temp2+(FLOAT(t)-xAvg)*(FLOAT(t)-xAvg);
  END;
  b := temp/temp2;
  (*find a in regression equation*)
  a := yAvg-(b*xAvg);
  (*computer coefficent of correlation*)
  FOR t := 1 TO num DO
    data2[t] := FLOAT(t)
  END; (*copy data*)
  cor := temp/FLOAT(num);
  cor := cor/(StdDev(data, num)*StdDev(data2, num));
  WriteString('Regression equation is: Y = ');
  WriteReal(a, 15);
  Write('+');
  WriteReal(b, 15);
  WriteString('* X');
  WriteLn;
  WriteString('Correlation Coefficient: ');
  WriteReal(cor, 15);
  WriteLn;
  WriteString('Plot data and regression line? (y/n) ');
```

```
Read(ch);
WriteLn;
ch := CAP(ch);
IF ch <> 'N' THEN
  FOR t := 1 TO num*2 DO
    data2[t] := a+(b*FLOAT(t))
  END; (*regression array*)
  min := GetMin(data, num)*2;
  max := GetMax(data, num)*2;
  CLR;
  ScatterPlot(data, num, min, max, num*2);
  ScatterPlot(data2, num*2, min, max, num*2);
  Read(ch);
  CLR;
END;
END Regress; (*regress*)
```

Figure 6-6 shows a scatter plot of both the sample life expectancy data and the regression line.

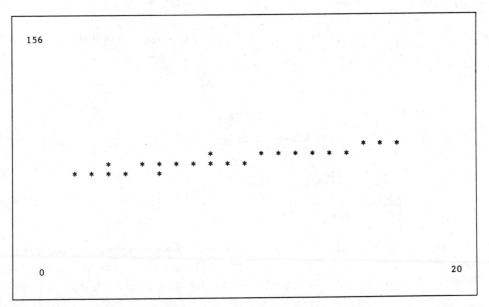

Figure 6-6. The regression line for life expectancy

Making a Complete Statistics Program

So far, this chapter has developed several functions that perform statistics on one variable. In this section, you put the functions together to form a complete program that you can use to analyze data, print bar charts or scatter plots, and make projections. Before you can create a complete program, you must define a data record to hold the information and a few support routines.

First, you need an array to hold the sample information. This section uses a single-dimension floating-point array called **data** of size MAX. MAX is defined to fit the largest sample that you need, which is 100 in this case. Here are the import statements, constant and type definitions, and the global data.

```
MODULE stats;

  FROM SYSTEM
    IMPORT WORD, ADR, TSIZE, CODE;
  FROM MathLib0 IMPORT arctan, cos, exp, ln, sin, sqrt;
  FROM Strings IMPORT Pos, Copy, Concat, Length, CompareStr;
  FROM RealInOut IMPORT ReadReal, WriteReal;
  FROM InOut IMPORT ReadInt, ReadCard, Read, ReadString, Write,
    WriteInt, WriteCard, WriteString, WriteLn;
  FROM FileSystem IMPORT File, SetRead, SetWrite, Close,
    ReadNBytes,WriteNBytes, WriteWord, ReadWord, Response,
    Reset, Lookup;

  CONST
    MAX = 100;

  TYPE
    str80 = ARRAY [0..79] OF CHAR;
    DataItem = REAL;
    DataArray = ARRAY [1..MAX] OF DataItem;

  VAR
    data: DataArray;
    a, m, md, std: REAL;
    num: INTEGER;
    ch: CHAR;
    datafile: File;
```

Aside from the statistical functions that have been developed already, you need routines to save and load data. The **Save** routine must also store the number of data elements, and the **Load** routine must read back that number.

```
PROCEDURE Save(data: DataArray;
               num: INTEGER);
  VAR
    f: File;
    t: INTEGER;
    w: CARDINAL;
    fname: ARRAY [0..80-1] OF CHAR;
    temp: REAL;
BEGIN
  REPEAT
    WriteString('Enter Filename: ');
    ReadString(fname);  WriteLn;
    Lookup(f,fname ,TRUE); (* create if not there *)
  UNTIL f.res = done;

  Reset(f);  (* rewrite from the beginning *)
  SetWrite(f);  (* enable write *)

  WriteWord(f,WORD(num));
  FOR t := 1 TO num DO
    WriteNBytes(f,ADR(data[t]), TSIZE(REAL), w);
    IF w<>TSIZE(REAL) THEN WriteString('write error'); END;
  END;
  Close(f);
END Save; (*save*)

PROCEDURE Load;
  VAR
    f: File;
    t: INTEGER;
    temp: WORD;
    w: CARDINAL;
    fname: ARRAY [0..80-1] OF CHAR;
BEGIN
  REPEAT
    WriteString('Enter Filename: ');
    ReadString(fname);  WriteLn;
    Lookup(f,fname ,FALSE); (* don't create if not there *)
  UNTIL f.res = done;
  SetRead(f);  (* enable write *)

  ReadWord(f,temp);
  num:=INTEGER(temp);

  FOR t := 1 TO num DO
    ReadNBytes(f,ADR(data[t]), TSIZE(REAL), w);
    IF w<>TSIZE(REAL) THEN WriteString('write error'); END;
  END;
  Close(f);
END Load; (*Load;*)
```

For your convenience, the entire statistics program is given next.

```
MODULE stats;

  FROM SYSTEM
    IMPORT WORD, ADR, TSIZE, CODE;
  FROM MathLib0 IMPORT arctan, cos, exp, ln, sin, sqrt;
  FROM Strings IMPORT Pos, Copy, Concat, Length, CompareStr;
  FROM RealInOut IMPORT ReadReal, WriteReal;
  FROM InOut IMPORT ReadInt, ReadCard, Read, ReadString, Write,
    WriteInt, WriteCard, WriteString, WriteLn;
  FROM FileSystem IMPORT File, SetRead, SetWrite, Close,
    WriteNBytes, WriteWord, ReadWord, Response, ReadNBytes,
    Reset, Lookup;

  CONST
    MAX = 100;

  TYPE
    str80 = ARRAY [0..79] OF CHAR;
    DataItem = REAL;
    DataArray = ARRAY [1..MAX] OF DataItem;

  VAR
    data: DataArray;
    a, m, md, std: REAL;
    num: INTEGER;
    ch: CHAR;
    datafile: File;


PROCEDURE CLR; (* clear the screen *)
BEGIN
  CODE(55H,        (* push bp *)
    0B9H,0,0,       (* mov cx,0 *)
    0B6H,18H,       (* mov dh,24 *)
    0B2H,4FH,       (* mov dl,79 *)
    0B4H,6,         (* mov ah,6 *)
    0B0H,0,         (* mov al,0 *)
    0B7H,7,         (* mov bh,7 *)
    0CDH,10H,       (* int 10h *)
    5DH);           (* pop bp *)
END CLR;


PROCEDURE GotoXY(x,y:INTEGER);
(* go to specified XY position *)
BEGIN
  CODE(8AH,76H,4H,       (* get x *)
    8AH,56H,6,            (* get y *)
    0B4H,2,              (* xy function call *)
    0B7H,0,              (* video page is 0 *)
    0CDH,10H);           (* int 10h *)
END GotoXY;


PROCEDURE QuickSort(VAR item: DataArray;
                    count: INTEGER);

  PROCEDURE qs(l, r: INTEGER;
               VAR it: DataArray);
```

```
    VAR
      i, j: INTEGER;
      x, y: DataItem;
  BEGIN
    i := l;
    j := r;
    x := it[(l+r) DIV 2];
    REPEAT
      WHILE it[i] < x DO
        INC(i, 1)
      END;
      WHILE x < it[j] DO
        DEC(j, 1)
      END;
      IF i <= j THEN
        y := it[i];
        it[i] := it[j];
        it[j] := y;
        INC(i, 1);
        DEC(j, 1);
      END;
    UNTIL i > j;
    IF l < j THEN
      qs(l, j, it)
    END;
    IF l < r THEN
      qs(i, r, it)
    END
  END qs;
BEGIN
  qs(1, count, item);
END QuickSort;


PROCEDURE IsIn(ch: CHAR;
              s: str80): BOOLEAN;
  VAR
    t: INTEGER;
BEGIN
  FOR t := 0 TO Length(s) DO
    IF s[t] = ch THEN
      RETURN TRUE
    END
  END;
  RETURN FALSE
END IsIn;


PROCEDURE Menu(): CHAR;
  VAR
    ch: CHAR;
BEGIN
  WriteLn; WriteLn;
  REPEAT
    WriteString('Enter data');
    WriteLn;
    WriteString('Display data');
    WriteLn;
    WriteString('Basic statistics');
```

```
      WriteLn;
      WriteString('Regression line and scatter Plot');
      WriteLn;
      WriteString('Plot a bar graph');
      WriteLn;
      WriteString('Save');
      WriteLn;
      WriteString('Load');
      WriteLn;
      WriteString('Quit');
      WriteLn;
      WriteLn;
      WriteString('choose one (E, D, B, R, P, S, L, D, Q): ');
      Read(ch);
      WriteLn;
      ch := CAP(ch);
    UNTIL IsIn(ch, 'EBRPSLDQD');
    RETURN ch;
END Menu;


PROCEDURE Display(data: DataArray;
                  num: INTEGER);
  VAR
    t: INTEGER;
BEGIN
  FOR t := 1 TO num DO
    WriteInt(t,1);
    Write(':');
    WriteReal(data[t],6);
    WriteLn
  END;
  WriteLn;
END Display;


PROCEDURE Enter(VAR data: DataArray);
  VAR
    t: INTEGER;
BEGIN
  WriteString('number of items?: ');
  ReadInt(num);
  WriteLn;
  FOR t := 1 TO num DO
    WriteString('Enter item ');
    WriteInt(t,6);
    WriteString(': ');
    ReadReal(data[t]);
    WriteLn;
  END;
END Enter;


PROCEDURE Mean(data: DataArray;
               num: INTEGER): REAL;
```

```
   VAR
     t: INTEGER;
     avg: REAL;
BEGIN
   avg := 0.0;
   FOR t := 1 TO num DO
     avg := avg+data[t]
   END;
   RETURN avg/FLOAT(num);
END Mean;


PROCEDURE StdDev(data: DataArray;
                     num: INTEGER): REAL;
   VAR
     t: INTEGER;
     std, avg: REAL;
BEGIN
   avg := Mean(data, num);
   std := 0.0;
   FOR t := 1 TO num DO
     std := std+((data[t]-avg)*(data[t]-avg))
   END;
   std := std/FLOAT(num);
   RETURN sqrt(std);
END StdDev;


PROCEDURE FindMode(data: DataArray;
                     num: INTEGER): REAL;
   VAR
     t, w, count, oldcount: INTEGER;
     md, oldmd: REAL;
BEGIN
   oldmd := FLOAT(0);
   oldcount := 0;
   FOR t := 1 TO num DO
     md := data[t];
     count := 1;
     FOR w := t+1 TO num DO
       IF md = data[w] THEN
         INC(count, 1)
       END
     END;
     IF count > oldcount THEN
       oldmd := md;
       oldcount := count;
     END;
   END;
   RETURN oldmd;
END FindMode; (*FindMode*)


PROCEDURE Median(data: DataArray;
                num: INTEGER): REAL;
```

```
    VAR
      dtemp: DataArray;
      t: INTEGER;
BEGIN
  FOR t := 1 TO num DO
    dtemp[t] := data[t]
  END; (*copy data for sort*)
  QuickSort(dtemp, num);
  RETURN dtemp[num DIV 2]; (*middle element*)
END Median; (*Median*)


PROCEDURE GetMax(data: DataArray;
                  num: INTEGER): INTEGER;
  VAR
    t: INTEGER;
    max: REAL;
BEGIN
  max := data[1];
  FOR t := 2 TO num DO
    IF data[t] > max THEN
      max := data[t]
    END
  END;
  RETURN TRUNC(max);
END GetMax;


PROCEDURE GetMin(data: DataArray;
                  num: INTEGER): INTEGER;
  VAR
    t: INTEGER;
    min: REAL;
BEGIN
  min := data[1];
  FOR t := 2 TO num DO
    IF data[t] < min THEN
      min := data[t]
    END
  END;
  RETURN TRUNC(min);
END GetMin;


PROCEDURE Line(startx,starty,endx,endy:INTEGER);
(* draw a line *)
BEGIN
  REPEAT
    GotoXY(startx,starty);
    Write('*');
    INC(starty);
  UNTIL starty>=endy;
END Line;


(* Plots a bar graph of data on IBM PC display.*)
PROCEDURE BarPlot(data: DataArray;
                  num: INTEGER);
```

```
    VAR
        x, y, max, min, incr, t: INTEGER;
        a, norm, spread: REAL;
        ch: CHAR;
BEGIN
    (* first, find min and max value to enable normalization*)
    CLR;
    max := GetMax(data, num);
    min := GetMin(data, num);
    IF min > 0 THEN
        min := 0
    END;
    spread := FLOAT(max-min);
    norm := FLOAT(24)/spread;
    GotoXY(0, 24);
    WriteInt(min,5);
    GotoXY(0, 0);
    WriteInt(max,5);
    GotoXY(74,24);
    WriteInt(num,5);
    incr := 78 DIV num;
    FOR t := 1 TO num DO
        a := data[t]-FLOAT(min);
        a := a*norm;
        y := TRUNC(a);
        x := ((t-1)*incr)+10;
        IF y<>0 THEN Line(x,24-y,x,24); END;
    END;
    Read(ch);
    CLR;
END BarPlot;


PROCEDURE ScatterPlot(data: DataArray;
                        num, ymin, ymax, xmax: INTEGER);
    VAR
        x, y, t, incr: INTEGER;
        a, spread, norm: REAL;

BEGIN
(* first, find min and max value to enable normalization*)
    IF ymin > 0 THEN
        ymin := 0
    END;
    spread := FLOAT(ymax-ymin);
    norm := FLOAT(24)/spread;
    GotoXY(0,24);
    WriteInt(ymin,5);
    GotoXY(0,0);
    WriteInt(ymax,5);
    GotoXY(74,24);
    WriteInt(xmax,5);
    incr := 78 DIV xmax;
    FOR t := 1 TO num DO
        a := data[t]-FLOAT(ymin);
        a := a*norm;
        y := TRUNC(a);
        x := ((t-1)*incr)+10;
```

```
      IF y<>0 THEN
        GotoXY(x,24-y);
        Write('*');
      END;
    END;
  END;
END ScatterPlot;


(* Compute the regression equation and the coefficient of
 correlation - then plot the data and regress line.*)
PROCEDURE Regress(data: DataArray;
                  num: INTEGER);
   VAR
     a, b, xAvg, yAvg, temp, temp2, cor: REAL;
     data2: DataArray;
     t, min, max: INTEGER;
     ch: CHAR;
BEGIN
(*find Mean of x and y*)
  yAvg := FLOAT(0);
  xAvg := FLOAT(0);
  FOR t := 1 TO num DO
  yAvg := yAvg+data[t];
  xAvg := xAvg+FLOAT(t); (* because x is time*)
END;
xAvg := xAvg/FLOAT(num);
yAvg := yAvg/FLOAT(num);
(*find b fact in regress equation*)
temp := FLOAT(0);
temp2 := FLOAT(0);
FOR t := 1 TO num DO
  temp := temp+(data[t]-yAvg)*(FLOAT(t)-xAvg);
  temp2 := temp2+(FLOAT(t)-xAvg)*(FLOAT(t)-xAvg);
END;
b := temp/temp2;
(*find a in regression equation*)
a := yAvg-(b*xAvg);
(*computer coeffecent of correlation*)
FOR t := 1 TO num DO
  data2[t] := FLOAT(t)
END; (*copy data*)
cor := temp/FLOAT(num);
cor := cor/(StdDev(data, num)*StdDev(data2, num));
WriteString('Regression equation is: Y = ');
WriteReal(a, 15);
Write('+');
WriteReal(b, 15);
WriteString('* X');
WriteLn;
WriteString('Correlation Coefficient: ');
WriteReal(cor, 15);
WriteLn;
WriteString('Plot data and regression line? (y/n) ');
Read(ch);
WriteLn;
ch := CAP(ch);
IF ch <> 'N' THEN
  FOR t := 1 TO num*2 DO
```

```
      data2[t] := a+(b*FLOAT(t))
    END; (*regression array*)
    min := GetMin(data, num)*2;
    max := GetMax(data, num)*2;
    CLR;
    ScatterPlot(data, num, min, max, num*2);
    ScatterPlot(data2, num*2, min, max, num*2);
    Read(ch);
    CLR;
  END;
END Regress;


PROCEDURE Save(data: DataArray;
               num: INTEGER);
  VAR
    f: File;
    t: INTEGER;
    w: CARDINAL;
    fname: ARRAY [0..80-1] OF CHAR;
    temp: REAL;
BEGIN
  REPEAT
    WriteString('Enter Filename: ');
    ReadString(fname);  WriteLn;
    Lookup(f,fname ,TRUE); (* create if not there *)
  UNTIL f.res = done;

  Reset(f);  (* re-write from the beginning *)
  SetWrite(f);  (* enable write *)

  WriteWord(f,WORD(num));
  FOR t := 1 TO num DO
    WriteNBytes(f,ADR(data[t]), TSIZE(REAL), w);
    IF w<>TSIZE(REAL) THEN WriteString('write error'); END;
  END;
  Close(f);
END Save;


PROCEDURE Load;
  VAR
    f: File;
    t: INTEGER;
    temp: WORD;
    w: CARDINAL;
    fname: ARRAY [0..80-1] OF CHAR;
BEGIN
  REPEAT
    WriteString('Enter Filename: ');
    ReadString(fname);  WriteLn;
    Lookup(f,fname ,FALSE); (* create if not there *)
  UNTIL f.res = done;

  SetRead(f);  (* enable write *)

  ReadWord(f,temp);
  num:=INTEGER(temp);
```

```
    FOR t := 1 TO num DO
      ReadNBytes(f,ADR(data[t]), TSIZE(REAL), w);
      IF w<>TSIZE(REAL) THEN WriteString('write error'); END;
    END;
    Close(f);
  END Load;


  BEGIN
    REPEAT
      ch := CAP(Menu());
      CASE ch OF
        'E':
          Enter(data) |
        'B':
          a := Mean(data, num);
          m := Median(data, num);
          std := StdDev(data, num);
          md := FindMode(data, num);
          WriteString('Mean: ');
          WriteReal(a, 15);
          WriteLn;
          WriteString('Median: ');
          WriteReal(m, 15);
          WriteLn;
          WriteString('standard deviation: ');
          WriteReal(std, 15);
          WriteLn;
          WriteString('mode: ');
          WriteReal(md, 15);
          WriteLn;
          WriteLn; |
        'D':
          Display(data, num) |
        'P':
          BarPlot(data, num) |
        'R':
          Regress(data, num) |
        'S':
          Save(data, num) |
        'L':
          Load
        ELSE
      END;
    UNTIL ch = 'Q';
  END stats.
```

Using the Statistics Program

To see how you might use the statistics program that is developed in this chapter, here is a simple stock-market-analysis example that uses Widget,

Inc. As an investor, you will be trying to decide whether the time is right to invest in Widget by buying stock; to *sell short* (the process of selling shares that you do not have in the hope of a rapid price drop so that you can buy them later at a cheaper price); or to invest elsewhere.

For the past 24 months, Widget's stock price has been as follows:

Month	Stock Price
1	$10
2	10
3	11
4	9
5	8
6	8
7	9
8	10
9	10
10	13
11	11
12	11
13	11
14	11
15	12
16	13
17	14
18	16
19	17
20	15
21	15
22	16
23	14
24	16

You should first determine whether Widget's stock price has established a trend. After entering the figures, you find the following basic statistics:

Mean	$12.08
Median	$11.00
Standard deviation	2.68
Mode	$11.00

Next, you should plot a bar graph of the stock price as shown in Figure 6-7. There may be a trend, but you should perform a formal regression

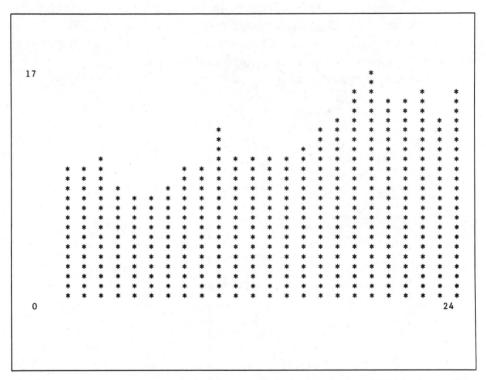

Figure 6-7.   A bar graph of the statistical information on Widget's profits over the last 24 months

analysis. The regression equation is

$$Y = 7.90 + 0.33 * X$$

with a correlation coefficient of 0.86, or about 74%. This is quite good — in fact, a definite trend is clear. Printing a scatter graph, as shown in Figure 6-8, makes this string growth readily apparent. Such results could cause an investor to throw caution to the winds and buy 1000 shares as quickly as possible!

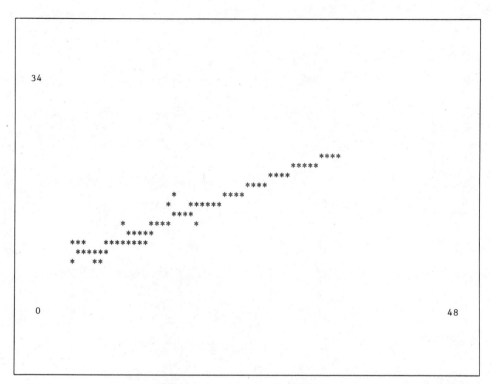

Figure 6-8. A scatter graph showing the growth of Widget, Incorporated

Final Thoughts

The correct use of statistics requires a general understanding of how the results are derived and what the numbers really mean. As with the Widget example, many people forget that past events do not necessary predict the future (except in some general way). Blindly relying on statistical evidence can cause disturbing results. Statistics can be used to reflect nature—but nature cannot be expected to reflect statistics!

Codes and Data Compression

C H A P T E R 7

Often, people who like computers and programming like to play with codes and ciphers. Perhaps the reason for this is that all codes involve algorithms — just as programs do. Or perhaps these persons have an affinity for cryptic things that most people cannot understand. All programmers seem to receive a great deal of satisfaction when a nonprogrammer looks at a program listing and says something like, "My God, that looks complicated!" After all, the act of writing a program is called "coding."

Closely associated with the subject of cryptography is *data compression*. Data compression means compacting information into a smaller space than is usually used. Because data compaction can play a role in encryption and uses many of the same principles as encryption, this chapter includes a discussion of it.

Computer-based cryptography is important for two primary reasons. The most obvious is the need to keep sensitive data on shared systems secure. Although password protection is adequate for many situations, important, confidential files are routinely coded to provide greater protection. The second reason to use computer-based codes is in data transmission. Not only are governments using codes for such matters as secret information, but broadcasters are also beginning to use them to protect sky-to-earth station transmissions. Because these types of coding procedures are so complex, they are usually handled by computers.

Data compression is also commonly used to increase the storage capacity of various storage devices. Although the cost of storage devices has fallen sharply in recent years, there still can be the need to fit more information into smaller areas.

A Short History of Cryptography

Although no one knows when secret writing began, a cuneiform tablet made around 1500 B.C. is one of the earliest known examples. The tablet contains a coded formula for making pottery glaze. The Greeks used codes as early as 475 B.C., and the upper class in Rome frequently used simple ciphers during the reign of Julius Caesar. During the Dark Ages, interest in cryptography waned (like many other intellectual pursuits) except among monks, who used it occasionally. With the birth of the Italian Renaissance, the art of cryptography again began to flourish. By the reign of Louis XIV of France, a code that was based on 587 randomly selected keys was used for government messages.

In the 1800s, two events helped move cryptography forward. The first was Edgar Allan Poe's stories, such as "The Gold Bug," which featured coded messages and excited the imagination of many readers. The second was the invention of the telegraph and the Morse code. Morse code was the first binary representation (dots and dashes) of the alphabet that was widely used.

By World War I, several nations had constructed mechanical "code machines" that permitted easy encoding and decoding of text by sophisticated, complex ciphers. At this point in history, the story of cryptography changes slightly to the story of code-breaking.

Before mechanical devices were used to encode and decode messages, complex ciphers were not used often because of the amount of time and effort that was required both for encoding and decoding. Hence, most codes could be broken within a relatively short period of time. However, the art of code-breaking became much more difficult when code machines were used. Although modern computers could break even those codes easily, these computers cannot dwarf the incredible talent of Herbert Yardley, who is still considered the master code-breaker of all time. He not only broke the U.S. diplomatic code in 1915 in his spare time, but he also broke the Japanese diplomatic code in 1922—even though he did not know Japanese! He accomplished this by using frequency tables of the Japanese language.

By World War II, the major method of breaking codes was to steal the code machine of the enemy—thereby avoiding the tedious, but intellectually satisfying, process of code-breaking. In fact, the Allies' possession of a German code machine (unknown to the Germans) contributed greatly to the outcome of the war.

With the advent of computers—especially multiuser computers—the need for secure, unbreakable codes has become even more important. Not only do computer files occasionally need to be confidential, but also access to the computer itself must be managed and regulated. Numerous methods of encrypting data files have been developed, and the DES (Data Encryption Standard) algorithm, which is accepted by the National Bureau of Standards, is generally considered to be secure from code-breaking efforts. However, DES is difficult to implement and may not be suitable for all situations.

The Basic Ciphers

Of the more traditional coding methods, there are two basic types: *substitution* and *transposition*. A substitution cipher replaces one character with another character, but leaves the message in the proper order. A transposition cipher essentially scrambles the characters of a message according to some rule. Both types of codes can be carried on to whatever level of complexity is desired and can even be intermixed. The digital computer adds a third basic type of encryption called *bit manipulation*, which alters the computerized representation of data by some algorithm.

All three methods may make use of a *key*. Generally, a key is some string of characters that is needed to decode a message. However, do not confuse the key with the method, because knowing only the key is never sufficient to decode a message—you must also know the encryption algorithm. The key "personalizes" a coded message so that only the people that know the key can decode it, even though the method used to encode the message may be accessible.

Two terms that you should become familiar with are *plaintext* and *ciphertext*. The plaintext of a message is the text that you can read; the ciphertext is the encoded version.

This chapter presents computerized methods that use each of the three basic methods to code text files. You will study several short programs that encode and decode text files. With one exception, all of these programs have both a **Code** and a **Decode** function. The **Decode** function always reverses the **Code** process that creates the ciphertext. In this chapter, for the sake of simplicity, all letters in a message will be coded and decoded in uppercase.

Substitution Ciphers

One of the simplest forms of the substitution cipher offsets the alphabet by a specified amount. For example, if you offset each letter by three, then

abcdefghijklmnopqrstuvwxyz

becomes

defghijklmnopqrstuvwxyzabc

Notice that the letters *abc* that were shifted off the front would be added to the end. To encode a message with this method, you simply substitute the shifted alphabet for the real one. For example, the message

meet me at sunset

becomes

phhw ph dw vxqvhw

With this program you can code any text message by any offset:

```
MODULE subs1;
(*A simple substitution cipher *)

   FROM InOut IMPORT ReadString, WriteLn, WriteString,
      ReadInt, Read;
   FROM FileSystem IMPORT File, SetRead, SetWrite, Close,
      ReadChar, WriteChar, Response, Reset, Lookup;


   TYPE
      str80 = ARRAY [0..79] OF CHAR;

   VAR
      fname: str80;
      inf, outf: File;
      start: INTEGER;
      ch: CHAR;

   PROCEDURE Code(inf, outf: File;
                     start: INTEGER);
      VAR
        ch: CHAR;
        t: INTEGER;
   BEGIN
     REPEAT
       ReadChar(inf, ch);
       ch := CAP(ch);
       IF (ch >= 'A') AND (ch <= 'Z') THEN
         t := INTEGER(ORD(ch))+start;
         IF t > INTEGER(ORD('Z')) THEN
           DEC(t, 26)
         END; (*wrap around*)
         ch := CHR(t);
       END;
       WriteChar(outf, ch);
```

```
            UNTIL inf.eof;
            WriteString('file coded');
            WriteLn;
            Close(inf);
            Close(outf);
    END Code;


    PROCEDURE Decode(inf, outf: File;
                        start: INTEGER);
        VAR
          ch: CHAR;
          t: INTEGER;

    BEGIN
        REPEAT
          ReadChar(inf, ch);
            ch := CAP(ch);
            IF (ch >= 'A') AND (ch <= 'Z') THEN
              t := INTEGER(ORD(ch))-start;
              IF t < INTEGER(ORD('A')) THEN
                INC(t, 26)
              END; (*wrap around*)
              ch := CHR(t);
            END;
            WriteChar(outf, ch);
          UNTIL inf.eof;
          WriteString('file decoded');
          WriteLn;
          Close(inf);
          Close(outf);
        END Decode;



    BEGIN
        REPEAT
          WriteString('Enter input filename: ');
          ReadString(fname);   WriteLn;
          Lookup(inf,fname ,FALSE); (* must be there *)
        UNTIL inf.res = done;


        REPEAT
          WriteString('Enter output filename: ');
          ReadString(fname);   WriteLn;
          Lookup(outf,fname ,TRUE); (* create it *)
        UNTIL outf.res = done;

        SetWrite(outf);  (* enable write *)
        SetRead(inf);   (* enable read *)

        WriteString('Enter starting position (1-26): ');
        ReadInt(start);   WriteLn;
        WriteString('Code or Decode (C or D): ');
        Read(ch);
        IF CAP(ch) = 'C' THEN
```

```
    Code(inf, outf, start)
  ELSIF CAP(ch) = 'D' THEN
    Decode(inf, outf, start)
  END;
END subs1.
```

Although a substitution cipher that is based on a constant offset can fool grade schoolers, it is generally not suitable for most situations because it is too easy to crack. After all, there are only 26 possible offsets, and it is simple to try all of them within a short period of time. An improved substitution cipher uses a scrambled alphabet instead of a simple offset.

A second failing of the simple substitution cipher is that it preserves the spaces between words, which makes it easier for code-breakers to crack. Another improvement would encode spaces. (Actually, all punctuation should be encoded but, for simplicity, the examples will not do this.) For example, you could map this randomized string that contains every letter of the alphabet and the space

abcdefghijklmnopqrstuvwxyz<space>

into this string:

qazwsxedcrfvtgbyhnujm ikolp

You may wonder if there is significant improvement in the security of a message that is encoded by using a randomized version of the alphabet in comparison to a simple offset version. The answer is yes—because there are 26 factorial (26!) ways to arrange the alphabet; with the space, that number becomes 27 factorial (27!) ways. The factorial of a number is that number times every whole number smaller than it, down to 1. For example, 6! is $6*5*4*3*2*1 = 720$. Therefore, 26! is a very large number.

The program shown here is an improved substitution cipher that uses the randomized alphabet just given. If you encoded the message

meet me at sunset

by using the improved substitution cipher program, it would look like

tssjptspqjpumgusj

which is a harder code to break.

```
MODULE subs2;
(*Improved substitution cipher*)

  FROM InOut IMPORT ReadString, WriteLn, WriteString,
    ReadInt, Read;
  FROM FileSystem IMPORT File, SetRead, SetWrite, Close,
    ReadChar, WriteChar, Response, Reset, Lookup;


  TYPE
    str80 = ARRAY [0..79] OF CHAR;

  VAR
    fname: str80;
    inf, outf: File;
    alphabet, sub: str80;
    ch: CHAR;

  (*this function returns the index into the alphabet*)
  PROCEDURE Find(alphabet: str80;
                 ch: CHAR): INTEGER;
    VAR
      t: INTEGER;
  BEGIN
    FOR t := 0 TO 26 DO
      IF ch = alphabet[t] THEN
        RETURN t
      END
    END;
    RETURN -1;
  END Find; (*Find*)


  (*returns TRUE if ch is a letter of the alphabet*)
  PROCEDURE IsAlpha(ch: CHAR): BOOLEAN;
  BEGIN
    RETURN (CAP(ch) >= 'A') AND (CAP(ch) <= 'Z');
  END IsAlpha; (* IsAlpha *)


  PROCEDURE Code(inf, outf: File);
    VAR
      ch: CHAR;
  BEGIN
    REPEAT
      ReadChar(inf, ch);
      ch := CAP(ch);
      IF IsAlpha(ch) OR (ch = ' ') THEN
        ch := sub[Find(alphabet, ch)]; (*Find substitution*)
      END;
      WriteChar(outf, ch);
    UNTIL inf.eof;
    WriteString('file coded');
    WriteLn;
```

```
      Close(inf);
      Close(outf);
   END Code;



   PROCEDURE Decode(inf, outf: File);
      VAR
         ch: CHAR;
   BEGIN
      REPEAT
         ReadChar(inf, ch);
         ch := CAP(ch);
         IF IsAlpha(ch) OR (ch = ' ') THEN
            ch := alphabet[Find(sub, ch)]; (*replace with real
                                                alphabet again*)
         END;
         WriteChar(outf, ch);
            UNTIL inf.eof;
      WriteString('file decoded');
      WriteLn;
      Close(inf);
      Close(outf);
   END Decode;



BEGIN
   REPEAT
      WriteString('Enter input filename: ');
      ReadString(fname);  WriteLn;
      Lookup(inf,fname ,FALSE); (* must be there *)
   UNTIL inf.res = done;

   REPEAT
      WriteString('Enter output filename: ');
      ReadString(fname);  WriteLn;
      Lookup(outf,fname ,TRUE); (* create it *)
   UNTIL outf.res = done;

   SetWrite(outf);  (* enable write *)
   SetRead(inf);  (* enable read *)

   WriteString('Code or Decode (C or D): ');
   Read(ch);

   alphabet := 'ABCDEFGHIJKLMNOPQRSTUVWXYZ ';
   sub := 'QAZWSXEDCRFVTGBYHNUJM IKOLP'; (*substitution alphabet*)

   IF CAP(ch) = 'C' THEN
      Code(inf, outf)
   ELSIF CAP(ch) = 'D' THEN
      Decode(inf, outf)
   END;
END subs2.
```

Although this chapter examines code-breaking later, you should know that even this improved substitution code can still be easily broken if you use a *frequency table* of the English language, which records the statistical information of the use of each letter of the alphabet. (This type of substitution is used in the "cryptograms" next to the crossword puzzles in many newspapers.) As you can see by looking at the coded message, *s* almost certainly has to be *e*, which is the most common letter in the English language, and *p* must be a space. The rest of the message can be decoded with a little effort. The larger the coded message is, the easier it is to crack with a frequency table. To impede the progress of a code-breaker who uses frequency tables to break a coded message, you can use a *multiple substitution cipher.* The same letter in the plaintext message will not necessarily have the same letter in the coded form. You can make a multiple substitution cipher easily by adding a second randomized alphabet and by switching between it and the first alphabet. While there are many possible schemes that you can use to switch between the two alphabets, this example makes the switch each time that a space is encountered. For the second randomized alphabet, use

poi uytrewqasdfghjklmnbvcxz

With this approach, the message

meet me at sunset

becomes

tsslzsspplpumguuj

To see how this works, set up the ordered alphabet and the two randomized alphabets (called **sub** and **sub2**) over one another.

alphabet	abcdefghijklmnopqrstuvwxyz<space>
sub	qazwsxedcrfvtgbyhnujm ikolp
sub2	poi uytrewqasdfghjklmnbvcxz

When the program starts, it codes the first word, *meet*, by using **sub**. The space after *meet* causes the program to use **sub2** to code the word *me*. The next spaces cause the program to code *at* with **sub**. Finally, the last space causes *sunset* to be coded with **sub2**.

Using multiple substitution ciphers makes utilizing frequency tables to break codes much more difficult because, at different times, different letters can stand for the same letter. It would be possible to use several different randomized alphabets and a more complex shifting routine in order to have all letters in the coded text occur equally as often. In this way, a frequency table would be useless in breaking the code.

The multiple substitution cipher shown here works only with the letters of the alphabet and spaces.

```
MODULE subs3;
(*Multiple substitution cipher*)

  FROM InOut IMPORT ReadString, WriteLn, WriteString,
    ReadInt, Read, Write;
  FROM FileSystem IMPORT File, SetRead, SetWrite, Close,
    ReadChar, WriteChar, Response, Reset, Lookup;

  TYPE
    str80 = ARRAY [0..79] OF CHAR;

  VAR
    fname: str80;
    inf, outf: File;
    alphabet, sub, sub2: str80;
    t: INTEGER;
    ch: CHAR;

  (*this function returns the index into the alphabet*)
  PROCEDURE Find(alphabet: str80;
                 ch: CHAR): INTEGER;
    VAR
      t: INTEGER;
  BEGIN
    FOR t := 0 TO 26 DO
      IF ch = alphabet[t] THEN
        RETURN t
      END
    END;
    RETURN -1;
  END Find;


  (*returns TRUE if ch is a letter of the alphabet*)
  PROCEDURE IsAlpha(ch: CHAR): BOOLEAN;
  BEGIN
    RETURN (CAP(ch) >= 'A') AND (CAP(ch) <= 'Z');
  END IsAlpha;

  PROCEDURE Code(inf, outf: File);
```

```
      VAR
        ch: CHAR;
        change: BOOLEAN;
    BEGIN
      change := TRUE;
      REPEAT
        ReadChar(inf, ch);
        ch := CAP(ch);
        IF IsAlpha(ch) THEN
          IF change THEN
            ch := sub[Find(alphabet, ch)]; (*Find substitution*)
            ELSE
            ch := sub2[Find(alphabet, ch)]; (*second sub*)
          END
        ELSIF ch=' ' THEN change:=NOT change; END;
        WriteChar(outf, ch);
      UNTIL inf.eof;
      WriteString('file coded');
      WriteLn;
      Close(inf);
      Close(outf);
    END Code;


    PROCEDURE Decode(inf, outf: File);
      VAR
        ch: CHAR;
        change: BOOLEAN;
    BEGIN
      change := TRUE;
      REPEAT
        ReadChar(inf, ch);
        ch := CAP(ch);
        IF IsAlpha(ch) THEN
          IF change THEN
            ch := alphabet[Find(sub, ch)]; (*Find substitution*)
            ELSE
            ch := alphabet[Find(sub2, ch)]; (*second sub*)
          END
        ELSIF ch=' ' THEN change:=NOT change END;
        WriteChar(outf, ch);
      UNTIL inf.eof;
      WriteString('file decoded');
      WriteLn;
      Close(inf);
      Close(outf);
    END Decode;


BEGIN
  REPEAT
    WriteString('Enter input filename: ');
    ReadString(fname);  WriteLn;
    Lookup(inf,fname ,FALSE); (* must be there *)
  UNTIL inf.res = done;
```

```
REPEAT
  WriteString('Enter output filename: ');
  ReadString(fname);  WriteLn;
  Lookup(outf,fname ,TRUE); (* create it *)
UNTIL outf.res = done;

SetWrite(outf); (* enable write *)
SetRead(inf);  (* enable read *)

WriteString('Code or Decode (C or D): ');
Read(ch);
alphabet := 'ABCDEFGHIJKLMNOPQRSTUVWXYZ ';
sub :=      'QAZWSXEDCRFVTGBYHNUJM IKOLP'; (*substitution alphabet*)
sub2 :=     'POI UYTREWQASDFGHJKLMNBVCXZ'; (*substitution #2*)

IF CAP(ch) = 'C' THEN
  Code(inf, outf)
ELSIF CAP(ch) = 'D' THEN
  Decode(inf, outf)
END;
END subs3.
```

Transposition Ciphers

One of the earliest-known transposition codes was created by the Spartans around 475 B.C. It used a device called a *skytale*, which is basically a strap that is wrapped around a cylinder upon which a message is written crossways. The strap is then unwound and delivered to the recipient of the message, who also has a cylinder of equal size. Theoretically, without the cylinder, the recipient cannot read the strap because the letters are out of order. However, in actual practice, this method is not completely effective because you could continue to try different-sized cylinders until the message begins to make sense.

You can create a computerized version of a skytale by placing the plaintext message into an array a certain way, and writing it out a different way. To do this, use a one-dimensional string to hold the message to be encoded, but write the message to the disk file as a two-dimensional array. For this version, the plaintext single-dimension array is 100 bytes long, and is written to disk as a 5×20 two-dimensional array. However, you could use any dimensions that you want. Because a fixed-size array holds the message, it is very likely that not every element of the array will be used. This situation makes it necessary for you to initialize the array before you place the plaintext into it. In actual practice, you should initialize the array with random characters;

however, for simplicity, this chapter uses the # sign — but any other character would do.

If you place the message

meet me at sunset

into the array **skytale** and view it as the two-dimensional array, it would look like this:

m	e	e	t	
m	e		a	t
	s	u	n	s
e	t	#	#	#
#	#	#	#	#

.
.
.

If you wrote the array out by column, the message would look like this:

mm e...eest...e u...tan... ts...

Here, the periods indicate the appropriate number of # signs. To decode the message, you fill columns in **skytale** so that you can display **skytale** in normal order. The program **skytale** uses this method to code and decode messages:

```
MODULE skytale;
(*skytale cipher*)

(*The largest message that can be coded is 100 characters*)

   FROM InOut IMPORT ReadString, WriteLn, WriteString,
      ReadInt, Read, Write;
   FROM FileSystem IMPORT File, SetRead, SetWrite, Close,
      ReadChar, WriteChar, Response, Reset, Lookup;

   TYPE
      sktl100 = ARRAY [1..100] OF CHAR;
      str80 = ARRAY [0..79] OF CHAR;
```

```
VAR

  inf, outf: File;
  fname: str80;
  skytale: sktl100;
  t: INTEGER;
  ch: CHAR;

(*returns TRUE if ch is a letter of the alphabet*)
PROCEDURE IsAlpha(ch: CHAR): BOOLEAN;
BEGIN
  RETURN (CAP(ch) >= 'A') AND (CAP(ch) <= 'Z');
END IsAlpha;


(*Read in text file, output 2-dimensional array*)
PROCEDURE Code(inf, outf: File);
  VAR
    ch: CHAR;
    t, t2: INTEGER;

BEGIN
  t := 1;
  REPEAT
    ReadChar(inf, skytale[t]);
    INC(t);
  UNTIL inf.eof OR (t=100);

  (*now Write out the array as 5x20 2-dimensional*)
  FOR t := 1 TO 5 DO
    FOR t2 := 0 TO 19 DO
      WriteChar(outf, skytale[t+(t2*5)])
    END
  END;
  WriteString('file coded');
  WriteLn;
  Close(inf);
  Close(outf);


END Code;


(*Read in as 5x20 2-dimensional - output as 1-dimensional*)
PROCEDURE Decode(inf, outf: File);
  VAR
    ch: CHAR;
    t, t2: INTEGER;

BEGIN
  FOR t := 1 TO 5 DO
    FOR t2 := 0 TO 19 DO
      ReadChar(inf, skytale[t+(t2*5)])
    END
  END;
```

```
      (*Write out normally*)
      FOR t := 1 TO 100 DO
        WriteChar(outf, skytale[t])
      END;
      WriteString('file decoded');
      WriteLn;
      Close(inf);
      Close(outf);
   END Decode;


BEGIN
  (* initialize the skytale array *)
  FOR t := 1 TO 100 DO
    skytale[t] := '#'
  END;

  REPEAT
    WriteString('Enter input filename: ');
    ReadString(fname);  WriteLn;
    Lookup(inf,fname ,FALSE); (* must be there *)
  UNTIL inf.res = done;

  REPEAT
    WriteString('Enter output filename: ');
    ReadString(fname);  WriteLn;
    Lookup(outf,fname ,TRUE); (* create it *)
  UNTIL outf.res = done;

  SetWrite(outf);  (* enable write *)
  SetRead(inf);  (* enable read *)

  WriteString('Code or Decode (C or D): ');
  Read(ch);

  IF CAP(ch) = 'C' THEN
    Code(inf, outf)
  ELSIF CAP(ch) = 'D' THEN
    Decode(inf, outf)
    END;
  END skytale.
```

There are other methods of obtaining transposed messages. One method that is particularly suited for use by computer swaps letters within the message as defined by some algorithm. For example, here is one that transposes letters:

```
MODULE transpose;
(*transposition cipher*)
(*Up to 100 character messages may be coded.*)

  FROM InOut IMPORT ReadString, WriteLn, WriteString,
    ReadInt, Read, Write;
  FROM FileSystem IMPORT File, SetRead, SetWrite, Close,
    ReadChar, WriteChar, Response, Reset, Lookup;
```

```
TYPE
  code100 = ARRAY [1..100] OF CHAR;
  str80 = ARRAY [0..79] OF CHAR;

VAR
  inf, outf: File;
  fname: str80;
  message: code100;
  ch: CHAR;
  t: INTEGER;


PROCEDURE Code(inf, outf: File);
  VAR
    temp: CHAR;
    t, t2: INTEGER;

BEGIN
  t := 1;
  REPEAT
    ReadChar(inf, message[t]);
    INC(t, 1);
  UNTIL inf.eof OR (t>100);
  message[t-1] := '#'; (*remove EOF*)

  (*now, transpose the characters*)
  FOR t2 := 0 TO 4 DO
    FOR t := 1 TO 10 DO
      temp := message[t+t2*20];
      message[t+t2*20] := message[t+10+t2*20];
      message[t+10+t2*20] := temp;
    END
  END;

  (*now Write it out*)
  FOR t := 1 TO 100 DO
    WriteChar(outf, message[t])
  END;
  WriteString('file coded');
  WriteLn;
  Close(inf);
  Close(outf);
END Code;



PROCEDURE Decode(inf, outf: File);
  VAR
    temp: CHAR;
    t, t2: INTEGER;

BEGIN
  t := 1;
  REPEAT
    ReadChar(inf, message[t]);
    INC(t, 1);
  UNTIL inf.eof OR (t>100);
  message[t-1] := '#'; (*remove EOF*)
```

```
(*now, transpose the characters*)
FOR t2 := 0 TO 4 DO
  FOR t := 1 TO 10 DO
    temp := message[t+t2*20];
    message[t+t2*20] := message[t+10+t2*20];
    message[t+10+t2*20] := temp;
  END
END;
(*now Write it out*)
FOR t := 1 TO 100 DO
  WriteChar(outf, message[t])
END;
WriteString('file decoded');
WriteLn;
Close(inf);
Close(outf);
END Decode;


BEGIN
  (* init the code array *)
  FOR t := 1 TO 100 DO
    message[t] := '#'
  END;

  REPEAT
    WriteString('Enter input filename: ');
    ReadString(fname);  WriteLn;
    Lookup(inf,fname ,FALSE); (* must be there *)
  UNTIL inf.res = done;

  REPEAT
    WriteString('Enter output filename: ');
    ReadString(fname);  WriteLn;
    Lookup(outf,fname ,TRUE); (* create it *)
  UNTIL outf.res = done;

  SetWrite(outf);  (* enable write *)
  SetRead(inf);  (* enable read *)

  WriteString('Code or Decode (C or D): ');
  Read(ch);

  IF CAP(ch) = 'C' THEN
    Code(inf, outf)
  ELSIF CAP(ch) = 'D' THEN
    Decode(inf, outf)
  END;
END transpose.
```

Although transposition codes can be effective, the algorithms become very complex if you need a high degree of security.

Bit-Manipulation Ciphers

The digital computer has given rise to a new method of encoding through the manipulation of the bits that compose the actual characters of the plaintext. Although the purist will claim that bit manipulation (or *alteration*, as it is sometimes called) is simply a variation on the substitution cipher, the concepts, methods, and options differ so significantly that it must be considered to be a cipher method in its own right.

Bit-manipulation ciphers are popular for two reasons. First, they are well-suited for use on a computer because they employ operations that the system can easily perform. Second, the ciphertext tends to look completely unintelligible—that is, like complete garbage—which makes the data look like unused or crashed files, thereby confusing anyone who tries to gain access to the file.

Generally, bit-manipulation ciphers are only applicable to computer-based files and cannot be used to create a hardcopy message because the bit manipulations tend to produce nonprinting characters. For this reason, you should assume that any file coded by bit-manipulation methods will remain a computer file.

Bit-manipulation ciphers convert plaintext into ciphertext by altering the bit pattern of each character by using one or more of these bitwise operators:

AND
OR
NOT
XOR

(Do not confuse these operations with those that have the same names that Modula-2 uses for logical operations.) Frankly, Modula-2 is not one of the best languages for creating bit-manipulation ciphers because it does not support bitwise operators directly. Using Modula-2 to perform bitwise operations on character data types requires that you create special procedures that use inline assembly code to perform the manipulations. This chapter will develop these routines as necessary. When they are applied to character or integer variables, the operations occur on a bit-by-bit basis. These operators make altering the state of bits within a byte simple.

The simplest bit-manipulation cipher, which is also the least secure, uses only **NOT**, the 1's complement operator. (Remember that **NOT** causes each bit within a byte to be inverted: a 1 becomes a 0, and a 0 becomes a 1.) Therefore, a byte complemented twice is the same as the original. The following program, **complement**, codes any text file by inverting the bits within each character. Notice that the procedure **comp** uses inline assembly code to perform the complement operation. This code only works for the 8086/8088 family of processors.

```
MODULE complement;
(*1's complement cipher*)

  FROM SYSTEM IMPORT CODE, GETREG, BX;
  FROM InOut IMPORT ReadString, WriteLn, WriteString,
    ReadInt, Read, Write;
  FROM FileSystem IMPORT File, SetRead, SetWrite, Close,
    ReadChar, WriteChar, Response, Reset, Lookup;

  TYPE
    str80 = ARRAY [0..79] OF CHAR;


  VAR
    inf, outf: File;
    fname: str80;
    ch: CHAR;
    t: INTEGER;


  PROCEDURE comp(ch: CHAR):CHAR;
    VAR CompResult: CHAR;
  BEGIN
    CODE(8BH, 46H, 4,     (* mov ax, [bp]+4 - get arg *)
      0F7h, 0D0H,         (* not ax *)
      8BH, 0D8H);         (* mov bx, ax *)
      GETREG(BX,CompResult);
      RETURN CompResult;
  END comp;

  PROCEDURE Code(inf, outf: File);
    VAR
      ch: CHAR;

  BEGIN
    REPEAT
      ReadChar(inf, ch);
      ch := comp(ch);
      WriteChar(outf, ch);
    UNTIL inf.eof;
    WriteString('file coded');
    WriteLn;
    Close(inf);
    Close(outf);
  END Code;
```

```
PROCEDURE Decode(inf, outf: File);
  VAR
    ch: CHAR;

BEGIN
  REPEAT
    ReadChar(inf, ch);
    ch := comp(ch);
    WriteChar(outf, ch);
  UNTIL inf.eof;
  WriteString('file decoded');
  WriteLn;
  Close(inf);
  Close(outf);
END Decode;


BEGIN
  REPEAT
    WriteString('Enter input filename: ');
    ReadString(fname);  WriteLn;
    Lookup(inf,fname ,FALSE); (* must be there *)
  UNTIL inf.res = done;

  REPEAT
    WriteString('Enter output filename: ');
    ReadString(fname);  WriteLn;
    Lookup(outf,fname ,TRUE); (* create it *)
  UNTIL outf.res = done;

  SetWrite(outf);  (* enable write *)
  SetRead(inf);  (* enable read *)
  WriteString('Code or Decode (C or D): ');
  Read(ch);

  IF CAP(ch) = 'C' THEN
    Code(inf, outf)
  ELSIF CAP(ch) = 'D' THEN
    Decode(inf, outf)
  END;
END complement.
```

It is difficult to show what the ciphertext of a message would look like because the bit manipulation that is used in this program generally creates nonprinting characters. Try it on your computer and examine the file—it will look quite cryptic.

There are two problems with this simple coding scheme. First, the encryption program does not use a key to decode, so anyone who has access to the program can decode an encoded file. Second, and perhaps more importantly, any experienced computer programmer would easily spot this method.

An improved method of bit-manipulation coding uses the XOR operator.

The XOR operator has the following TRUTH table:

XOR	0	1
0	0	1
1	1	0

The outcome of the XOR operation is TRUE if and only if one operand is TRUE and the other is FALSE. This characteristic gives XOR a unique property: if you XOR a byte with another byte called the *key*, and XOR the outcome of that operation again with the key, the result will be the original byte, as shown here:

```
      1  1  0  1      1  0  0  1
   ^  0  1  0  1      0  0  1  1   (key)
   ─────────────────────────────
      1  0  0  0      1  0  1  0


      1  0  0  0      1  0  1  0
   ^  0  1  0  1      0  0  1  1   (key)
   ─────────────────────────────
      1  1  0  1      1  0  0  1
```

If you use this process to code a file, the process solves the two problems of the method that uses the simple 1's complement. First, because it uses a key, the encryption program alone cannot decode a file; second, because using a key makes each file unique, the method that was used on the file is not obvious to someone who is schooled only in computer science.

The key does not need to be just one byte long. In fact, you could use a key of several characters and alternate the characters through the file. However, this example uses a single-character key to keep the program uncluttered. Notice that the procedure **xor** performs the bitwise XOR function.

```
MODULE XorWithKey;
(* xor with key for security *)

   FROM SYSTEM IMPORT CODE, GETREG, BX;
   FROM InOut IMPORT ReadString, WriteLn, WriteString,
      ReadInt, Read, Write;
   FROM FileSystem IMPORT File, SetRead, SetWrite, Close,
      ReadChar, WriteChar, Response, Reset, Lookup;

   TYPE
      str80 = ARRAY [0..79] OF CHAR;
```

```
VAR
  inf, outf: File;
  fname: str80;
  ch: CHAR;
  key: CHAR;
  t: INTEGER;


PROCEDURE xor(arg, key: CHAR):CHAR;
  VAR XorResult: CHAR;
BEGIN
  CODE(8BH, 46H, 4,     (* mov ax, [bp]+4 - 1st arg *)
       33H, 46H, 6,     (* xor ax, [bp]+6 - 2nd arg *)
       8BH, 0D8H);      (* mov bx, ax *)
    GETREG(BX,XorResult);
    RETURN XorResult;
END xor;

PROCEDURE Code(inf, outf: File; key: CHAR);
  VAR
    ch: CHAR;
BEGIN
  REPEAT
    ReadChar(inf, ch);
    IF NOT inf.eof THEN
      ch := xor(key,ch);
      WriteChar(outf, ch);

      END;
    UNTIL inf.eof;
    WriteString('file coded');
    WriteLn;
    Close(inf);
    Close(outf);
  END Code;




  PROCEDURE Decode(inf, outf: File; key: CHAR);
    VAR
      ch: CHAR;
  BEGIN
    REPEAT
      ReadChar(inf, ch);
      IF NOT inf.eof THEN
        ch := xor(key, ch);
        WriteChar(outf, ch);
      END;
    UNTIL inf.eof;
    WriteString('file decoded');
    WriteLn;
    Close(inf);
    Close(outf);
  END Decode;


BEGIN
  REPEAT
    WriteString('Enter input filename: ');
```

```
    ReadString(fname);  WriteLn;
    Lookup(inf,fname ,FALSE); (* must be there *)
UNTIL inf.res = done;

REPEAT
  WriteString('Enter output filename: ');
  ReadString(fname);  WriteLn;
  Lookup(outf,fname ,TRUE); (* create it *)
UNTIL outf.res = done;

SetWrite(outf);  (* enable write *)
SetRead(inf);   (* enable read *)

WriteString('Code or Decode (C or D): ');
Read(ch);
WriteLn;

WriteString('enter one character key: ');
Read(key);
WriteLn;

IF CAP(ch) = 'C' THEN
  Code(inf, outf, key)
ELSIF CAP(ch) = 'D' THEN
  Decode(inf, outf, key)
  END;
END XorWithKey.
```

Data Compression

Data-compression techniques essentially squeeze a certain amount of information into a smaller space. They are often used in computer systems to
increase the storage of the system effectively, to save transfer time (especially
over phone lines), and to provide a level of security. Although there are many
data-compression schemes available, this section examines only two of them.
The first is *bit compression*, in which more than one character is stored into a
single byte, and the second is *character deletion*, in which actual characters
from the file are deleted.

Eight into Seven

All computers use byte sizes that are even powers of two because of the binary representation of data in the machine. The uppercase and lowercase letters and punctuation only require about 63 different codes that need only 6-bit bytes. (A 6-bit byte could have values of 0 through 63.) However, most computers use an 8-bit byte; hence, 25% of the byte's storage is wasted. You could, therefore, actually compact 4 characters into 3 bytes if you could use the last 2 bits in each byte. The only problem is that there are more than 63 different ASCII character codes so that the uppercase and lowercase alphabet falls somewhere in the middle. This means that some necessary characters require at least 7 bits.

You could use a non-ASCII representation (which is done on rare occasions), but it is not generally advisable. However, an easier method is to compact 8 characters into 7 bytes to make use of the fact that no letter or common punctuation mark uses the eighth bit of a byte. Therefore, you can use the eighth bit of each of the 7 bytes to store the eighth character. This method still saves 12.5%. However, many computers, including the IBM PC, do use 8-bit characters to represent special or graphics characters. Also, some word processors use the eighth bit to indicate text-processing instructions. Therefore, using this type of data compaction only works on "straight" ASCII files that do not use the eighth bit for anything.

To see how this would work, consider the following 8 characters represented as 8-bit bytes:

Byte 1	0	1	1	1	0	1	0	1
Byte 2	0	1	1	1	1	1	0	1
Byte 3	0	0	1	0	0	0	1	1
Byte 4	0	1	0	1	0	1	1	0
Byte 5	0	0	0	1	0	0	0	0
Byte 6	0	1	1	0	1	1	0	1
Byte 7	0	0	1	0	1	0	1	0
Byte 8	0	1	1	1	1	0	0	1

As shown, the eighth bit is always zero, which is always the case unless it is used for parity checking on straight text files. The easiest way to compress 8 characters into 7 bytes is to distribute the 7 significant bits of byte 1 into the 7 unused eighth-bit positions of bytes 2 through 8. If you do this, the 7 remaining bytes will look like this:

```
                        ┌───────────────────── Byte 1 - read down
                        │
Byte 2      1  1  1  1      1  1  0  1
Byte 3      1  0  1  0      0  0  1  1
Byte 4      1  1  0  1      0  1  1  0
Byte 5      0  0  0  1      0  0  0  0
Byte 6      1  1  1  0      1  1  0  1
Byte 7      0  0  1  0      1  0  1  0
Byte 8      1  1  1  1      1  0  0  1
```

To reconstruct byte 1, you only need to take the eighth bit off of each of the 7 bytes.

As stated, this compression technique compresses any text file by 1/8, or 12.5%, which is a substantial savings. For example, if you were transmitting the source code for your favorite program to a friend over long-distance telephone lines, then you would save 12.5% of the expense of transmission. (Remember that the object code, or executable version of the program, needs the full 8 bits!)

The program **compress** shown here compresses a text file as described earlier. Four bitwise operations are required: shift-right, shift-left, OR, and AND. These are coded by using inline assembly language near the top of the program. As with previous programs, these procedures only work for the 8086/8088 family of processors.

```
MODULE compress;
(* fit characters into 7 bit words *)

   FROM SYSTEM IMPORT CODE, GETREG, BX;
   FROM InOut IMPORT ReadString, WriteLn, WriteString,
     ReadInt, Read, Write, WriteInt;
   FROM FileSystem IMPORT File, SetRead, SetWrite, Close,
     ReadChar, WriteChar, Response, Reset, Lookup;


   TYPE
     str80 = ARRAY [0..79] OF CHAR;
```

```
VAR
  inf, outf: File;
  fname: str80;
  ch: CHAR;
  t: INTEGER;


PROCEDURE and(arg1: CHAR; arg2: CHAR):CHAR;
  VAR result: CHAR;
BEGIN
  CODE(8BH, 46H, 4,     (* mov ax, [bp]+4 - 1st arg *)
     23H, 46H, 6,       (* and ax, [bp]+6 - 2nd arg *)
     8BH, 0D8H);        (* mov bx, ax *)
     GETREG(BX,result);
     RETURN result;
END and;


PROCEDURE or(arg1: CHAR; arg2: CHAR):CHAR;
  VAR result: CHAR;
BEGIN
  CODE(8BH, 46H, 4,     (* mov ax, [bp]+4 - 1st arg *)
     0BH, 46H, 6,       (* or ax, [bp]+6 - 2nd arg *)
     8BH, 0D8H);        (* mov bx, ax *)
     GETREG(BX,result);
     RETURN result;
END or;


PROCEDURE shr(arg1, arg2: CHAR):CHAR;
  VAR result: CHAR;
BEGIN
  CODE(8BH, 46H, 6,     (* mov ax, [bp]+6 - 1st arg *)
     8BH, 4EH, 4,       (* mov cx, [bp]+4 - 2nd arg *)
     0D3H, 0E8H,        (* shr ax, cl *)
     8BH, 0D8H);        (* mov bx, ax *)
  GETREG(BX,result);
  RETURN result;
END shr;


PROCEDURE shl(arg1, arg2: CHAR):CHAR;
  VAR result: CHAR;
BEGIN
  CODE(8BH, 46H, 6,     (* mov ax, [bp]+6 - 1st arg *)
     8BH, 4EH, 4,       (* mov cx, [bp]+4 - 2nd arg *)
     0D3H, 0E0H,        (* shl ax, cl *)
     8BH, 0D8H);        (* mov bx, ax *)
  GETREG(BX,result);
  RETURN result;
END shl;


PROCEDURE Compress(inf, outf: File);
```

```
    VAR
      ch, ch2, ch3: CHAR;
      done: BOOLEAN;
      i:INTEGER;
BEGIN
  done := FALSE;
  REPEAT
    ReadChar(inf, ch);
    IF inf.eof THEN
      done := TRUE
    ELSE
      ch:=shl(ch,CHR(1)); (*shift off unused bit*)
      FOR t := 0 TO 6 DO
        IF inf.eof THEN
          ch2 := CHAR(0);
          done := TRUE;
        ELSE
          ReadChar(inf, ch2)
        END;
        ch2:=and(ch2,CHR(127)); (* turn off top bit *)
        ch3:=shl(ch,CHR(t)); (* get then next bit *)
        ch3:=and(ch3,CHR(128));
        ch2:=or(ch2,ch3); (*pack bits*)
        WriteChar(outf, ch2);
      END;
    END; (*else*)
  UNTIL done;
  WriteString('file compressed');
  WriteLn;
  Close(inf);
  Close(outf);
END Compress; (*Compress*)


PROCEDURE Decompress(inf, outf: File);
  VAR
    ch, ch2: CHAR;
    s: ARRAY [1..7] OF CHAR;
    done: BOOLEAN;
    i:INTEGER;
BEGIN
  done := FALSE;
  REPEAT
    ch := CHAR(0);
    t:=1;
    REPEAT
      IF inf.eof THEN
        done := TRUE
      ELSE
        ReadChar(inf, ch2);
        s[t] := and(ch2,CHR(127)); (*turn off top bit *)
        ch2 := and(ch2,CHR(128)); (*clear lower bits*)
        ch2:=shr(ch2,CHR(t)); (*de-pack*)
        ch := or(ch,ch2); (*build up 8th byte*)
      END;
      INC(t);
    UNTIL (t=8) OR done;
    DEC(t);
```

```
        WriteChar(outf, ch);
        FOR i := 1 TO t DO
          WriteChar(outf, s[i])
        END;

    UNTIL done;
    WriteString('file decompressed');
    WriteLn;
    Close(inf);
    Close(outf);
  END Decompress;

BEGIN
  REPEAT
    WriteString('Enter input filename: ');
    ReadString(fname);  WriteLn;
    Lookup(inf,fname ,FALSE); (* must be there *)
  UNTIL inf.res = done;

  REPEAT
    WriteString('Enter output filename: ');
    ReadString(fname);  WriteLn;
    Lookup(outf,fname ,TRUE); (* create it *)
  UNTIL outf.res = done;

  SetWrite(outf);  (* enable write *)
  SetRead(inf);  (* enable read *)
  WriteString('Compress or Decompress (C or D): ');
  Read(ch);
  WriteLn;

  IF CAP(ch) = 'C' THEN
    Compress(inf, outf)
  ELSIF CAP(ch) = 'D' THEN
    Decompress(inf, outf)
  END;
END compress.
```

Here, the code is fairly complex because the program must shift various bits around. If you remember what is being done with the first byte of each 8-byte group, then the code becomes easier to follow.

The 16-Character Language

Although unsuitable for most situations, an interesting method of data compression deletes unnecessary letters from words—in essence, changing most words into abbreviations. Data compression is accomplished because the unused characters are not stored. Saving space by using abbreviations is very common—that is the reason that you use "Mr." instead of "Mister." Instead of using actual abbreviations, the approach that is presented here automatically removes certain letters from a message. To do this, you need a *minimal alphabet*. A minimal alphabet is one in which several seldom-used letters have been removed, leaving only those letters that are necessary to form most words or to avoid ambiguity. Therefore, the method extracts any character that is not in the minimal alphabet from any word in which that character appears. Exactly how many characters are in a minimal alphabet is a matter of choice. However, this section uses the 14 most common letters, plus spaces and carriage returns. The next few paragraphs will explain how.

To automate the abbreviation process requires that you know what letters are used most frequently in the alphabet so that you can create a minimal alphabet. In theory, you could count the letters in each word in a dictionary; however, different writers use different frequency mixes, so a frequency chart that is based just on the words that make up the English language may not reflect the actual usage frequency of letters. (It would take a long time to count the letters!) As an alternative, you can count the frequency of the letters in this chapter and use them as a basis for your minimal alphabet. You need a program that will do this. The following program is quite simple:

```
MODULE count;
(*count the number of each type of characters in a file*)

   FROM InOut IMPORT ReadString, WriteLn, WriteString,
      WriteCard, Read, Write;
   FROM FileSystem IMPORT File, SetRead, SetWrite, Close,
      ReadChar, WriteChar, Response, Reset, Lookup;

   TYPE
      str80 = ARRAY [0..79] OF CHAR;

   VAR
      inf: File;
      fname:str80;
      t: CARDINAL;
      alpha: ARRAY [0..25] OF CARDINAL;
      space, period, comma: CARDINAL;


   (*returns TRUE if ch is a letter of the alphabet*)
   PROCEDURE IsAlpha(ch: CHAR): BOOLEAN;
   BEGIN
      RETURN (CAP(ch) >= 'A') AND (CAP(ch) <= 'Z');
   END IsAlpha;


   PROCEDURE Count(inf: File);
      VAR
         ch: CHAR;
```

```
BEGIN
  REPEAT
    ReadChar(inf, ch);
    ch := CAP(ch);
    IF IsAlpha(ch) THEN
      alpha[ORD(ch)-ORD('A')] := alpha[ORD(ch)-ORD('A')]+1
      ELSE
        CASE ch OF
          ' ': INC(space) |
          '.': INC(period) |
          ',': INC(comma)
        ELSE (* do nothing *)
        END;
      END;
  UNTIL inf.eof;
  Close(inf);
END Count;


BEGIN
  REPEAT
    WriteString('Enter input filename: ');
    ReadString(fname);  WriteLn;
    Lookup(inf,fname ,FALSE); (* must be there *)
  UNTIL inf.res = done;

  FOR t := 0 TO 25 DO
    alpha[t] := 0
  END;
  space := 0;
  comma := 0;
  period := 0;
  Count(inf);
  FOR t := 0 TO 25 DO
    Write(CHR(t+ORD('A')));
    WriteString(': ');
    WriteCard(alpha[t], 5);
    WriteLn;
  END;
  WriteString('space: ');
  WriteCard(space, 0);
  WriteLn;
  WriteString('period: ');
  WriteCard(period, 0);
  WriteLn;
  WriteString('comma: ');
  WriteCard(comma, 0);
  WriteLn;
END count.
```

The program skips all punctuation except periods, commas, and spaces. If you run this program on the text of this chapter, you get the following frequency.

A	2525
B	532
C	838
D	1145
E	3326
F	828
G	529
H	1086
I	2242
J	39
K	94
L	1103
M	1140
N	2164
O	1767
P	697
Q	62
R	1656
S	1672
T	3082
U	869
V	376
W	370
X	178
Y	356
Z	20
SPACE	5710
PERIOD	234
COMMA	513

The frequency of letters in this chapter compares well with the standard English mix, and is offset only by the repeated use of the Modula-2 keywords in the programs.

To achieve significant data compression, you need to cut the alphabet substantially by removing the letters that are used least frequently. Although there are many ideas about exactly what a workable minimum alphabet is, the 14 most common letters and the space comprise around 85% of all characters in this chapter. Because the carriage-return character is also necessary to preserve word breaks, you must include it also. Therefore, this chapter uses a minimal alphabet that consists of 14 characters, a space, and a carriage return:

A B D E H I L M N O R S T U <space> <CR>

Here is a program that removes all characters except the 16 selected characters. The program writes the carriage-return/linefeed combination, if it is present. This makes the output readable—it is not necessary to store the linefeed because it could be reconstructed at a later time.

```
MODULE Compres2;
(*16 character language*)

   FROM InOut IMPORT ReadString, WriteLn, WriteString,
     ReadInt, Read, Write, WriteCard;
FROM FileSystem IMPORT File, SetRead, SetWrite, Close,
   ReadChar, WriteChar, Response, Reset, Lookup;
FROM Strings IMPORT Pos;

TYPE
   str80 = ARRAY [0..79] OF CHAR;


VAR
   inf, outf: File;
   fname: str80;
   ch: CHAR;
   t: INTEGER;


PROCEDURE Comp2(inf, outf: File);
   VAR
     ch: CHAR;
     done: BOOLEAN;

BEGIN
   done := FALSE;
   REPEAT
     IF  NOT inf.eof THEN
        ReadChar(inf, ch);
        ch := CAP(ch);
        IF Pos(ch, 'ABCDEILMNORSTU ') < 16 THEN
          WriteChar(outf, ch)
        END;
        IF ORD(ch) = 13 THEN
          WriteChar(outf, ch)
        END; (*cr*)
        IF ORD(ch) = 10 THEN
          WriteChar(outf, ch)
        END; (*lf*)
     ELSE
        done := TRUE
     END;
   UNTIL done;
   WriteString('file compressed');
   WriteLn;
   Close(inf);
   Close(outf);
END Comp2;
```

```
BEGIN
  REPEAT
    WriteString('Enter input filename: ');
    ReadString(fname);  WriteLn;
    Lookup(inf,fname ,FALSE); (* must be there *)
  UNTIL inf.res = done;

  REPEAT
    WriteString('Enter output filename: ');
    ReadString(fname);  WriteLn;
    Lookup(outf,fname ,TRUE); (* create it *)
  UNTIL outf.res = done;

  SetWrite(outf);  (* enable write *)
  SetRead(inf);  (* enable read *)

  Comp2(inf, outf);
END Compres2.
```

The program uses the **Pos** function to determine if each character that is read is in the minimal alphabet. **Pos** returns a value greater than the length of the string if there is no match, or the position of the first match if found.

If you use this program on the message

> Attention High Command:
>
> > Attack successful. Please send additional supplies and fresh troops. This is essential to maintain our foothold.
>
> > General Frashier

the compressed message would look like this:

> Attention i Command
> > Attac successul lease send additional sulies and
> > res troos Tis is essential to maintain our
> > ootold
> > eneral rasier

As you can see, the message is largely readable, although some ambiguity is present. Ambiguity is the chief drawback to this method of data compression. However, if you knew the vocabulary of the writer of the message, you could probably select a better minimal alphabet that would remove some ambiguity. In spite of the potential for ambiguity, this method saved quite a bit of space. While the original message was 168 bytes long, the compacted message was 142 bytes long—a savings of about 16%.

If both character deletion and bit compression were applied to the message, then about 28% less storage would have been needed, which could be important. For example, if you were a submarine captain and wanted to send a message to headquarters but did not want to give away your position, you might want to compress the message using both methods so that it would be as short as possible.

Both the bit compression method and the character deletion method of data compression have uses in encryption. Bit compression further encrypts the information and makes decoding harder than character deletion. The character deletion method has one wonderful advantage: if you use it before using encryption, it disguises the character frequency of the source language.

Code-Breaking

No chapter on encryption methods is complete without a brief look at code-breaking. The art of code-breaking is essentially one of trial and error. With the use of digital computers, you can break relatively simple ciphers easily through exhaustive testing. However, more complex codes either cannot be broken or require techniques and resources that are not commonly available. For simplicity, this section focuses on breaking the more straightforward codes.

If you wish to break a message that was ciphered by using a simple substitution method with only an offset alphabet, then all you need do is try all 26 possible offsets to see which one fits. A program to do this is shown here:

```
MODULE brksub;
(*Code breaker program for simple substitution
  ciphers.  Messages can be as long as 1000
  characters.*)

  FROM InOut IMPORT ReadString, WriteLn, WriteString,
    WriteInt, Read, Write;
  FROM FileSystem IMPORT File, SetRead, SetWrite, Close,
    ReadChar, WriteChar, Response, Reset, Lookup;

  TYPE
    str80 = ARRAY [0..79] OF CHAR;

  VAR
    fname: str80;
    inf: File;
```

```
    message: ARRAY [0..1000] OF CHAR; (*holds input message*)
    ch: CHAR;


(*returns TRUE if ch is a letter of the alphabet*)
PROCEDURE IsAlpha(ch: CHAR): BOOLEAN;
BEGIN
   RETURN (CAP(ch) >= 'A') AND (CAP(ch) <= 'Z');
END IsAlpha;


PROCEDURE Break(inf: File);
   VAR
     ch: CHAR;
     done: BOOLEAN;
     sub, t, t2, l: INTEGER;

BEGIN
   done := FALSE;
   l := 0;
   REPEAT
     ReadChar(inf, message[l]);
     message[l] := CAP(message[l]);
     INC(l);
     UNTIL inf.eof;
     DEC(l); (*clear EOF char*)

     t := 0;
     sub := -1; (*not Decoded*)
     REPEAT
       FOR t2 := 0 TO l DO
         ch := message[t2];
         IF IsAlpha(ch) THEN
           ch := CHR((INTEGER(ORD(ch))-t));
           IF ch < 'A' THEN
             ch := CHR((INTEGER(ORD(ch))+26))
           END;
         END;
         Write(ch);
       END;
       WriteLn;
       WriteString('Decoded? (Y/N): ');
       WriteLn;
       Read(ch);
       WriteLn;
       IF CAP(ch) = 'Y' THEN
         sub := t
       END;
       INC(t);
     UNTIL (t = 26) OR (CAP(ch) = 'Y');
     IF sub <> -1 THEN
       WriteString('offset is ');
       WriteInt(sub, 0)
     END;
     Close(inf);
   END Break;
```

```
BEGIN
  REPEAT
    WriteString('Enter input filename: ');
    ReadString(fname);  WriteLn;
    Lookup(inf,fname ,FALSE); (* must be there *)
  UNTIL inf.res = done;

  Break(inf);
END brksub.
```

With only a slight variation, you could use the same program to break ciphers that use a random alphabet. In this case, you would substitute manually entered alphabets as shown in this program:

```
MODULE brksub2;
(*Code Breaker program for random substitution
  ciphers.  Messages can be as long as 1000
  characters.*)
FROM InOut IMPORT ReadString, WriteLn, WriteString,
  WriteInt, Read, Write;
FROM FileSystem IMPORT File, SetRead, SetWrite, Close,
  ReadChar, WriteChar, Response, Reset, Lookup;

TYPE
  str80 = ARRAY [0..79] OF CHAR;

VAR
  inf: File;
  fname: str80 ;
  sub: ARRAY [0..25] OF CHAR;
  message: ARRAY [0..1000] OF CHAR; (*holds input message*)
  ch: CHAR;


(*returns TRUE if ch is a letter of the alphabet*)
PROCEDURE IsAlpha(ch: CHAR): BOOLEAN;
BEGIN
  RETURN (CAP(ch) >= 'A') AND (CAP(ch) <= 'Z');
END IsAlpha;



PROCEDURE Break2(inf: File);
  VAR
    ch: CHAR;
    done: BOOLEAN;
    t, l: INTEGER;

BEGIN
  done := FALSE;
  l := 0;
  REPEAT
    ReadChar(inf, message[l]);
    message[l] := CAP(message[l]);
```

```
          INC(l);
      UNTIL inf.eof;
      DEC(l); (*clear EOF*)

      REPEAT
        WriteString('enter substitution alphabet: ');
        ReadString(sub);
        WriteLn;
        FOR t := 0 TO l DO
          ch := message[t];
          IF IsAlpha(ch) THEN
            ch := sub[ORD(ch)-ORD('A')];
          END;
          Write(ch);
        END;
        WriteLn;
        WriteString('Decoded? (Y/N): ');
        Read(ch);
        WriteLn;
        IF CAP(ch) = 'Y' THEN
          done := TRUE
        END;
      UNTIL done;
      WriteString('substitution alphabet is: ');
      WriteString(sub);
      WriteLn;
      Close(inf);
    END Break2;


BEGIN
  REPEAT
    WriteString('Enter input filename: ');
    ReadString(fname);  WriteLn;
    Lookup(inf,fname ,FALSE); (* must be there *)
  UNTIL inf.res = done;

  Break2(inf);
END brksub2.
```

Unlike the substitution ciphers, the transposition and bit-manipulation ciphers are harder to break by using the trial-and-error methods that are shown here. If you have to break such complex codes, good luck!

Oh, and by the way —*hsaovbno wlymljapvu pz haahpuhisl, pa vjjbyz vusf hz hu hjjpklua.*

Random
Number Generators
and Simulations

CHAPTER 8

Random number sequences are used in a variety of programming situations, ranging from simulations (which are the most common) to games and other recreational software. Since there is no built-in random number generator in Modula-2, it is possible that you do not have one with your compiler. For some applications, you may need to have available two or more different generators to provide different sets of random numbers for different tasks. Also, certain simulations require a *skewed*, or unbalanced, random number generator, which produces a sequence that is weighted toward one end or the other. The first part of this chapter is devoted to constructing and testing random number generators.

The second part of this chapter covers the use of random numbers in real-world simulations. The first is a grocery store check-out simulation, and the second is a "random-walk" stock portfolio manager. Both simulations illustrate fundamental aspects of simulation programming.

Random Number Generators

Technically, the term *random number generator* is absurd; numbers, in and of themselves, are not random! For example, is 100 a "random number"? Is 25? What is really meant by *random number generator* is something that creates a *sequence* of numbers that appears to be in random order. This raises a more complex question: What is a random sequence of numbers? The only correct answer is that a random sequence of numbers is a sequence in which all elements are completely unrelated. This definition leads to the paradox that any sequence can be both random and nonrandom, depending upon the way that the sequence was obtained. For example, this list of numbers

$$1\ 2\ 3\ 4\ 5\ 6\ 7\ 8\ 9\ 0$$

was created by typing, in order, the top row of keys on the keyboard, so the sequence certainly cannot be construed as randomly generated. However, what if you happened to draw this sequence from a barrel of numbered tennis balls? Then, the sequence *would* be randomly generated. Thus, the randomness of a sequence depends on the *way that it was generated,* and not on what the actual sequence is.

Keep in mind that sequences of numbers that are generated by a computer are *deterministic*: each number, other than the first number, depends on the number that precedes it. Technically, this means that you can only create a *quasi-random sequence* of numbers by using a computer. However, this situation is usually good enough for most problems and, for the purposes of this book, the sequences are simply called random.

Generally, it is best if a sequence is *uniformly* distributed. (Do not confuse this distribution with the normal distribution or the bell-shaped curve.) In a uniform distribution, all events are equally probable, so a graph of a uniform distribution tends to be a flat line rather than a curve.

Before the widespread use of computers, whenever random numbers were needed, they were produced by either throwing dice or pulling numbered balls from a jar. In 1955, the RAND Corporation published a table of one million random digits that were obtained with the help of a computer-like machine. In the early days of computer science, many methods were devised to generate random numbers, although most were discarded. One particularly interesting method that almost worked was developed by John von Neumann, the father of the modern computer. Often referred to as the *middle-square method*, it squares the previous random number and then extracts its middle digits. For example, if you were creating three-digit numbers and the previous value was 121, then you would square it to make 14641. By extracting the middle three digits, the next number would become 464. The problem with this method is that it tends to lead to a short repeating pattern called a *cycle*, especially after a zero has entered the pattern. For this reason, this method is not used today.

Currently, the most common way to generate random numbers is by using the equation

$$R_{n+1} = (aR_n + c) \bmod m$$

where

$$R >= 0$$
$$a >= 0$$
$$c >= 0$$
$$m > R_{0,} a, c$$

Note that R_n is the previous number and R_{n+1} is the next number. This method is sometimes referred to as the *linear congruential method*. This formula is so simple that you might think that random number generation is easy. However, there is a catch: how well this equation performs depends heavily upon the values of a, c, and m. Choosing these values is sometimes more of an art than a science. There are some complex rules that can help you choose those values; however, this discussion only covers a few simple rules and experiments.

The modulus, m, should be fairly large because it determines the range of the random numbers. Remember that the modulus operation produces the remainder of a division that uses the same operands. Hence,

10 **MOD** 4

is 2 because 4 goes into 10 twice with a remainder of 2. Therefore, if the modulus is 12, then the randomizing equation can only produce the numbers

0 through 11, whereas, if the modulus is 21,425, the equation can generate the numbers 0 through 21,424. Remember that a small modulus does not actually affect randomness—it only affects the range. Choosing the multiplier, *a*, and the increment, *c*, is much harder. Usually, the increment is fairly small and the multiplier is fairly large. You need a lot of testing to confirm that you have created a good generator.

Here is one of the more common random number generators. The equation in **Ran1** has been used as the basis for the random number generator in many popular languages.

```
VAR
   a1: CARDINAL;  (* initialize to 1 prior
                     to calling Ran1  *)
PROCEDURE Ran1(): REAL;
   VAR
     t: REAL;
BEGIN
   t := FLOAT((a1*32749+3) MOD 32749);
   a1 := TRUNC(t);
   RETURN ABS(t/FLOAT(32749));
END Ran1;
```

This function has three important features. First, the random number is actually a **CARDINAL**, even though the function returns a **REAL**. Integers are necessary for the linear congruential method, but random number generators, by convention, are expected to return a number between 0 and 1, which means that it is a floating-point number. Second, the *seed*, or starting value, is set by using the global variable **a1**. Prior to the first call to **Ran**, **a1** must be initialized to 1. Third, to obtain a number between 0 and 1, the random number is divided by the modulus prior to the return. If you study this process, you will see that the value of **a1** prior to the return line must be a value between 0 and 32748. Therefore, when that number is divided by 32749, a number equal to or greater than 0 but less than 1 is produced.

Part of the linear congruential method is based upon the occasional occurrence of integer overflow. Some Modula-2 compilers have options that either allow this overflow to occur or repeat a runtime error. If your compiler can check range, you must deselect that option in order to use this method. (For example, the R- compiler option on the Logitech compiler is an example of this type of option.)

Many random number generators are not useful because they either produce nonuniform distributions or have short, repeating sequences. Even though these problems may appear to be slight at first, using the same random number generator over and over again can produce biased results that are based on these problems. The solution is to create several different generators and use them either individually or jointly to obtain more random numbers. Using several generators helps smooth the distribution of the sequence by reducing small biases in each generator. Here are two more generators—called **Ran2** and **Ran3**—that produce good distributions:

```
VAR
  a2, a3: CARDINAL;

PROCEDURE Ran2(): REAL;
  VAR
    t: REAL;
BEGIN
  t := FLOAT((a2*1001+3) MOD 17417);
  a2 := TRUNC(t);
  RETURN ABS(t/FLOAT(17417));
END Ran2;


PROCEDURE Ran3(): REAL;
  VAR
    t: REAL;
BEGIN
  t := FLOAT((a3*125+7) MOD 1717);
  a3 := TRUNC(t);
  RETURN ABS(t/FLOAT(1717));
END Ran3;
```

The global variable **a2** must be initialized to 203 prior to using **Ran2**, and **a3** initialized to 1001 prior to using **Ran3**.

Each of the random number generators produces a fairly good sequence of random numbers. Yet, the questions remain: How "random" are the sequences? How good are these generators?

Determining the Quality of a Generator

You can use several tests to determine the randomness of a sequence of numbers. None of these tests can tell you if a sequence is random; rather, they tell you if it is not. These tests can identify a nonrandom sequence, but just because a specific test does not find a problem does not mean that a given sequence is indeed random. However, a test can raise your confidence in the random number generator that produced the sequence. For the purposes of this chapter, most of these tests are either too complicated or too time-consuming in their most rigorous forms. However, this section looks briefly at a few simple ways that you can test a sequence.

To begin, here is a way to find out how closely the distribution of the numbers in a sequence conforms to what you would expect a random distribution to be. For example, imagine that you are attempting to generate random sequences of the digits 0 through 9. The probability of each digit occurring is 1/10 because there are 10 possibilities for each number in the sequence, all of which are equally possible. Assume that the sequence

$$9\ 1\ 8\ 2\ 4\ 6\ 3\ 7\ 5\ 8\ 2\ 9\ 0\ 4\ 2\ 4\ 7\ 8\ 6\ 2$$

was actually generated. If you count the number of times that each digit occurs, the result is

Digit	Occurrences
0	1
1	1
2	4
3	1
4	3
5	1
6	2
7	2
8	3
9	2

Next, you should ask if this distribution of the digits is sufficiently similar to the expected distribution.

Remember that, if a random number generator is good, it generates sequences randomly. In a truly random state, all sequences are possible. This implies that any generated sequence should qualify as a valid random sequence. So, how can you tell if the sequence just given is random? In fact, how could any sequence of the 10 digits be nonrandom since any sequence is possible? The answer is that some sequences are *less likely* to be random than others. You can determine the *probability* of a given sequence being random by using the *chi-square test*.

	$p=99\%$	$p=95\%$	$p=75\%$	$p=50\%$	$p=25\%$	$p=5\%$
$n=5$	0.5543	1.1455	2.675	4.351	6.626	11.07
$n=10$	2.558	3.940	6.737	9.342	12.55	18.31
$n=15$	5.229	7.261	11.04	14.34	18.25	25.00
$n=20$	8.260	10.85	15.45	19.34	23.83	31.41
$n=30$	14.95	18.49	24.48	29.34	34.80	43.77

Figure 8-1.   Selected chi-square values

Basically, the chi-square test subtracts the expected number of occurrences for all numbers generated from the observed number of occurrences. The result is called V, which you can use to find a percentage in a table of chi-square values. This percentage represents the likelihood that a random sequence has been produced. Figure 8-1 presents a small table of chi-square values. (You can find complete tables in most books on statistics.)

The formula to obtain V is

$$V = \sum_{i=1}^{N} \frac{(O_i - E_i)^2}{E_i}$$

where O_i is the number of observed occurrences, E_i is the number of expected occurrences, and N is the number of discrete elements. The value for E_i is determined by multiplying the probability of that element occurring by the number of observations. In this case, because each digit is expected to occur 10% of the time and 20 samples were taken, the value for E is 2 for all digits. N is 10 because there are 10 possible elements, which are the digits 0 through 9. Therefore,

$$V = \frac{(1-2)^2}{2} + \frac{(1-2)^2}{2} + \frac{(4-2)^2}{2} + \frac{(1-2)^2}{2} + \frac{(3-2)^2}{2} +$$

$$\frac{(1-2)^2}{2} + \frac{(2-2)^2}{2} + \frac{(2-2)^2}{2} + \frac{(3-2)^2}{2} + \frac{(2-2)^2}{2}$$

$$= \frac{1}{2} + \frac{1}{2} + \frac{4}{2} + \frac{1}{2} + \frac{1}{2} + \frac{1}{2} + 0 + 0 + \frac{1}{2} + 0$$

$$= 5$$

To determine the likelihood that the sequence is not random, find the row in the table in Figure 8-1 that equals the number of observations; in this case, the number is 20. Then read across until you find a number that is greater than V. In this case, it is column 1. This means that there is a 99% likelihood that a sample of 20 elements will have a V greater than 8.260. This situation also implies that there is only a 1% likelihood that the tested sequence was randomly generated. To "pass" the chi-square test, the probability of V must fall between 75% and 25%. (This range is derived by using mathematics that is beyond the scope of this book.)

However, you might counter that conclusion by asking, Since all sequences are possible, how can this sequence have only a 1% chance of being legitimate? The answer is that it is just a probability—the chi-square test is actually not a test at all, only a confidence builder. In fact, if you use the chi-square test, you should obtain several different sequences and average the results to avoid rejecting a good random number generator. Any single sequence might be rejected, but several sequences that are averaged together should provide a good test.

However, a sequence could pass the chi-square test and still not be random. For example, the sequence

$$1\ 3\ 5\ 7\ 9\ 9\ 7\ 5\ 3\ 1$$

would pass the chi-square test, but does not appear to be random. In this case, a *run* has been generated. A run is simply a strictly ascending or descending sequence of numbers that is at evenly spaced intervals. Runs can also be separated by "noise" digits: the digits that make up the run can be interspersed throughout an otherwise random sequence. It is possible to design a test for these situations, but it is beyond the scope of this book.

Another feature to test for is the length of the *period;* that is, how many numbers can be generated before the sequence begins to repeat—or worse, to degenerate into a short cycle. All computer-based random number generators eventually repeat a sequence. The longer the period, the better the generator. Even though the frequency of the numbers within the period is uniformly distributed, the numbers do not constitute a random series because a truly random series does not repeat itself consistently. Generally, a period of several thousand numbers is sufficient for most applications. (Again, a test for this can be performed, but the test is beyond the scope of this book.)

Several other tests can be applied to determine the quality of a random number generator. In fact, there has probably been more code written to test random number generators than to construct them. Here is yet another test that lets you "visually" test random number generators by using a graph to show you how the sequence is generated. Ideally, the graph should be based on the frequency of each number. Because random number generators can produce thousands of different numbers, this is impractical. Instead, you will create a graph that is grouped by the tenths digit of each number: for example, since all random numbers produced are between 0 and 1, the number 0.9365783 is grouped under 0.9, and 0.34523445 is grouped under 0.3. This means that the graphic representation of the output of the generator has 10 lines, with each line representing the number of times that a number in that group occurred. The program prints the mean of each sequence, which you can use to detect a bias in the numbers. To display the output, this program uses the text mode graphics procedures that were developed earlier in Chapter 6.

```
MODULE RanGenerator;

(*Comparison of three random number
                        generators*)
  FROM SYSTEM IMPORT CODE, GETREG, BX, WORD;
  FROM InOut IMPORT WriteString, WriteLn, Write, Read;
  FROM RealInOut IMPORT WriteReal;

  CONST
    COUNT = 100;

  VAR

    freq1, freq2, freq3: ARRAY [0..9] OF CARDINAL;
    a3, a2, a1: CARDINAL;
    f, f2, f3: REAL;
```

```
      r, r2, r3: REAL;
      y, x: CARDINAL;
      ch: CHAR;

PROCEDURE CLR; (* clear the screen *)
BEGIN
  CODE(55H,         (* push bp *)
    0B9H,0,0,        (* mov cx,0 *)
    0B6H,18H,        (* mov dh,24 *)
    0B2H,4FH,        (* mov dl,79 *)
    0B4H,6,          (* mov ah,6 *)
    0B0H,0,          (* mov al,0 *)
    0B7H,7,          (* mov bh,7 *)
    0CDH,10H,        (* int 10h *)
    5DH);            (* pop bp *)
END CLR;


PROCEDURE GotoXY(x,y:CARDINAL);
(* go to specified XY position *)
BEGIN
  CODE(8AH,76H,4H,      (* get x *)
    8AH,56H,6,          (* get y *)
    0B4H,2,             (* xy function call *)
    0B7H,0,             (* video page is 0 *)
    0CDH,10H);          (* int 10h *)
END GotoXY;

PROCEDURE Line(startx,starty,endx,endy:CARDINAL);
(* draw a line *)
BEGIN
  REPEAT
    GotoXY(startx,starty);
    Write('*');
    INC(starty);
  UNTIL starty>endy;
END Line;


PROCEDURE Display;
  VAR
    t: CARDINAL;
BEGIN
  FOR t := 0 TO 9 DO
    Line(t*2, 23-freq1[t], t*2, 23);
    Line(t*2+25, 23-freq2[t], t*2+25, 23);
    Line(t*2+50, 23-freq3[t], t*2+50, 23);
  END;
END Display; (*Display*)


PROCEDURE Ran1(): REAL;
  VAR
    t: REAL;
BEGIN
  t := FLOAT((a1*32749+3) MOD 32749);
  a1 := TRUNC(t);
  RETURN ABS(t/FLOAT(32749));
END Ran1;
```

```
PROCEDURE Ran2(): REAL;
  VAR
    t: REAL;
BEGIN
  t := FLOAT((a2*1001+3) MOD 17417);
  a2 := TRUNC(t);
  RETURN ABS(t/FLOAT(17417));
END Ran2;


PROCEDURE Ran3(): REAL;
  VAR
    t: REAL;
BEGIN
  t := FLOAT((a3*125+7) MOD 1717);
  a3 := TRUNC(t);
  RETURN ABS(t/FLOAT(1717));
END Ran3;


BEGIN
  CLR;
  GotoXY(25, 0);
  WriteString('Comparison of Random');
  GotoXY(27, 1);
  WriteString('Number Generators');
  GotoXY(8, 24);   WriteString('Ran1');
  GotoXY(32, 24); WriteString('Ran2');
  GotoXY(57, 24); WriteString('Ran3');

  a1 := 1;
  a2 := 1001; (*initialize random generator variables *)
  a3 := 203;

  f := 0.0;
  f2 := 0.0;
  f3 := 0.0;
  FOR x := 0 TO 9 DO

  (* initialize frequency arrays *)
  freq1[x] := 0;
  freq2[x] := 0;
  freq3[x] := 0;
END;
FOR x := 1 TO COUNT DO
  r := Ran1(); (* get a random number *)
  f := f+r; (* add for computation of mean *)
  y := TRUNC(r*10.0); (* convert to an integer between 0 and 9*)
  freq1[y] := freq1[y]+1; (* increment frequency count*)

  r2 := Ran2(); (* get a random number *)
  f2 := f2+r2; (* add for computation of mean *)
  y := TRUNC(r*10.0); (* convert to an integer between 0 and 9*)
  freq2[y] := freq2[y]+1; (* increment frequency count*)

  r3 := Ran3(); (* get a random number *)
  f3 := f3+r3; (* add for computation of mean *)
  y := TRUNC(r*10.0); (* convert to an integer between 0 and 9*)
  freq3[y] := freq3[y]+1; (* increment frequency count*)
```

```
   Display; (* graph frequency counts *)
  END;
  Read(ch); WriteLn;
  WriteString('mean of Ran1 is: ');
  WriteReal(f/FLOAT(COUNT), 18);
  WriteLn;
  WriteString('mean of Ran2 is: ');
  WriteReal(f2/FLOAT(COUNT), 18);
  WriteLn;
  WriteString('mean of Ran3 is: ');
  WriteReal(f3/FLOAT(COUNT), 18);
  WriteLn;
END RanGenerator.
```

In the program, the functions **Ran1**, **Ran2**, and **Ran3** are displayed side-by-side for easy comparison. Each function generates 100 numbers and, based on the digit in the tenths position, the appropriate frequency array is updated. The procedure **Display** plots all three frequency arrays on the screen after each number, so that you can watch the display grow. Figure 8-2 shows the output from each of the random number generators at the end of the 100 numbers. The mean is 0.5008 for **Ran1**, 0.4301 for **Ran2**, and 0.5028 for **Ran3**. These are acceptable.

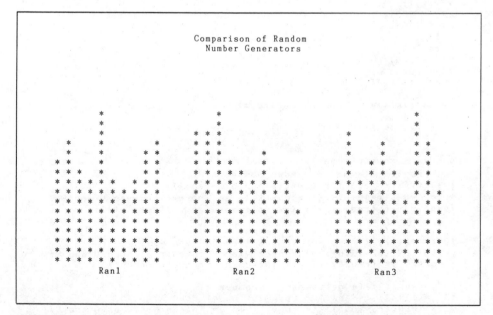

Figure 8-2.   Output from the random number generator program

To use the display program effectively, you must watch both the shape of the graph and the way that it grows in order to check for any short repeating cycles. For example, **Ran2** generates significantly fewer numbers between 0.9 and 0.999999 (the far-right bar of **Ran2**) than either **Ran1** or **Ran3**.

Of course, this "test" is not conclusive, but it does provide insight into the way that a generator produces its numbers, and it can speed up the testing process by allowing obviously poor generators to be rejected quickly. (It also makes a great program to run when someone asks you to show them your computer!)

Using Multiple Generators

One simple technique that improves the randomness of the sequences produced by the three generators is to combine them under the control of one master function. This function selects between two of them based on the result of the third. With this method, you can obtain long periods and diminish the effects of any cycle or bias.

The function called **CombRandom**, shown here, combines **Ran1**, **Ran2**, and **Ran3**:

```
PROCEDURE CombRan():REAL;
(* random selection of generators *)
VAR
    f: REAL;
BEGIN
    f:=Ran2();
    IF f>0.5 THEN RETURN Ran1();
    ELSE RETURN Ran3();     (* random selection of generators *)
    END;
END CombRan;
```

The result of **Ran2** is used to decide whether **Ran1** or **Ran3** becomes the value of the master function **CombRan**. With this method, the period of **CombRan** is equal to or greater than the sum of the period of **Ran1** and **Ran3**. Thus, this method makes it possible to produce sequences with long periods. Feel free to alter the mix between **Ran1** and **Ran3** by changing the constant in the **IF** to obtain the exact distribution between them that you like. You can also add additional generators and select between them for even longer periods. The next program displays the graph of **CombRan** and its mean, and Figure 8-3 shows the final graph after 100 random numbers have been computed. The mean of **CombRan** is 0.5516.

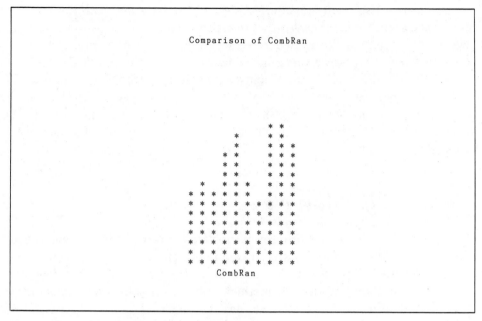

Figure 8-3. The final graph of **CombRan**

```
MODULE CombRanGenerator;

(*Comparison of three random number
                      generators*)
   FROM SYSTEM IMPORT CODE, GETREG, BX, WORD;
   FROM InOut IMPORT WriteString, WriteLn, Write, Read;
   FROM RealInOut IMPORT WriteReal;

   CONST
     COUNT = 100;

   VAR

     freq1 : ARRAY [0..9] OF CARDINAL;
     a3, a2, a1: CARDINAL;
     f, f2, f3: REAL;
     r: REAL;
     y, x: CARDINAL;
     ch: CHAR;

PROCEDURE CLR; (* clear the screen *)
```

```
BEGIN
  CODE(55H,         (* push bp *)
    0B9H,0,0,        (* mov cx,0 *)
    0B6H,18H,        (* mov dh,24 *)
    0B2H,4FH,        (* mov dl,79 *)
    0B4H,6,          (* mov ah,6 *)
    0B0H,0,          (* mov al,0 *)
    0B7H,7,          (* mov bh,7 *)
    0CDH,10H,        (* int 10h *)
    5DH);            (* pop bp *)
END CLR;


PROCEDURE GotoXY(x,y:CARDINAL);
(* go to specified XY position *)
BEGIN
  CODE(8AH,76H,4H,      (* get x *)
    8AH,56H,6,          (* get y *)
    0B4H,2,             (* xy function call *)
    0B7H,0,             (* video page is 0 *)
    0CDH,10H);          (* int 10h *)
END GotoXY;

PROCEDURE Line(startx,starty,endx,endy:CARDINAL);
(* draw a line *)
BEGIN
  REPEAT
    GotoXY(startx,starty);
    Write('*');
    INC(starty);
  UNTIL starty>endy;
END Line;


PROCEDURE Display;
  VAR
    t: CARDINAL;
BEGIN
  FOR t := 0 TO 9 DO
    Line(t*2+25, 23-freq1[t], t*2+25, 23);
  END;
END Display; (*Display*)


PROCEDURE Ran1(): REAL;
  VAR
    t: REAL;
BEGIN
  t := FLOAT((a1*32749+3) MOD 32749);
  a1 := TRUNC(t);
  RETURN ABS(t/FLOAT(32749));
END Ran1;


PROCEDURE Ran2(): REAL;
  VAR
    t: REAL;
```

```
BEGIN
   t := FLOAT((a2*1001+3) MOD 17417);
   a2 := TRUNC(t);
   RETURN ABS(t/FLOAT(17417));
END Ran2;


PROCEDURE Ran3(): REAL;
   VAR
      t: REAL;
BEGIN
   t := FLOAT((a3*125+7) MOD 1717);
   a3 := TRUNC(t);
   RETURN ABS(t/FLOAT(1717));
END Ran3;

PROCEDURE CombRan():REAL;
(* random selection of generators *)
VAR
   f: REAL;
BEGIN
   f:=Ran2();
   IF f>0.5 THEN RETURN Ran1();
   ELSE RETURN Ran3();      (* random selection of generators *)
   END;
END CombRan;

BEGIN
   CLR;
   GotoXY(25, 0);
   WriteString('Comparison of CombRan');
   GotoXY(30, 24); WriteString('CombRan');

   a1 := 1;
   a2 := 1001; (*initialize random generator variables *)
   a3 := 203;

   f := 0.0;
   f2 := 0.0;
   f3 := 0.0;
   FOR x := 0 TO 9 DO
      (* initialize frequency array *)
      freq1[x] := 0;
   END;
   FOR x := 1 TO COUNT DO
      r := CombRan(); (* get a random number *)
      f := f+r; (* add for computation of mean *)
      y := TRUNC(r*10.0); (* convert to an integer between 0 and 9*)
      freq1[y] := freq1[y]+1; (* increment frequency count*)

      Display;
   END;
   Read(ch); WriteLn;
   WriteString('mean of CombRan is: ');
   WriteReal(f/FLOAT(COUNT), 18);
   WriteLn;
END CombRanGenerator.
```

Simulations

The remainder of this chapter examines two applications of random number generators to *simulations*. A simulation is a computerized model of some real-world situation. Anything can be simulated; the success of a simulation depends primarily upon how well the programmer understands the event being simulated. Because real-world situations often have thousands of variables, many events are difficult to simulate meaningfully. However, there are several events that lend themselves to simulations.

Simulations are important for two reasons. The first reason is that they let you alter the parameters of a situation to observe the results, even though in reality such experimentation might be either too costly or dangerous. For example, a simulation of a nuclear power plant can test the effects of certain types of failures without danger. The second reason is that simulations let you create situations that cannot occur in the real world. For example, a psychologist might want to study the effects of gradually increasing the intelligence of a mouse to that of a human to find out at what point the mouse runs a maze the fastest. Although this cannot be done in real life, a simulation may provide insight into the nature of intelligence versus instinct.

Simulating a Check-out Line

The first example simulates a check-out line in a grocery store. The store is open for 10 hours a day, with peak hours being from 12 noon to 1 P.M. and from 5 P.M. to 6 P.M. The 12 noon to 1 P.M. slot is twice as busy as the rest of the day and the 5 P.M. to 6 P.M. slot is three times as busy. As the simulation runs, one random number generator "creates" customers, another generator determines how long it will take to check out, and a third generator decides which of the open lines the customers will go to. The goal of the simulation is to help management find the optimal number of check-out lines that should be available over a typical shopping day so that the number of people in line at any time is limited to 10 or less, and cashiers do not have to wait for customers to serve.

This program appears to be simultaneous because each procedure used inside the main program loop does some work and then returns — in essence, each performs manual time-slicing. For example, the procedure that simulates the check-out only checks out part of each order each time that it is called. In this way, each procedure inside the main loop continues to execute. You could obtain a similar effect by using Modula-2's multiprocessing capabilities; however, in this simple situation, they would have created more overhead and inefficiency than the process shown here. (In general, you should only use multiple processes when they are necessary or simplify a program.) The main program to the **CheckOut** program is shown here:

```
BEGIN
  CLR;

  a1 := 1;
  a2 := 203; (*initialize random generator variables *)
  a3:= 1001;

  change := FALSE;
  cust := 0;
  time := 0;
  FOR x := 0 TO 9 DO
    queues[x] := 0; (*initialize queues*)
    open[x] := FALSE; (*no customers or check-outs at start of day*)
    count[x] := 0; (*line count*)
  END;
  GotoXY(30, 24);
  WriteString('1                    10');

  GotoXY(30, 23);
  WriteString("o o o o o o o o o o");
  GotoXY(1, 24);
  WriteString('Check-out lines:');
  (*now start day by opening up the first check-out station*)
  open[0] := TRUE;
  REPEAT
    AddCust;
    AddQueue;
    Display;
    CheckOut;
    Display;
    IF (time > 30) AND (time < 50) THEN
      AddCust
    END;
    IF (time > 70) AND (time < 80) THEN
      AddCust;
      AddCust;
    END;
    INC(time);
  UNTIL time > 100; (*end of day*)
  Read(ch);

END checkout.
```

The main loop drives the entire simulation:

```
REPEAT
   AddCust;
   AddQueue;
   Display;
   CheckOut;
   Display;
   IF (time > 30) AND (time < 50) THEN
      AddCust
   END;
   IF (time > 70) AND (time < 80) THEN
      AddCust;
      AddCust;
   END;
   INC(time);
UNTIL time > 100; (*end of day*)
```

```
        queue 1: 7      time: 28
        queue 2: 4
        queue 3: 0
        queue 4: 0
        queue 5: 0
        queue 6: 0
        queue 7: 0
        queue 8: 0
        queue 9: 0
        queue 10: 0




                           *
                           *
                           *
                           * *
                           * *
                           * *
                           * *
                           o o o o o o o o o o
  Check-out lines:         1                 10
```

Figure 8-4. The state of the check-out line when **time** = 28

The procedure **AddCust** uses either the **Ran1** function or the **Ran3** function to generate the amount of customers who arrive at the check-out lines at each request. **AddQueue** both places the customers into an open check-out line, based on the results of **Ran2**, and opens a new line if all currently open lines are full. **Display** shows a graphic representation of the simulation; **Check-Out** uses **Ran2** to assign each customer a check-out count, while each call decrements that count by 1. When a customer's count is 0, the customer leaves the check-out line.

In order to match the peak hours of the store, the **time** variable alters the rate at which customers are generated. In essence, each pass through the loop is one-tenth of an hour.

Figures 8-4, 8-5, and 8-6 show the state of the check-out lines at **time**=28, **time**=60, and **time**=88, which correspond to normal time, the end of the first peak, and the end of the second peak. Notice that, at the end of the second peak, a maximum of five check-out lines is needed. If the simulation is programmed properly, this means that the grocery store does not need to operate the remaining five lines.

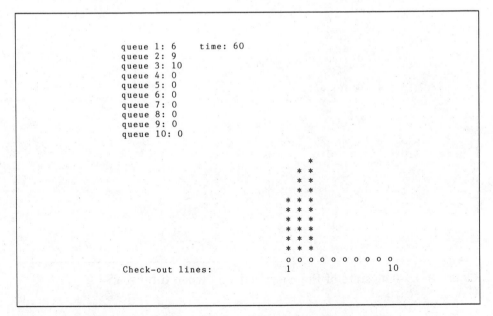

Figure 8-5. The state of the check-out line when **time** = 60

```
              queue 1: 7      time: 88
              queue 2: 8
              queue 3: 8
              queue 4: 9
              queue 5: 6
              queue 6: 0
              queue 7: 0
              queue 8: 0
              queue 9: 0
              queue 10: 0




                                      *
                                  *   *   *
                              *   *   *   *
                              *   *   *   *   *
                              *   *   *   *   *
                              *   *   *   *   *
                              *   *   *   *   *
                              *   *   *   *   *
                              *   *   *   *
                              o o o o o o o o o o
         Check-out lines:     1                 10
```

Figure 8-6.   The state of the check-out line when **time** = 88

You can control several variables directly in the program. First, you can alter the way and the amount of customers that arrive. Second, you could change **AddCust** to return gradually more or less customers as the peak hours approach and wane. The program assumes that customers will randomly choose which line to stand in. Although this may be true of some customers, others will obviously choose the shortest line. You could account for this by altering the **AddQueue** procedure to put a customer into the shortest line sometimes and to place customers randomly at other times. The simulation does not account for the occasional accident—such as a dropped ketchup bottle—or an unruly customer at the check-out, both of which would cause that line to stall temporarily.

Here is the entire program for your convenience:

```
MODULE checkout;
(*Simulation of grocery store check-out lines*)
FROM SYSTEM IMPORT CODE, GETREG, BX, WORD;
FROM InOut IMPORT WriteString, WriteLn, Write, Read,
   WriteInt;
FROM RealInOut IMPORT WriteReal;

VAR
```

```
    queues, count: ARRAY [0..9] OF INTEGER;
    open: ARRAY [0..9] OF BOOLEAN;
    cust, time: INTEGER;
    a1, a2, a3: CARDINAL;
    y, x: INTEGER;
    change: BOOLEAN;
    ch: CHAR;

PROCEDURE CLR; (* clear the screen *)
BEGIN
  CODE(55H,        (* push bp *)
    0B9H,0,0,       (* mov cx,0 *)
    0B6H,18H,       (* mov dh,24 *)
    0B2H,4FH,       (* mov dl,79 *)
    0B4H,6,         (* mov ah,6 *)
    0B0H,0,         (* mov al,0 *)
    0B7H,7,         (* mov bh,7 *)
    0CDH,10H,       (* int 10h *)
    5DH);           (* pop bp *)
END CLR;


PROCEDURE GotoXY(x,y:CARDINAL);
(* go to specified XY position *)
BEGIN
  CODE(8AH,76H,4H,        (* get x *)
    8AH,56H,6,            (* get y *)
    0B4H,2,               (* xy function call *)
    0B7H,0,               (* video page is 0 *)
    0CDH,10H);            (* int 10h *)
END GotoXY;

PROCEDURE Ran1(): REAL;
  VAR
    t: REAL;
BEGIN
  t := FLOAT((a1*32749+3) MOD 32749);
  a1 := TRUNC(t);
  RETURN ABS(t/FLOAT(32749));
END Ran1;


PROCEDURE Ran2(): REAL;
  VAR
    t: REAL;
BEGIN
  t := FLOAT((a2*1001+3) MOD 17417);
  a2 := TRUNC(t);
  RETURN ABS(t/FLOAT(17417));
END Ran2;


PROCEDURE Ran3(): REAL;
  VAR
    t: REAL;
BEGIN
  t := FLOAT((a3*125+7) MOD 1717);
  a3 := TRUNC(t);
  RETURN ABS(t/FLOAT(1717));
END Ran3;
```

```
PROCEDURE Line(startx,starty,endx,endy:CARDINAL);
(* draw a line *)
  VAR
    y: CARDINAL;
BEGIN
  (* first clear previous line *)
  y:=10;
  REPEAT
    GotoXY(startx,y);
    Write(' ');
    INC(y);
  UNTIL y>=endy;

  (* now draw line *)
  WHILE starty<endy DO
    GotoXY(startx,starty);
    Write('*');
    INC(starty);
  END;
END Line;


PROCEDURE AddCust;
  VAR
    f, r: REAL;
BEGIN
  IF change THEN
    (*alternate between two*)
    f := Ran1();
  ELSE
    f := Ran2();
  END; (*generators*)
  IF f > 0.5 THEN
    IF f < 0.6 THEN
      (*add one customer*)
      INC(cust, 1)
    ELSIF f < 0.7 THEN
      (*two customers*)
      INC(cust, 2)
    ELSIF f < 0.8 THEN
      (*three customers*)
      INC(cust, 3)
    ELSE
      INC(cust, 4)
    END
  END; (*four customers*)
END AddCust;


PROCEDURE CheckOut;
  VAR
    t: INTEGER;
BEGIN
  FOR t := 0 TO 9 DO
    IF queues[t] <> 0 THEN
      (*get check out-time*)
      WHILE count[t] = 0 DO
        count[t] := TRUNC(Ran1()*5.0)
      END; (*a new customer needs to get check-out time*)
      count[t] := count[t]-1;
```

```
        IF count[t] = 0 THEN
          queues[t] := queues[t]-1
        END; (*remove the customer*)
      END;
      IF queues[t] = 0 THEN
        open[t] := FALSE
      END; (*close line down*)
    END;
END CheckOut; (*CheckOut*)


(*See if there is any spare check-out capacity*)
PROCEDURE AllFull(): BOOLEAN;
  VAR
    t: CARDINAL;

BEGIN
  FOR t := 0 TO 9 DO
    IF (queues[t] < 10) AND open[t] THEN
      RETURN FALSE
    END
  END;
  RETURN TRUE
END AllFull; (*AllFull*)


(*open a check-out line*)
PROCEDURE AddQueue;
  VAR
    t, line: INTEGER;
    done: BOOLEAN;
BEGIN
  done := FALSE;
  WHILE cust <> 0 DO
    IF AllFull() THEN
      t := 0;
      REPEAT
        IF  NOT open[t] THEN
          open[t] := TRUE;
          done := TRUE;
        END;
        INC(t, 1);
      UNTIL done OR (t = 9);
    ELSE
      line := TRUNC(Ran2()*10.0);
      IF open[line] AND (queues[line] < 10) THEN
        queues[line] := queues[line]+1;
        DEC(cust, 1);
      END;
    END;
    IF AllFull() AND open[9] THEN
      cust := 0
    END; (*all full*)
  END;
END AddQueue;


PROCEDURE Display;
  VAR
    t: INTEGER;
```

```
BEGIN
  GotoXY(15, 1);
  WriteString('time: ');
  WriteInt(time,0);
  FOR t := 0 TO 9 DO
    Line((t*2)+30, 23-queues[t], (t*2)+30, 23);
    GotoXY(1, 1+t);
    WriteString('queue ');
    WriteInt(t+1, 0);
    WriteString(': ');
    WriteInt(queues[t],0);
    Write(' ');
  END;
END Display; (*Display*)



BEGIN
  CLR;

  a1 := 1;
  a2 := 203; (*initialize random generator variables *)
  a3:= 1001;


  change := FALSE;
  cust := 0;
  time := 0;
  FOR x := 0 TO 9 DO
    queues[x] := 0; (*initialize queues*)
    open[x] := FALSE; (*no customers or check-outs at start of day*)
    count[x] := 0; (*line count*)


END;
GotoXY(30, 24);
WriteString('1                  10');
GotoXY(30, 23);
WriteString("o o o o o o o o o o");
GotoXY(1, 24);
WriteString('Check-out lines:');
(*now start day by opening up the first check-out station*)
open[0] := TRUE;
REPEAT
  AddCust;
  AddQueue;
  Display;
  CheckOut;
  Display;
  IF (time > 30) AND (time < 50) THEN
    AddCust
  END;
  IF (time > 70) AND (time < 80) THEN
    AddCust;
    AddCust;
  END;
  INC(time, 1);
UNTIL time > 100; (*end of day*)
Read(ch);

END checkout.
```

Random-Walk Portfolio Management

The art of stock portfolio management is generally based on various theories and assumptions about many factors, some of which cannot be easily known unless you are an insider. There are buying and selling strategies that are based on statistical analyses of stock prices, PE ratios, the price of gold, the GNP, and even the cycles of the moon! The computer scientist's revenge is to use the computer to simulate the free marketplace—the stock exchange—and without all of the real-life worry!

You may think that the stock exchange is simply too hard to simulate—that it has too many variables and too many unknowns, and that it swings widely at times and coasts smoothly at others. However, the problem itself is the solution: because the marketplace is so complex, you can think of it as being composed of *randomly occurring events*. This means that you can simulate the stock exchange as a series of disconnected random occurrences. This simulation is affectionately referred to as the *random-walk method* of portfolio management. The term is derived from the classic thought experiment that involves a drunk wandering a street, weaving randomly from lamppost to lamppost. With the random-walk theory, you let chance be your guide, because it is as good as any other method.

Before you go on, be warned: the random-walk method is generally discredited by professional money managers. It is presented here for fun and enjoyment, and not to help you make actual investment decisions.

To implement the random-walk method, you first select 10 companies from the *Wall Street Journal* by some chance method—for example, throw darts at it and use the companies whose names you hit. After you have selected 10 companies, feed their names into the random-walk simulation program so that it can tell you what to do with them.

The program can tell you basically five things that you can do with the stock of each company:

- Sell
- Buy
- Sell short
- Buy on margin
- Hold (do nothing)

The operations of selling, buying, and holding stocks are self-explanatory. When you *sell short*, you sell stock that you do not own in the hopes that soon you can buy it cheaper and deliver it to the person you sold it to. Selling short is a way to make money when the stock market is going down. When you *buy on margin*, you use—for a small fee—the money of the brokerage house to finance part of the cost of the stock that you purchased. The idea behind buying on margin is that, if the stock increases enough, you make more money than you could have made if you had bought only a smaller amount of stock with cash. This makes money only in a bull, or rising, market.

The random-walk program is shown here. The **KeyPressed** function in **Terminal** checks for keyboard status to wait for a key press. This function allows you to use at a random point the sequence that the random number generator produces. In essence, you create a random seed value, which prevents the program from always producing the same advice.

```
MODULE stock;
(*Random-walk portfolio program*)

   FROM InOut IMPORT WriteString, WriteLn,
     ReadString, Read;
   FROM RealInOut IMPORT WriteReal;
   FROM Terminal IMPORT KeyPressed;
   FROM Strings IMPORT Length;

   TYPE
      str80 = ARRAY [0..79] OF CHAR;
      action = (buy, sell, hold, short, margin);

   VAR
      a1, t: CARDINAL;
      stock: ARRAY [1..10] OF str80;
      ch: CHAR;
      act: action;
      f: REAL;

   PROCEDURE Ran1(): REAL;
      VAR
         t: REAL;
   BEGIN
      t := FLOAT((a1*32749+3) MOD 32749);
      a1 := TRUNC(t);
      RETURN ABS(t/FLOAT(32749));
   END Ran1;


   (*input the company names*)
   PROCEDURE Enter;
      VAR
         t: CARDINAL;
   BEGIN
      FOR t := 1 TO 10 DO
```

```
      WriteString('Enter company name: ');
      ReadString(stock[t]);   WriteLn;
    END;
END Enter;


PROCEDURE NextAction(): action;
  VAR
    f: REAL;
    NextActionResult: action;
BEGIN
  NextActionResult := hold;
  CASE TRUNC(Ran1()*10.0) OF
    1:
      NextActionResult := sell |
    2:
      NextActionResult := buy  |
    3:
      NextActionResult := short |
    4:
      NextActionResult := margin
    ELSE
  END;
  RETURN NextActionResult
END NextAction;


BEGIN
  FOR t:=1 TO 10 DO
    stock[t]:="";
  END;
  WriteString('Wait a while, then strike any key ');
  REPEAT
    f := Ran1(); (*Randomize the generator*)
  UNTIL KeyPressed();
  Read(ch);
  a1:=1;
  WriteLn;
  WriteString('Enter New Companies? (Y/N) ');
  WriteLn;
  Read(ch);
  IF CAP(ch) = 'Y' THEN
    Enter
  END;
  REPEAT
    FOR t := 1 TO 10 DO
      act := NextAction();
      IF Length(stock[t]) > 0 THEN
        WriteString(stock[t]);
        WriteString(': ');
        CASE act OF
            buy:
            WriteString('buy');
            WriteLn               |
          sell:
            WriteString('sell');
            WriteLn               |
          short:
            WriteString('sell short');
            WriteLn               |
```

```
    margin:
      WriteString('buy on margin');
      WriteLn            |
    hold:
      WriteString('hold');
      WriteLn
    ELSE
  END;
 END;
END;
WriteString('Again (Y/N) ');
Read(ch);  WriteLn;
UNTIL CAP(ch) = 'N';
END stock.
```

The program requires you to interpret its instructions in the following manner:

Instruction	Interpretation
Buy	Buy as much of the specified stock as you can afford without borrowing.
Sell	Sell all of the stock if any is owned. Then randomly select a new company to take its place.
Sell short	Sell 100 shares of the specified company even though you don't own it in the hopes that you can buy it cheaper in the future.
Buy on margin	Borrow money to buy shares of the specified stock.
Hold	Do nothing.

For example, if you were to run this program and used the fictitious company names of Com1 through Com10, the first day's advice might look like this:

Com1: sell
Com2: buy
Com3: buy on margin
Com4: sell short
Com5: hold
Com6: hold
Com7: hold
Com8: buy
Com9: hold
Com10: sell short

The second day's advice might be

> Com1: hold
> Com2: hold
> Com3: sell
> Com4: sell short
> Com5: hold
> Com6: hold
> Com7: buy
> Com8: buy on margin
> Com9: hold
> Com10: sell

Remember that, because the program waits for you to type a key, your output will differ from that shown here. You might prefer to run the program weekly or monthly, instead of daily.

Feel free to alter the program in any way. For example, you could have the program give you amounts of stock to buy and sell, depending on your available funds. However, remember that this program is for fun only and is not recommended as a way to make actual investments in the market. However, it is interesting to create a portfolio on paper and to track its performance.

Expression Parsing and Evaluation

CHAPTER 9

How do you write a program that takes as input any string containing an algebraically correct numeric expression—such as 10−5*3—and properly computes the answer, which in this case is −5? If a "high priesthood" still exists among programmers, then it must be made up of those few who know how to do this. Almost everyone who uses a computer is mystified by the way that a high-level language converts such complex expressions as 10*3−(4+*COUNT*)/12 into instructions that a computer can execute. This conversion process is called *expression parsing*. It forms the backbone of all language compilers, interpreters, and spreadsheet programs. Few programmers know how to write an expression parser; this realm of programming is generally thought of as off limits except to the enlightened few.

However, this should not be the situation. Expression parsing is actually very straightforward and is similar to other programming tasks. In some ways it is easier because it works with the strict rules of algebra. This chapter develops what is commonly referred to as a *recursive descent parser*, as well as all of the necessary support routines that enable you to evaluate complex numeric expressions. After you have mastered using the parser, you can enhance and modify it to suit your needs—and join the "high priesthood" yourself!

Expressions

Although expressions can be made up of all types of information, you will be studying only one type: *numeric expressions*. For the purposes of this chapter, assume that numeric expressions can be made up of the following:

- Numbers
- The operators $+ - / * \char94 =$
- Parentheses
- Variables

The $\char94$ symbol indicates exponentiation, as in BASIC, and the $=$ symbol represents the assignment operator. All of these items follow the rules of algebra with which you are familiar. Some examples of expressions are

$$10-8$$
$$(100-5) * 14/6$$
$$a+b-c$$
$$10\char94 5$$
$$a=10-b$$

Assume the following precedence for the operators:

$$
\begin{array}{ll}
\text{Highest} & \char94 \\
& * / \\
& + - \\
\text{Lowest} & =
\end{array}
$$

Operators of equal precedence evaluate from left to right.

For the examples in this chapter, the following assumptions will be made: All variables are single letters, which means that 26 variables—the letters A through Z—are available. All numbers are reals and the routines process them as such. (You could easily write the routines to handle any type of number.) Finally, the routines include only a minimal amount of error-checking in order to keep the logic clear and uncluttered.

Try to evaluate this expression:

$$10-2*3$$

This expression has the value 4. Although you could easily create a program that would compute that specific expression, the point is to create a computer program that gives the correct answer for any arbitrary expression. At first, you might think that you could use a routine something like this:

```
a := get first operand
while(operands present) do
begin
    op := get operator;
    b := get second operand;
    a := a op b
end;
```

With this routine, you could get the first operand, the operator, and the second operand; perform the operation; get the next operator and operand, if any; perform that operation; and so on. If you use this basic concept, the expression $10-2*3$ would evaluate to 24 (that is, 8*3) instead of the correct answer, 4, because this procedure neglects the precedence of the operators. You cannot simply perform the operations in order from left to right because you must complete the multiplication before the subtraction. A beginner may think that this could be easily overcome—and sometimes, in restrictive cases, it can—but the problem only gets worse and worse when parentheses, exponentiation, variables, function calls, and the like are added in.

Although there are a few ways to write a set of procedures that evaluate expressions of this sort, you will study one that is easily written and is also the most common. (Some of the other methods to write parsers employ complex tabes that almost require another computer program to generate them.

These are sometimes called *table-driven parsers*.) The method that you will study is called a *recursive descent parser* and, in this chapter, you will see how it got its name.

Dissecting an Expression

Before you can develop a parser to evaluate expressions, you must get pieces of the expression easily. For example, given the expression

$$A*B-(W+10)$$

you need to get the operands A, B, W, and 10, the parentheses, and the operators $*$ + and $-$. In general, you need a routine that returns each item in the expression individually. The routine must also be able to skip over spaces and tabs, and know when it reaches the end of the expression.

Formally, each piece of an expression is called a *token*. Therefore, the procedure that returns the next token in the expression is called **GetToken**. You need a global string to hold the expression string. In **GetToken**, this string is called **prog**. The **prog** variable is global because it must maintain its value between calls to **GetToken**, and it must allow other procedures to use it. In addition to **prog**, the global integer t is used to index into **prog**, which allows **GetToken** to advance through the expression one token at a time. **GetToken** assumes that **prog** is terminated by a $. You must make certain that this is the case because the $ signals the end of the expression.

Besides returning a token, you also need to know what type of token you are getting. The parser that is developed in this chapter only needs three types: **VARIABLE**, **NUMBER**, and **DELIMITER**, where **DELIMITER** is used for both operators and parentheses. Here is **GetToken** with its necessary globals and support procedures:

```
TYPE
  str80 = ARRAY [0..79] OF CHAR;
  TType = (DELIMITER, VARIABLE, NUMBER);

VAR
  token, prog: str80;
  TokType: TType;
  t: INTEGER;
  result: REAL;
```

```
(*returns TRUE if ch is a letter of the alphabet*)
PROCEDURE IsAlpha(ch: CHAR): BOOLEAN;
BEGIN
  RETURN (CAP(ch) >= 'A') AND (CAP(ch) <= 'Z');
END IsAlpha;


(*True if newline, space or tab*)
PROCEDURE IsWhite(ch: CHAR): BOOLEAN;
BEGIN
  RETURN (ch = ' ') OR (ch = CHR(9)) OR (ch = CHR(13));
END IsWhite;


(*TRUE if is a delimiter*)
PROCEDURE IsDelim(ch: CHAR): BOOLEAN;
BEGIN
  IF Pos(ch, ' +-/*%^=()$') < 11 THEN
    RETURN TRUE
  ELSE
    RETURN FALSE
  END;
END IsDelim;


(*TRUE if a digit between 0 and 9*)
PROCEDURE IsDigit(ch: CHAR): BOOLEAN;
BEGIN
  RETURN (ch >= '0') AND (ch <= '9');
END IsDigit;


PROCEDURE GetToken;
  VAR
    temp: str80;
BEGIN
  token := ''; (*null string*)
  WHILE (IsWhite(prog[t])) DO
    INC(t)
  END; (*strip leading spaces*)
  IF prog[t] = '$' THEN
    token := '$'
  END;

  IF Pos(prog[t], '+-*/%^=()') < 9 THEN
    TokType := DELIMITER;
    token[0] := prog[t]; (*is an operator*)
    token[1] := CHR(0);
    INC(t);
  ELSIF IsAlpha(prog[t]) THEN
    WHILE (NOT IsDelim(prog[t])) DO
      Concat(token, prog[t], token); (*build token*)
      INC(t);
    END;
    TokType := VARIABLE;
  ELSIF IsDigit(prog[t]) THEN
```

```
      WHILE (NOT IsDelim(prog[t])) DO
        Concat(token, prog[t], token); (*build number*)
        INC(t);
        TokType := NUMBER;
      END;
    END;
  END GetToken;
```

Before you can use **GetToken**, you must set the global variable, **t**, to zero. Remember that this variable is used to index into the array **prog**, which holds the input expression. Upon entry into **GetToken**, the routine checks for the $ terminator, which indicates the end of the expression string. Next, the routine skips leading spaces. Because spaces are added to expressions to add clarity, the parser allows them but ignores them.

After the routine skips the spaces, **prog[t]** points to either a number, a variable, an operator, or a $ if trailing spaces end the expression. If the next character is an operator, the routine returns it as a string in the global variable **token**, and places the type of **DELIMITER** in **TokType**. However, if the next character is a letter, then the routine assumes it to be one of the variables, and returns it as a string in **token**; **TokType** is assigned the value **VARIABLE**. If the next character is a number, then the routine returns that integer as a string in **token** with a type of **NUMBER**. Finally, if the next character is none of these, then the routine assumes that it has reached the end of the expression, and that **token** is a $.

To keep the code of this procedure clean, a certain amount of error-checking has been omitted and some assumptions have been made. For example, the routine discards any unrecognized character. Also, in this version, variables may be any length, but only the first letter is significant. However, you can fill in these and other details according to your specific application. You can easily modify or enhance **GetToken** to enable character strings, floating-point numbers, or whatever you want to return from an input string token.

To understand how **GetToken** works, study what it returns for each token and type for the expression $A + 100 - (B*C)/2$.

Token	Token type
A	**VARIABLE**
+	**DELIMITER**
100	**NUMBER**
−	**DELIMITER**
(	**DELIMITER**

B	VARIABLE
*	DELIMITER
C	VARIABLE
)	DELIMITER
/	DELIMITER
2	NUMBER
$	$

Expression Parsing

Remember that there are several possible ways to parse and evaluate an expression. For the purposes of this chapter think of expressions as *recursive data structures* that are defined in terms of themselves. If, for the moment, expressions are restricted to allow only $+ - * /$ and parentheses, then you can define all expressions by using the rules

expression => *term* [+ *term*] [− *term*]
term => *factor* [* *factor*] [/ *factor*]
factor => *variable, number,* or (*expression*)

where any part of these can be null. The square brackets indicate optional parts, and the => means "produces." In fact, these rules are usually called the *production rules* of the expression. Therefore, you would read the second rule as "term produces factor times factor, or factor divided by factor." The precedence of the operators is implicit in the way that an expression is defined.

The expression

$$10+5*B$$

has two terms: 10 and 5*B. However, it has three factors: 10, 5, and B. These factors consist of two numbers and one variable.

On the other hand, the expression

$$14*(7-C)$$

has two terms: 14 and (7−C), which is one number and one parenthesized expression. The parenthesized expression evaluates to one number and one variable.

This process forms the basis for a recursive descent parser, which is basically a set of mutually recursive routines that work in a chain-like fashion. At each appropriate step, the parser can perform the specified operations in the algebraically correct sequence. To see how this process works, parse the expression 10/3−(100+56) and perform the arithmetic operations at the right time:

Step 1.   Get the first term: 10/3.
Step 2.   Get each factor and divide integers. That value is 3.
Step 3.   Get the second term: (100+56). At this point, you must recursively analyze the second expression.
Step 4.   Get each factor and add. The result is 156.
Step 5.   Return from the recursive call and subtract 156 from 3, which yields an answer of −153.

If you are confused at this point, do not worry. This is a complex concept, which takes getting used to. There are two things to remember about this recursive view of expressions: first, the precedence of the operators is *implicit* in the way that the production rules are defined; second, this method of parsing and evaluating expressions is similar to the way that people do the same thing without a computer.

A Simple
Expression Parser

In the remainder of this chapter, two parsers are developed. The first one parses and evaluates only constant expressions—those expressions with no variables. This is the parser in its simplest form. The second parser includes the 26 user-defined variables A through Z, and allows assignments to those variables.

Here is the entire simple version of the recursive descent parser. It assumes the same global data shown for the **GetToken** procedure that was given earlier.

```
(* ********** Expression Parser ************* *)
PROCEDURE GetExp(VAR result: REAL);
BEGIN
  GetToken;
  IF  Length(token) <> 0 THEN
    Level2(result)
  ELSE
    Serror(3)
  END;
END GetExp;


PROCEDURE Level2(VAR result: REAL);
  VAR
    op: CHAR;
    hold: REAL;
BEGIN
  Level3(result);
  op := token[0];
  WHILE ((op = '+') OR (op = '-')) DO
    GetToken;
    Level3(hold);
    Arith(op, result, hold);
    op := token[0]
  END;
END Level2;


PROCEDURE Level3(VAR result: REAL);
  VAR
    op: CHAR;
    hold: REAL;
BEGIN
  Level4(result);
  op := token[0];
  WHILE ((op = '*') OR (op = '/')) DO
    GetToken;
    Level4(hold);
    Arith(op, result, hold);
    op := token[0];
  END;
END Level3;


PROCEDURE Level4(VAR result: REAL);
  VAR
    hold: REAL;
BEGIN
  Level5(result);
  IF token[0] = '^' THEN
    GetToken;
    Level4(hold);
    Arith('^', result, hold); (*exponents*)
  END;
END Level4;
```

```
PROCEDURE Level5(VAR result: REAL);
  VAR
    op: CHAR;
BEGIN
  op := ' ';
  IF ((TokType = DELIMITER) AND
    ((token[0] = '+') OR (token[0] = '-'))) THEN
    (*unary plus or minus*)
    op := token[0];
    GetToken;
  END;
  Level6(result);
  IF op = '-' THEN
    result := (-result)
  END;
END Level5;



PROCEDURE Level6(VAR result: REAL);
BEGIN
  IF (token[0] = '(') AND (TokType = DELIMITER) THEN
    (*parenthesized expression*)
    GetToken;
    Level2(result);
    IF token[0] <> ')' THEN
      Serror(2)
    END; (*parentheses unbalanced*)
    GetToken;
  ELSE
    Primitive(result)
  END;
END Level6; (*Level6*)



PROCEDURE Primitive(VAR result: REAL);
  VAR
    code: BOOLEAN;
BEGIN
  IF TokType = NUMBER THEN
    StringToReal(token, result, code)
  ELSE
    Serror(1)
  END;
  GetToken;
END Primitive;
```

The parser as shown can handle the operators $+ - *$ and $/$, as well as exponentiation ($^\wedge$), the unary minus, and parentheses. It has six levels as well as the **primitive** procedure, which returns the value of a number.

In addition to the parser code just given, there are several special routines: **Serror**, which reports syntax errors, and **Arith** and **Pwr**, which perform various arithmetic operations. These routines are shown here:

```
(*print error messages*)
PROCEDURE Serror(i: INTEGER);
BEGIN
  CASE i OF
    1:
      WriteString('Syntax Error');
      WriteLn |
    2:
      WriteString('Unbalanced Parentheses');
      WriteLn |
    3:
      WriteString('No Expression Present');
      WriteLn
    ELSE
  END;
END Serror;


(*raise a to b power*)
PROCEDURE Pwr(a, b: REAL): REAL;
  VAR
    t: INTEGER;
    temp: REAL;
    PwrResult: REAL;
BEGIN
  IF a = 0.0 THEN
    PwrResult := 1.0
  ELSE
    temp := a;
    FOR t := TRUNC(b) TO 2 BY -1 DO
      a := a*temp
    END;
    PwrResult := a;
  END;
  RETURN PwrResult
END Pwr;


(*perform arithmetic functions*)
PROCEDURE Arith(op: CHAR;
                VAR result, operand: REAL);
BEGIN
  CASE op OF
    '+':
      result := result+operand |
    '-':
      result := result-operand |
```

```
    '*':
      result := result*operand |
    '/':
      result := result/operand |
    '^':
      result := Pwr(result, operand)
    ELSE
  END;
END Arith; (*Arith*)
```

As shown earlier, the two globals, **token** and **TokType**, return the next token and its type from the expression string, and the **prog** string holds the expression.

Here is the entire parser and all support routines, with a simple main program that you can use to demonstrate the parser:

```
MODULE parser;
(* parser for reals and operators - no
   variables *)

  FROM Strings
    IMPORT Pos, Copy, Concat, Length, CompareStr;
  FROM InOut IMPORT ReadString, WriteString, WriteLn;
  FROM RealInOut IMPORT WriteReal;
  FROM RealConversions IMPORT StringToReal;

  TYPE
    str80 = ARRAY [0..79] OF CHAR;
    TType = (DELIMITER, VARIABLE, NUMBER);

  VAR
    token, prog: str80;
    TokType: TType;
    t: INTEGER;
    result: REAL;


  (*returns TRUE if ch is a letter of the alphabet*)
  PROCEDURE IsAlpha(ch: CHAR): BOOLEAN;
  BEGIN
    RETURN (CAP(ch) >= 'A') AND (CAP(ch) <= 'Z');
  END IsAlpha;


  (*True if newline, space or tab*)
  PROCEDURE IsWhite(ch: CHAR): BOOLEAN;
  BEGIN
    RETURN (ch = ' ') OR (ch = CHR(9)) OR (ch = CHR(13));
  END IsWhite;
```

```
(*TRUE if is a delimiter*)
PROCEDURE IsDelim(ch: CHAR): BOOLEAN;
BEGIN
  IF Pos(ch, ' +-/*%^=()$') < 11 THEN
    RETURN TRUE
  ELSE
    RETURN FALSE
  END;
END IsDelim;


(*TRUE if a digit between 0 and 9*)
PROCEDURE IsDigit(ch: CHAR): BOOLEAN;
BEGIN
  RETURN (ch >= '0') AND (ch <= '9');
END IsDigit;

PROCEDURE GetToken;
  VAR
    temp: str80;
BEGIN
  token := ''; (*null string*)
  WHILE (IsWhite(prog[t])) DO
    INC(t)
  END; (*strip leading spaces*)
  IF prog[t] = '$' THEN
    token := '$'
  END;

  IF Pos(prog[t], '+-*/%^=()') < 9 THEN
    TokType := DELIMITER;
    token[0] := prog[t]; (*is an operator*)
    token[1] := CHR(0);
    INC(t);
  ELSIF IsAlpha(prog[t]) THEN
    WHILE (NOT IsDelim(prog[t])) DO
      Concat(token, prog[t], token); (*build token*)
      INC(t);
    END;
    TokType := VARIABLE;
  ELSIF IsDigit(prog[t]) THEN
    WHILE (NOT IsDelim(prog[t])) DO
      Concat(token, prog[t], token); (*build number*)
      INC(t);
      TokType := NUMBER;
    END;
  END;
END GetToken;


(*print error messages*)
PROCEDURE Serror(i: INTEGER);
BEGIN
```

```
    CASE i OF
      1:
        WriteString('Syntax Error');
        WriteLn |
      2:
        WriteString('Unbalanced Parentheses');
        WriteLn |
      3:
        WriteString('No Expression Present');
        WriteLn
      ELSE
    END;
END Serror;


(*raise a to b power*)
PROCEDURE Pwr(a, b: REAL): REAL;
  VAR
    t: INTEGER;
    temp: REAL;
    PwrResult: REAL;
BEGIN
  IF a = 0.0 THEN
    PwrResult := 1.0
  ELSE
    temp := a;
    FOR t := TRUNC(b) TO 2 BY -1 DO
      a := a*temp
    END;
    PwrResult := a;
  END;
  RETURN PwrResult
END Pwr;


(*perform arithmetic functions*)
PROCEDURE Arith(op: CHAR;
                VAR result, operand: REAL);
BEGIN
  CASE op OF
    '+':
      result := result+operand |
    '-':
      result := result-operand |
    '*':
      result := result*operand |
    '/':
      result := result/operand |
    '^':
      result := Pwr(result, operand)
    ELSE
  END;
END Arith; (*Arith*)
```

```
(* ********* Expression Parser ************ *)
PROCEDURE GetExp(VAR result: REAL);
BEGIN
  GetToken;
  IF INTEGER(Length(token)) <> 0 THEN
    Level2(result)
  ELSE
    Serror(3)
  END;
END GetExp;


PROCEDURE Level2(VAR result: REAL);
  VAR
    op: CHAR;
    hold: REAL;
BEGIN
  Level3(result);
  op := token[0];
  WHILE ((op = '+') OR (op = '-')) DO
    GetToken;
    Level3(hold);
    Arith(op, result, hold);
    op := token[0]
  END;
END Level2;


PROCEDURE Level3(VAR result: REAL);
  VAR
    op: CHAR;
    hold: REAL;
BEGIN
  Level4(result);
  op := token[0];
  WHILE ((op = '*') OR (op = '/')) DO
    GetToken;
    Level4(hold);
    Arith(op, result, hold);
    op := token[0];
  END;
END Level3;



PROCEDURE Level4(VAR result: REAL);
  VAR
    hold: REAL;
BEGIN
  Level5(result);
  IF token[0] = '^' THEN
    GetToken;
    Level4(hold);
```

```
      Arith('^', result, hold); (*exponents*)
    END;
END Level4;



PROCEDURE Level5(VAR result: REAL);
   VAR
     op: CHAR;
BEGIN
  op := ' ';
  IF ((TokType = DELIMITER) AND
     ((token[0] = '+') OR (token[0] = '-'))) THEN
     (*unary plus or minus*)
     op := token[0];
     GetToken;
   END;
   Level6(result);
   IF op = '-' THEN
     result := (-result)
   END;
END Level5;



PROCEDURE Level6(VAR result: REAL);
BEGIN
   IF (token[0] = '(') AND (TokType = DELIMITER) THEN
     (*Parenthesized expression*)
     GetToken;
     Level2(result);
     IF token[0] <> ')' THEN
       Serror(2)
     END; (*parentheses unbalanced*)
     GetToken;
   ELSE
     Primitive(result)
   END;
END Level6; (*Level6*)



PROCEDURE Primitive(VAR result: REAL);
   VAR
     code: BOOLEAN;
BEGIN
   IF TokType = NUMBER THEN
     StringToReal(token, result, code)
   ELSE
     Serror(1)
   END;
   GetToken;
END Primitive;
```

```
BEGIN (*main*)
  REPEAT
    t := 0; (*initialize token counter*)
    WriteString('enter an expression: ');
    ReadString(prog);
    WriteLn;
    Concat(prog, '$', prog);
    IF CompareStr(prog, "quit$") <> 0 THEN
      GetExp(result);
      WriteReal(result, 18);
      WriteLn;
    END;
  UNTIL CompareStr(prog, "quit$") = 0;
END parser.
```

To understand exactly how the parser evaluates an expression, work through the following expression, which you can assume is contained in **prog**:

$$10-3*2$$

When **GetExp**, the entry routine into the parser, is called, it gets the first token and, if that token is null, it prints the message **no expression present** and returns. If a token is present, then **Level2** is called. (**Level1** will be added when the assignment operator is used, but it is not needed here.)

The token now contains the number 10. **Level2** calls **Level3**, and **Level3** calls **Level4**, which in turn calls **Level5**. **Level5** checks to see if the token is a unary + or a unary −, which it is not in this case, so **Level6** is called. **Level6** either recursively calls **Level2** in the case of a parenthesized expression, or calls **primitive** to find the value of the integer. Finally, when **primitive** is executed and the value 10 is placed in **result**, **GetToken** obtains another token. The procedures then begin to return up the chain. At this time, the token is now the operator − and the procedures return up to **Level2**.

The next step is very important. Because the token is a −, **GetToken** saves it and obtains the new token 3; the descent down the chain begins again. **Primitive** is entered, the integer 3 is returned in **result**, and the token * is read. This causes a return back up the chain to **Level3**, where the final token 2 is read. At this point, the first arithmetic operation occurs with the multiplication of 2 and 3. This result is then returned to **Level2**, and the subtraction is performed to yield an answer of 4.

Although the process may seem complicated at first, you should work through some other examples to verify for yourself that the procedure works correctly every time.

You could use this parser as a desktop calculator, as the sample driver program illustrates. You could also use it in a database or a simple spreadsheet application. Before you can use the parser in a language or a sophisticated calculator, you would need to add the ability to handle variables, which is the subject of the next section.

Adding Variables to the Parser

All programming languages, and many calculaors and spreadsheets, use variables to store values for later use. The simple parser in the preceding section needs to be expanded to include variables before you can use it for this purpose. First, you must give the variables a place to reside. Since the parser is restricted to floating-point expressions, you can use an array of **REAL** variables. The parser can only recognize the variables A through Z, although you could expand it if you wanted to. Each variable uses one array location in a 26-element array. Therefore, you must add

```
vars:ARRAY[0..25] OF REAL;   (*26 variables*)
```

to the module declaration list. However, before you can use these variables, you should initialize them to zero.

You also need a routine to look up the value of a given variable. Because you are using the letters A through Z as variable names, you can also use them to index into the array **vars** directly by simply subtracting the ordinal value for A from each letter. Here is the procedure **FindVar**:

```
PROCEDURE FindVar(s: str80): REAL;
BEGIN
  RETURN vars[ORD(CAP(s[0]))-ORD('A')];
END FindVar;
```

As written, this procedure accepts long variable names, but only the first letter is significant. You may modify this procedure to fit your needs.

You must also modify the **primitive** procedure to handle both numbers and variables as primitives. Here is the new version:

```
PROCEDURE Primitive(VAR result: REAL);
  VAR
    code: BOOLEAN;
BEGIN
  IF TokType = NUMBER THEN
    StringToReal(token, result, code)
  ELSIF TokType = VARIABLE THEN
    result := FindVar(token)
  ELSE
    Serror(1)
  END;
  GetToken;
END Primitive; (*Primitive*)
```

Technically, these changes are all that you need for the parser to use variables correctly; however, there is no way for you to assign values to these variables. Often, you can assign values outside the parser, but, since you can treat the = sign as an assignment operator, you can make it part of the parser by using various methods. One method is to add a **Level1** to the parser, as shown here:

```
PROCEDURE Level1(VAR result: REAL);
  VAR
    hold: REAL;
    temp: TType;
    slot: INTEGER;
    TempToken: str80;
BEGIN
  IF TokType = VARIABLE THEN
    (*save old token*)
    TempToken := token;
    temp := TokType;
    slot := ORD(CAP(token[0]))-ORD('A');
    GetToken; (*see if there is = for assignment*)
    IF token[0] <> '=' THEN
      PutBack; (*replace the token*)
      (*restore old token*)
      token := TempToken;
      TokType := temp;
      Level2(result);
    ELSE
      (*is assignment*)
```

```
      GetToken;
      Level2(result);
      vars[slot] := result;
    END;
    (*if*)
  ELSE
    Level2(result)
  END;
END Level1;
```

When **Level1** encounters a variable as the first token in an expression, the variable may be either the target of an assignment, as in

$$A = B*10$$

or it may simply be part of an expression, such as

$$A - 123.23$$

For **Level1** to know which it is, **Level1** must perform a *look-ahead*. First, **Level1** must save the current token, and then read the next token to see what it is. If it is =, then the routine knows that an assignment is being made, and executes the proper routines. If the next token is not =, then **Level1** must return that token into the expression string, and recover the previous token. You can do this with the procedure **PutBack**, which returns a token to the input expression by simply decrementing the index **t** by the length of the token. Look-ahead can be a time-consuming process, and should be avoided except where absolutely necessary.

Here is the entire enhanced parser, support routines, and main program:

```
MODULE parser;
(* parser for reals and operators and
   variables *)

  FROM Strings
    IMPORT  Pos, Copy, Concat, Length, CompareStr;
  FROM InOut IMPORT ReadString, WriteString, WriteLn;
  FROM RealInOut IMPORT WriteReal;
  FROM RealConversions IMPORT StringToReal;

  TYPE
    str80 = ARRAY [0..79] OF CHAR;
    TType = (DELIMITER, VARIABLE, NUMBER);
```

```
VAR
  vars: ARRAY [0..25] OF REAL; (*26 variables*)
  token, prog: str80;
  TokType: TType;
  t: INTEGER;
  result: REAL;


(*returns TRUE if ch is a letter of the alphabet*)
PROCEDURE IsAlpha(ch: CHAR): BOOLEAN;
BEGIN
  RETURN (CAP(ch) >= 'A') AND (CAP(ch) <= 'Z');
END IsAlpha;


(*True if newline, space or tab*)
PROCEDURE IsWhite(ch: CHAR): BOOLEAN;
BEGIN
  RETURN (ch = ' ') OR (ch = CHR(9)) OR (ch = CHR(13));
END IsWhite;


(*TRUE if is a delimiter*)
PROCEDURE IsDelim(ch: CHAR): BOOLEAN;
BEGIN
  IF Pos(ch, ' +-/*%^=()$') < 11 THEN
    RETURN TRUE
  ELSE
    RETURN FALSE
  END;
END IsDelim;


(*TRUE if a digit between 0 and 9*)
PROCEDURE IsDigit(ch: CHAR): BOOLEAN;
BEGIN
  RETURN (ch >= '0') AND (ch <= '9');
END IsDigit;


PROCEDURE GetToken;
  VAR
    temp: str80;
BEGIN
  token := ''; (*null string*)
  WHILE (IsWhite(prog[t])) DO
    INC(t)
  END; (*strip leading spaces*)
  IF prog[t] = '$' THEN
    token := '$'
  END;

  IF Pos(prog[t], '+-*/%^=()') < 9 THEN
    TokType := DELIMITER;
    token[0] := prog[t]; (*is an operator*)
```

```
      token[1] := CHR(0);
      INC(t);
   ELSIF IsAlpha(prog[t]) THEN
     WHILE (NOT IsDelim(prog[t])) DO
       Concat(token, prog[t], token); (*build token*)
       INC(t);
     END;
     TokType := VARIABLE;
   ELSIF IsDigit(prog[t]) THEN
     WHILE (NOT IsDelim(prog[t])) DO
       Concat(token, prog[t], token); (*build number*)
       INC(t);
       TokType := NUMBER;
     END;
   END;
END GetToken;


(*print error messages*)
PROCEDURE Serror(i: INTEGER);
BEGIN
   CASE i OF
     1:
       WriteString('Syntax Error');
       WriteLn |
     2:
       WriteString('Unbalanced Parentheses');
       WriteLn |
     3:
       WriteString('No Expression Present');
       WriteLn
     ELSE
   END;
END Serror;
(*raise a to b power*)
PROCEDURE Pwr(a, b: REAL): REAL;
   VAR
     t: INTEGER;
     temp: REAL;
     PwrResult: REAL;
BEGIN
   IF a = 0.0 THEN
     PwrResult := 1.0
   ELSE
     temp := a;
     FOR t := TRUNC(b) TO 2 BY -1 DO
       a := a*temp
     END;
     PwrResult := a;
   END;
   RETURN PwrResult
END Pwr;


(*perform arithmetic functions*)
PROCEDURE Arith(op: CHAR;
                VAR result, operand: REAL);
```

```
BEGIN
  CASE op OF
    '+':
      result := result+operand |
    '-':
      result := result-operand |
    '*':
      result := result*operand |
    '/':
      result := result/operand |
    '^':
      result := Pwr(result, operand)
    ELSE
  END;
END Arith; (*Arith*)


PROCEDURE FindVar(s: str80): REAL;
BEGIN
  RETURN vars[ORD(CAP(s[0]))-ORD('A')];
END FindVar;


(* put a token back into the input stream *)
PROCEDURE PutBack;
BEGIN
  DEC(t, Length(token));
END PutBack;

(* ********** Expression Parser ************ *)
(* With variables and assignment *)
PROCEDURE GetExp(VAR result: REAL);
BEGIN
  GetToken;
  IF INTEGER(Length(token)) <> 0 THEN
    Level1(result)
  ELSE
    Serror(3)
  END;
END GetExp;


PROCEDURE Level1(VAR result: REAL);
  VAR
    hold: REAL;
    temp: TType;
    slot: INTEGER;
    TempToken: str80;
BEGIN
  IF TokType = VARIABLE THEN
    (*save old token*)
    TempToken := token;
    temp := TokType;
    slot := ORD(CAP(token[0]))-ORD('A');
    GetToken; (*see if there is = for assignment*)
    IF token[0] <> '=' THEN
      PutBack; (*replace the token*)
```

```
      (*restore old token*)
      token := TempToken;
      TokType := temp;
      Level2(result);
    ELSE
      (*is assignment*)
      GetToken;
      Level2(result);
      vars[slot] := result;
    END;
    (*if*)
  ELSE
    Level2(result)
  END;
END Level1;


PROCEDURE Level2(VAR result: REAL);
  VAR
    op: CHAR;
    hold: REAL;
BEGIN
  Level3(result);
  op := token[0];
  WHILE ((op = '+') OR (op = '-')) DO
    GetToken;
    Level3(hold);
    Arith(op, result, hold);
    op := token[0]
  END;
END Level2;


PROCEDURE Level3(VAR result: REAL);
  VAR
    op: CHAR;
    hold: REAL;
BEGIN
  Level4(result);
  op := token[0];
  WHILE ((op = '*') OR (op = '/')) DO
    GetToken;
    Level4(hold);
    Arith(op, result, hold);
    op := token[0];
  END;
END Level3;


PROCEDURE Level4(VAR result: REAL);
  VAR
    hold: REAL;
BEGIN
  Level5(result);
  IF token[0] = '^' THEN
    GetToken;
```

```
      Level4(hold);
      Arith('^', result, hold); (*exponents*)
   END;
END Level4;



PROCEDURE Level5(VAR result: REAL);
   VAR
     op: CHAR;
BEGIN
   op := ' ';
   IF ((TokType = DELIMITER) AND
     ((token[0] = '+') OR (token[0] = '-'))) THEN
     (*unary plus or minus*)
     op := token[0];
     GetToken;
   END;
   Level6(result);
   IF op = '-' THEN
     result := (-result)
   END;
END Level5;



PROCEDURE Level6(VAR result: REAL);
BEGIN
   IF (token[0] = '(') AND (TokType = DELIMITER) THEN
     (*Parenthesized expression*)
     GetToken;
     Level2(result);
     IF token[0] <> ')' THEN
       Serror(2)
     END; (*parentheses unbalanced*)
     GetToken;
   ELSE
     Primitive(result)
   END;
END Level6; (*Level6*)


PROCEDURE Primitive(VAR result: REAL);
   VAR
     code: BOOLEAN;
BEGIN
   IF TokType = NUMBER THEN
     StringToReal(token, result, code)
   ELSIF TokType = VARIABLE THEN
     result := FindVar(token)
   ELSE
     Serror(1)
   END;
   GetToken;
END Primitive; (*Primitive*)


BEGIN
```

```
REPEAT
  t := 0; (*initialize token counter*)
  WriteString('enter an expression: ');
  ReadString(prog);
  WriteLn;
  Concat(prog, '$', prog);
  IF CompareStr(prog, "quit$") <> 0 THEN
    GetExp(result);
    WriteReal(result, 18);
    WriteLn;
  END;
UNTIL CompareStr(prog, "quit$") = 0;
END parser.
```

With the enhanced parser, you can now enter expressions such as

$$A = 10/4$$
$$A - B$$
$$C = A*(F - 21)$$

and they will be properly evaluated.

Syntax-Checking
in a Recursive
Descent Parser

In expression parsing, a syntax error is a situation in which the input expression does not conform to the strict rules that the parser requires. Usually, a syntax error is caused by human error —generally, typing mistakes! For example, the following expressions will not be parsed correctly by the parsers in this chapter:

$$10**8$$
$$(10 - 5)*9)$$
$$/8$$

The first expression has two operators in a row, the second expression has unbalanced parentheses, and the last expression has a division sign that starts an expression. The parsers do not allow any of these conditions.

Because syntax errors can confuse the parser and cause it to give erroneous results, it is important—indeed necessary—to guard against them.

As you studied the code of the parsers, you have probably noticed that the procedure **Serror** is called under certain situations. Unlike many other parsers, the recursive descent method makes syntax-checking easy, because it generally occurs in either **primitive**, **FindVar**, or **Level6**, where parentheses are checked. The only problem with the syntax-checking as it now stands is that the entire parser is not aborted on syntax error. This can cause multiple error messages to be generated.

To add complete error recovery, you must add a global variable that is checked at each level. The variable would initially be FALSE, and any call to **Serror** would set it TRUE, which would cause the parser to abort one procedure at a time.

If you leave the code the way that it is, all that will happen is that multiple syntax error messages may be issued. While this could be an annoyance in some situations, it could be a blessing in others, because multiple errors will be caught in some cases. However, you will generally want to enhance the syntax-checking before you use it in commercial programs.

Converting BASIC
and C to Modula-2

CHAPTER 10

Most programmers spend much of their time converting programs from one language into another. The conversion process is called *translating*. You may find the process to be either easy or difficult, depending on the methods that you use to translate and how well you know the source and destination languages. This chapter presents some topics and techniques to help you convert C and BASIC programs into Modula-2.

Why would anyone want to translate a program that is written in one language into another? One reason is *maintainability:* a program that is written in an unstructured language like BASIC is difficult to maintain or enhance. Another reason is *speed* and *efficiency:* as a language, Modula-2 is very efficient, and some demanding tasks have been translated into Modula-2 for better performance. A third reason is *practicality:* a user may see a useful program in one language, but may own or use a compiler in a different language. You will probably want to translate a program into Modula-2 for one or more of these reasons.

C and BASIC were chosen from the field of nearly 100 computer languages because they are popular languages among microcomputer users, and because they represent opposite ends of the programming-language spectrum. C is a structured language that has many similarities to Modula-2, while BASIC is a nonstructured language that has virtually no similarities to Modula-2. While this chapter cannot cover the translation of these languages in every detail, it examines several of the most important problems that you will confront. You must already be familiar with either BASIC or C; this chapter does not teach either language.

Converting C to Modula-2

C and Modula-2 have many similarities—especially in their control structures and their use of stand-alone subroutines with local variables. This makes it possible to do a large amount of *one-to-one translating*, which is the process of substituting the Modula-2 keyword or function for its equivalent in C. With one-to-one translating, you can use the computer to help you with the translation process; this chapter develops a simple translation program later in this section.

Even though C and Modula-2 are similar, keep in mind the three major differences between them. First, Modula-2 uses strong type-checking while C does not. Therefore, you will have to modify some types of routines that are written in C to make all operand types agree; you can also use Modula-2's type-conversion functions. For example, in C, you may mix character and integer types freely, but in Modula-2, you may not mix them without using type-conversion functions.

Second, and more important, Modula-2 is formally *block structured*, while C is not. Block structured refers to a language's ability to create logically connected units of code that can be referenced together. The term also means that procedures can have other procedures—known only to the outer procedure—nested inside them. This concept also extends in Modula-2 to include **MODULE**s that are nested within other **MODULE**s. C is commonly referred to as block structured because it allows the easy creation of blocks of code; however, it does not allow functions to be defined inside other functions.

For example, if you assume that **B** is used only by **A**, then the following code in C must have two functions.

```
A()
{
        printf("starting A\n");
        B();
}

B()
{
        printf("inside function B\n");
}
```

However, if you translate this code into Modula-2, it looks like this:

```
PROCEDURE A;
VAR
   x:INTEGER;

   PROCEDURE B;
   BEGIN
      WriteString('inside proc b');
   END B;

BEGIN
   WriteString('starting A');
   B;
END A;
```

Here, **PROCEDURE B** is defined inside of **PROCEDURE A**. This means that **PROCEDURE B** is known only to **PROCEDURE A** and may only be used by **PROCEDURE A**. Outside of **PROCEDURE A**, you could define another **PROCEDURE B** without conflict. Also, in the C version, you would have to ensure that there were no other functions called **B** anywhere else in the program.

A third difference between C and Modula-2 is that, in C, all references to functions that are not found in a specific file are resolved at link time (when they are found in other link files), whereas Modula-2 resolves these references at compile time by using the **IMPORT** statement. In Modula-2, you must declare all variables, types, and procedures before you use them. This means that you must import any variable, type, or procedure that is in a different file.

An often-overlooked similarity between C and Modula-2 is that both support, and even encourage, separate compilation and linking. Although Modula-2 is built upon the concept of the **MODULE**, it is not very different from the way that most C compilers allow you to combine multiple files at link time. Therefore, you can generally convert the contents of a C file directly into a Modula-2 **MODULE** without substantial difficulties. However, remember that C lacks Modula-2's concept of **DEFINITION** and **IMPLE-MENTATION** modules, but creating these should be straightforward.

A Comparison Between C and Modula-2

Figure 10-1 compares Modula-2 keywords with C keywords and operators. As you can see, many Modula-2 keywords have no C equivalent. This is due in part to the fact that Modula-2 uses keywords in places where C uses opera-tors to accomplish the same process. At times, Modula-2 is simply "wordier" than C. (If you are only vaguely familar with C, you should know that it is famous for having only 28 keywords!)

In addition to the keywords, Modula-2 has several built-in *standard iden-tifiers*, which you can use directly in a program. These identifiers may be functions (such as **CAP**) or global values (such as **FALSE**). Modula-2 also uses standard identifiers to specify such data types as **REAL, INTEGER, BOOLEAN**, and **CHAR**. Figure 10-2 shows several of the more common standard Modula-2 identifiers with their C equivalents. In addition to those, there are other Modula-2 built-in procedures that have C equivalents, which are found in various library modules, but which may vary from compiler to compiler.

Modula-2 also differs from C in its operators. Figure 10-3 shows the C operators and the Modula-2 equivalents. As Figure 10-3 shows, the bitwise operators that C supports have no equivalents in Modula-2 and would require special functions—usually in assembly code—to support them. (You saw some of these functions in Chapter 7 when bit-manipulation ciphers were developed.)

Converting C Loops into Modula-2 Loops

Because program control loops are fundamental to most programs, this sec-tion compares C's loops to Modula-2's loops. C has three built-in loops: **for, while**, and **do/while**.

Modula-2	C
AND	&&
ARRAY	
BEGIN	{
BY	
CASE	switch
CONST	
DEFINITION	
DIV	\
DO	
ELSE	else
ELSIF	else if
END	}
EXIT	break
EXPORT	
FOR	for
IF	if
IMPORT	extern (on occasion)
IMPLEMENTATION	
IN	
LOOP	for(;;)
MOD	%
MODULE	
NIL	(sometimes \0)
NOT	!
OF	
OR	‖
POINTER	*
PROCEDURE	
QUALIFIED	
RECORD	struct
REPEAT	do
SET	
THEN	
TO	
TYPE	
UNTIL	while (as in do/while)
VAR	
WHILE	while
WITH	

Figure 10-1. A comparison of Modula-2 and C keywords

C	Modula-2
char	boolean
char	CHAR
EOF	EOF
0	FALSE
int	INTEGER
scanf( ) and others	Read, ReadString, ReadCard, and so on
float	REAL
any nonzero value	TRUE
printf( )	WRITE, WriteString, or WriteLn

Figure 10-2. Modula-2 equivalents of some C standard identifiers

C	Modula-2	Meaning
+	+	addition
−	−	subtraction
*	*	multiplication
/	/	division
/	DIV	integer division
%	MOD	modulus
=	:=	assignment
==	=	equals as a condition
<	<	less than
>	>	greater than
>=	>=	greater than or equals
<=	<=	less than or equals
!=	<>	not equal
&&	AND	logic AND
||	OR	logic OR
!	NOT	logical NOT
&		bitwise AND
|		bitwise OR
~		bitwise NOT (one's complement)

Figure 10-3. Modula-2 operators and C equivalents

C's **for** loop has the general form

for(*initialization*; *condition*; *increment*) *statement*;

The C **for** is a much more general statement than the Modula-2 **for/do**. The test condition does not need to be only a target value, as in Modula-2; rather, it can be any Boolean expression. The *increment* portion of the statement also does not need to increment anything; it could increment some variable that is unrelated to the test condition. In addition, there is no mechanism to tell you whether the loop is running positively or negatively because it does not use Modula-2's **BY** option. Both the *initialization* and *increment* sections can be compound—something that has no parallel in Modula-2. However, despite these differences, a C **for** loop often has the form of the standard Modula-2 **FOR/DO**, which makes translating a simple matter. For example, you can translate the C **for** loop

```
for(x=10;x<=100;++x) printf("%d\n",x);
```

into Modula-2 as

```
FOR x:=10 TO 100 DO WriteInt(x,0);
```

The C **while** and the Modula-2 **WHILE/DO** are virtually the same. However, the C **do/while** and the Modula-2 **REPEAT/UNTIL** differ not only in their keywords, but also in their loop test conditions, which are "reversed." The C **do/while** loops *while* the loop condition *is true*, whereas the Modula-2 **UNTIL** implies that a loop runs *until* something becomes true. Thus, the Modula-2 **REPEAT/UNTIL** loops while it is false. Here is a sample translation of both these types of loops.

```
C                           Modula-2

while(x<5)                  WHILE x<5 DO
{                           BEGIN
    printf("%d",x);            WriteCard(x, 3);
    x=getnum();                ReadCard(x);
}                           END;

do {                        REPEAT
    x=getnum();                ReadCard(x);
    printf("%d",x);            WriteCard(x, 3);
} while(x<=5);              UNTIL x>5;
```

Be careful when you translate the **do/while** to **REPEAT/UNTIL**: You must reverse the sense of the test condition. (There have been some philosophical discussions concerning the **do/while** versus the **REPEAT/UNTIL**. The **do/while** is considered to be positive because it loops while the condition is TRUE; the **REPEAT/UNTIL** has been called negative because the loop executes as long as the condition is FALSE. It has been suggested that choosing the easiest loop to use is based on whether you are a pessimist or an optimist—but this has yet to be proved!)

A Sample Translation

To give you a sense of the translation process, follow the steps of converting this simple C program into Modula-2.

```
float qwerty;

main()
{
        qwerty=0;
        printf("%f",qwerty);
        printf("hello there\n");
        tom(25);
        printf("%f\n",ken(10));
        printf("%2.4f\n",qwerty):
}

Tom(x)
int x;
{
        printf("%d", x*2);
}

float ken(w)
float w;
{
        qwerty=23.34;
        return w/3.1415;
}
```

The C program has three functions declared. (Keep in mind that all C subroutines are functions—whether or not the return value is used.) The first step in translating this program into Modula-2 is to determine which C functions will become Modula-2 functions (that is, which return a value), and which will simply be procedures. You can determine this by looking for the C keyword **return**. If it is present in a function, you can then assume that a value is going to be returned. (Technically, this may not always be the case, but it is sufficient for this example.) The only function that uses a **return** is **ken**. Therefore, the Modula-2 equivalent of **ken** is

```
PROCEDURE ken (w: REAL): REAL;
BEGIN
  qwerty:=23.34
  RETURN w/3.1415;
END ken;
```

The C function **tom** does not return a value, so it becomes a procedure in Modula-2:

```
PROCEDURE tom (x: INTEGER);
BEGIN
  WriteInt(x*2, 0);
END tom;
```

Next, you must convert the **main** function into the main **MODULE** code for the Modula-2 version, as shown here:

```
BEGIN
  qwerty:=0.0;
  WriteReal(qwerty, 0);
  WriteLn;
  WriteString('hello there');
  WriteLn;
  tom(25);
  WriteReal(ken(10), 0);
  WriteReal(qwerty, 0);
END test.
```

Finally, you must declare the global variable **qwerty** as a **REAL**, and add the **MODULE** header and the **IMPORT** lists. When you finish this process and put the pieces together, the Modula-2 translation of the C program looks like this:

```
MODULE test;
  FROM InOut IMPORT WriteString, WriteInt;
  FROM RealInOut IMPORT WriteReal;

  VAR qwerty: real;

PROCEDURE tom (x: INTEGER);
BEGIN
  WriteInt(x*2, 3);
END tom;
```

```
PROCEDURE ken (w: REAL): REAL;
BEGIN
  qwerty:=23.34
  RETURN w/3.1415;
END ken;

BEGIN
  qwerty:=0.0;
  WriteReal(qwerty);
  WriteLn;
  WriteString('hello there');
  WriteLn;
  tom(25);
  WriteReal(ken(10.0),0);
  WriteReal(qwerty,0);
END test.
```

Using the Computer to Help You Convert C to Modula-2

It is possible to construct a computer program that accepts source code in one language and outputs it in another. The best way to do this is to implement a complete language parser for the source language—but instead of generating machine-executable object code, the parser produces the destination language source code. You can occasionally find advertisements for such products in computer magazines, and their high prices reflect the complexity of the task. However, to help you in your conversion efforts, you can write a simple program that performs only some of the simpler translations. This "computer assist" can make conversion jobs much easier.

A computer-assist translator accepts as input a program in the source language, performs the one-to-one conversions into the destination language automatically, and leaves the harder conversions up to you. For example, to assign **count** the value of 10 in C, you would write

```
count=10;
```

In Modula-2, the statement is the same except that there is a colon next to the equal sign. Therefore, the computer-assist translator can change the = assignment statement in C to the := in Modula-2 for you. Another example is the C **while** loop: the Modula-2 loop construct, **WHILE/DO**, is used the same way.

However, C and Modula-2 access disk files in different ways, and there is no easy way to perform such a conversion automatically. You also cannot automate the conversion of the C **do/while** into the Modula-2 **REPEAT/ UNTIL** easily. Hence, these complicated translations are left to you.

Here are the steps to create a C-to-Modula-2 translator. First, you need a procedure that returns one token at a time from the C program. You can modify the procedure **GetToken** that was developed in Chapter 9 for this use, as shown here:

```
PROCEDURE GetToken;
  VAR
    temp: str80;
BEGIN
  token := ""; (*null string*)
  WHILE (IsWhite(prog[t])) DO
    INC(t);
  END; (*strip leading spaces*)

  IF prog[t]=EOL THEN
    token[0]:=EOL;
    token[1]:=CHR(0);
    TokType:=DELIMITER;
    INC(t);
  END;

  IF prog[t] = '$' THEN
    token := "$"
  END;

  IF Pos(prog[t], '.#:;,+|<>&~-*/!%^=(){}') < 22
    THEN
    IF (prog[t] = '{') OR (prog[t] = '}') THEN
      TokType := NAME;
      IF prog[t] = '{' THEN
        token := 'BEGIN';
        INC(indent);
      ELSE
        token := 'END';
        DEC(indent);
      END;
    ELSE
      TokType := DELIMITER;
      token[0] := prog[t]; (*is an delimiter*)
      token[1] := CHR(0);
    END;
    INC(t);
  ELSIF IsAlpha(prog[t]) THEN
    WHILE (NOT IsDelim(prog[t])) DO
      Concat(token, prog[t], token); (*build token*)
      INC(t);
    END;
    TokType := NAME;
```

```
    ELSIF IsDigit(prog[t]) THEN
      WHILE (NOT IsDelim(prog[t])) DO
        Concat(token, prog[t], token); (*build number*)
        INC(t);
        TokType := NUMBER;
      END;
    ELSIF (prog[t]='"') OR (prog[t]=CHR(39)) THEN
      (*is string*)
      INC(t);
      token := '"';
      WHILE (prog[t]<>'"') AND (prog[t]<>CHR(39)) DO
        Concat(token, prog[t], token);
        INC(t);
        TokType := STR;
      END;
      INC(t); (*go past closing quotes*)
      Concat(token, '"', token);
    END;
  END GetToken;
```

C's { and } are transformed into their Modula-2 equivalents **BEGIN** and **END** inside **GetToken** in order to simplify certain other areas of the program later on.

The second step in creating the translator is to provide a routine that translates elements of the C language into their Modula-2 counterparts. The procedure **Translate** shown here is not the best way to code such a routine, but it is sufficient for the translator's purposes. In its present form, **Translate** does not perform all possible one-to-one translations—the remainder of these translations is left to you.

```
(*translate C into Modula-2*)
PROCEDURE Translate;
BEGIN
CASE token[0] OF
  '~':
    token := "not" |
  '=': (*look ahead to see if double equals*)
    GetToken;
    IF CompareStr(token, "=") = 0 THEN
      token := "=="
    ELSE
      PutBack; (*restore token to stream*)
      token := ":="; (*assignment*)
    END; |
  '!': (*look ahead to see if <> or NOT*)
    GetToken;
    IF CompareStr(token, '=') = 0 THEN
      token := '<>'
    ELSE
      PutBack;
      token := "NOT";
    END; |
```

```
  '%':
    token := "MOD" |
  '|':
    GetToken;
    IF CompareStr(token, "|") <> 0 THEN
      PutBack
    END; (*not double or*)
    token := 'OR'; |
  '&':
    GetToken;
    IF CompareStr(token, "&") <> 0 THEN
      PutBack
    END; (*not double and*)
    token := "AND"
  ELSE
END;
(*now check for keywords*)
IF CompareStr(token, "switch")  = 0 THEN
  token := "CASE"
ELSIF CompareStr(token, "while")  = 0 THEN
  token := "WHILE"
ELSIF CompareStr(token, "struct")  = 0 THEN
  token := "RECORD"
ELSIF CompareStr(token, "int")  = 0 THEN
  token := "CARDINAL"
ELSIF CompareStr(token, "float")  = 0 THEN
  token := "REAL"
ELSIF CompareStr(token, "char")  = 0 THEN
  token := "CHAR"
ELSIF CompareStr(token, "printf")  = 0 THEN
  token := "WriteX"
ELSIF CompareStr(token, "extern")  = 0 THEN
  token:= "IMPORT"
ELSIF CompareStr(token, "for")  = 0 THEN
  token:= "FOR"
ELSIF CompareStr(token, "return")  = 0 THEN
  token:= "RETURN"
ELSIF CompareStr(token, "break")  = 0 THEN
  token:= "|"
ELSIF CompareStr(token, "case")  = 0 THEN
  token := ""
  END;
END Translate;
```

Notice that, in most cases, **Translate** passes C keywords and operators through because they are the same in both languages. However, for the C **while** and **do/while** loops, **Translate** cannot know whether a Modula-2 **WHILE/DO** or **REPEAT/UNTIL** loop is needed. The entire translation program is shown here:

```
MODULE CToModula;

(* A simple C-to-Modula converter *)
```

```
FROM InOut IMPORT EOL, WriteString, ReadString,
  WriteLn, Write, WriteCard;
FROM Strings
  IMPORT Pos, Copy, Concat, Length, CompareStr;
FROM FileSystem IMPORT File, SetRead, SetWrite, Close,
  ReadChar, WriteChar, Response, Reset, Lookup;


TYPE
  str80 = ARRAY [0..79] OF CHAR;
  TType = (DELIMITER, NAME, NUMBER, STR);

VAR
  token, prog: ARRAY [0..254] OF CHAR;
  TokType: TType;
  inf, outf: File;
  indent, t: CARDINAL;
  fname: str80;
  lf: CHAR;


(*returns TRUE if ch is a letter of the alphabet*)
PROCEDURE IsAlpha(ch: CHAR): BOOLEAN;
BEGIN
  RETURN (CAP(ch) >= 'A') AND (CAP(ch) <= 'Z');
END IsAlpha;

(*True if newline, space or tab*)
PROCEDURE IsWhite(ch: CHAR): BOOLEAN;
BEGIN
  RETURN (ch = ' ') OR (ch = CHR(9)) OR (ch = CHR(13));
END IsWhite;


(*TRUE if is a delimiter*)
PROCEDURE IsDelim(ch: CHAR): BOOLEAN;
BEGIN
  IF ch = CHR(39) THEN
    (*a ' *)
    RETURN TRUE
  ELSIF Pos(ch, ' #:.,;<>|&~+-/*%^=!()${}') < 24 THEN
    RETURN TRUE
  ELSE
    RETURN FALSE
  END;
END IsDelim;


(*TRUE if a digit between 0 and 9*)
PROCEDURE IsDigit(ch: CHAR): BOOLEAN;
BEGIN
  RETURN  (ch >= '0') AND (ch <= '9');
END IsDigit;


PROCEDURE GetToken;
  VAR
    temp: str80;
```

```
BEGIN
  token := ""; (*null string*)
  WHILE (IsWhite(prog[t])) DO
    INC(t);
  END; (*strip leading spaces*)

  IF prog[t]=EOL THEN
    token[0]:=EOL;
    token[1]:=CHR(0);
    TokType:=DELIMITER;
    INC(t);
  END;

  IF prog[t] = '$' THEN
    token := "$"
  END;

  IF Pos(prog[t], '.#:;,+|<>&~-*/!%^=(){}') < 22
    THEN
    IF (prog[t] = '{') OR (prog[t] = '}') THEN
      TokType := NAME;
      IF prog[t] = '{' THEN
        token := 'BEGIN';
        INC(indent);
      ELSE
        token := 'END';
        DEC(indent);
      END;
    ELSE
      TokType := DELIMITER;
      token[0] := prog[t]; (*is an delimiter*)
      token[1] := CHR(0);
    END;
    INC(t);
  ELSIF IsAlpha(prog[t]) THEN
    WHILE (NOT IsDelim(prog[t])) DO
      Concat(token, prog[t], token); (*build token*)
      INC(t);
    END;
    TokType := NAME;
  ELSIF IsDigit(prog[t]) THEN
    WHILE (NOT IsDelim(prog[t])) DO
      Concat(token, prog[t], token); (*build number*)
      INC(t);
      TokType := NUMBER;
    END;
  ELSIF (prog[t]='"') OR (prog[t]=CHR(39)) THEN
    (*is string*)
    INC(t);
    token := '"';
    WHILE (prog[t]<>'"') AND (prog[t]<>CHR(39)) DO
      Concat(token, prog[t], token);
      INC(t);
      TokType := STR;
    END;
    INC(t); (*go past closing quotes*)
    Concat(token, '"', token);
  END;
END GetToken;
```

```
(*put back unused token*)
PROCEDURE PutBack;
BEGIN
  DEC(t, Length(token));
END PutBack;


(*translate C into Modula-2*)
PROCEDURE Translate;
BEGIN
  CASE token[0] OF
    '~':
      token := "not" |
    '=': (*look ahead to see if double equals*)
      GetToken;
      IF CompareStr(token, "=") = 0 THEN
        token := "=="
      ELSE
        PutBack; (*restore token to stream*)
        token := ":="; (*assignment*)
      END; |
    '!': (*look ahead to see if <> or NOT*)
      GetToken;
      IF CompareStr(token, '=') = 0 THEN
        token := '<>'
      ELSE
        PutBack;
        token := "NOT";
      END; |
    '%':
      token := "MOD" |
    '|':
      GetToken;
      IF CompareStr(token, "|") <> 0 THEN
        PutBack
      END; (*not double or*)
      token := 'OR'; |
    '&':
      GetToken;
      IF CompareStr(token, "&") <> 0 THEN
        PutBack
      END; (*not double and*)
      token := "AND"
  ELSE
  END;
  (*now check for keywords*)
  IF CompareStr(token, "switch") = 0 THEN
    token := "CASE"
  ELSIF CompareStr(token, "while") = 0 THEN
    token := "WHILE"
  ELSIF CompareStr(token, "struct") = 0 THEN
    token := "RECORD"
  ELSIF CompareStr(token, "int") = 0 THEN
    token := "CARDINAL"
  ELSIF CompareStr(token, "float") = 0 THEN
    token := "REAL"
  ELSIF CompareStr(token, "char") = 0 THEN
    token := "CHAR"
```

```
  ELSIF CompareStr(token, "printf")  = 0 THEN
    token := "WriteX"
  ELSIF CompareStr(token, "extern")  = 0 THEN
    token:= "IMPORT"
  ELSIF CompareStr(token, "for")  = 0 THEN
    token:= "FOR"
  ELSIF CompareStr(token, "return")  = 0 THEN
    token:= "RETURN"
  ELSIF CompareStr(token, "break")  = 0 THEN
    token:= "|"
  ELSIF CompareStr(token, "case")  = 0 THEN
    token := ""
  END;
END Translate;


PROCEDURE WriteFileString(VAR f: File; str: ARRAY OF CHAR);
(* write a string to a disk file *)
  VAR
    t: CARDINAL;
BEGIN
  t:=0;
  WHILE str[t]<>CHR(0) DO
    WriteChar(f, str[t]);
    INC(t);
  END;
  WriteChar(f,' ');
END WriteFileString;


  PROCEDURE convert;
    VAR
      count: CARDINAL;
  BEGIN
    GetToken;
    (* now indent properly *)
    IF CompareStr(token,"BEGIN") = 0 THEN
      FOR count := 1 TO (indent-1)*2 DO
        WriteChar(outf, ' ')
      END;
    ELSE
      FOR count := 1 TO indent*3 DO
        WriteChar(outf, ' ')
      END;
    END;
    WHILE CompareStr(token, "$") <> 0 DO
      CASE TokType OF
        STR:
          WriteFileString(outf, token) |
        NAME:
          Translate;
          WriteFileString(outf, token);
          WriteChar(outf, " "); |
        DELIMITER:
          Translate;
          WriteFileString(outf, token);   |
        NUMBER:
          WriteFileString(outf, token)
```

```
        ELSE
      END;
      GetToken;
    END;
    WriteChar(outf,EOL);
  END convert;


BEGIN (*main*)
  REPEAT
    WriteString('Enter input filename: ');
    ReadString(fname);  WriteLn;
    Lookup(inf,fname ,FALSE); (* must be there *)
  UNTIL inf.res = done;

  REPEAT
    WriteString('Enter output filename: ');
    ReadString(fname);  WriteLn;
    Lookup(outf,fname ,TRUE); (* create it *)
  UNTIL outf.res = done;

  SetWrite(outf);  (* enable write *)
  SetRead(inf);  (* enable read *)

  indent := 0; (*indentation counter for each BEGIN and END*)
  WHILE  NOT inf.eof DO
    t := 0; (* reset index each time *)

    REPEAT
      ReadChar(inf, prog[t]);
      INC(t);
    UNTIL (prog[t-1]=EOL) OR inf.eof;  (* cr *)

    prog[t]:=CHR(0);
    Concat(prog, "$", prog);
    t:=0;  (* reset for indexing by GetToken *)
    convert;
  END;
  WriteChar(outf, '.');
  Close(inf);
  Close(outf);
END CToModula.
```

The program uses the global variable **indent** to indent the code two spaces for each **BEGIN**, and to remove the two spaces for each **END**. This step allows the pseudo-Modula-2 output to be properly formatted.

In essence, the C-to-Modula-2 conversion-assist program reads in a line of C source code, takes a token at a time from that line, performs any translations that it can, and writes out a Modula-2 version. To see how this simple program can make translating from C to Modula-2 easier, run this C program through the translator:

```
extern char t;
main()
{
  printf("this is a test");

  while c<0 {
    for (a=1; a<100; a++)
      b=s;
  }
}


int a;
{
  switch(a) {
    case 1: return 'a';
      break;
    case 2: return 'b';
  }
}
```

After you run this program through the translator program, the pseudo-C Modula-2 output is as follows:

```
IMPORT  CHAR  t  ;
main  ( )
BEGIN
    WriteX  ( "this is a test" ) ;

    WHILE  c  < 0 BEGIN
       FOR  ( a  := 1 ; a  < 100 ; a  + + )
       b  := s  ;
    END
END

test  ( a  )
CARDINAL  a  ;
BEGIN
    CASE  ( a  ) BEGIN
        1 : RETURN  "a" ;
      |  ;
        2 : RETURN  "b" ;
    END
END.
```

As you can see, this is not Modula-2 code, but this saves you a lot of typing. All that you need to do is edit this a line at a time to correct the differences, and add the appropriate **IMPORT** lists and module header.

Converting BASIC to Modula-2

The task of converting BASIC to Modula-2 is much more difficult than that of C to Modula-2. BASIC is not a structured language and bears little similarity to Modula-2. This means that BASIC lacks a complete set of control structures and, more important, it lacks stand-alone subroutines with local variables. The translation task is very tricky: generally, it requires extensive knowledge of both BASIC and Modula-2, and an understanding of the program because you will essentially rewrite the program in Modula-2 by using the BASIC version as a guide. Because of the complexity of this task, this section examines some of the more troublesome translations and offers suggestions.

Converting BASIC Loops into Modula-2 Loops

In many versions of BASIC, the **FOR/NEXT** loop is the only form of loop control. The overall form of the **FOR/NEXT** loop in BASIC is generally similar to the **FOR/DO** loop in Modula-2: the **FOR/DO** has an initialization, a target value, and a counterpart to BASIC's **STEP** option, which is the **BY**. The Modula-2 **FOR/DO** loop is much more sophisticated and flexible than the BASIC **FOR/NEXT** because it allows you to use any scalar type for loop control. Consider the BASIC **FOR/NEXT** loop

```
10 FOR X=1 TO 100
20    PRINT X
30 NEXT
```

which is equivalent to

```
FOR x:=1 TO 100 DO
  WriteCard(x,0);
  WriteLn;
END;
```

in Modula-2. As you can see, the conversion is essentially a one-to-one substitution. The trick in converting the **FOR/NEXT** loop is to check that the loop-control variable is not modified inside the loop. Many BASICs allow you to alter the control variable by code inside the loop, as shown next.

```
10 FOR COUNT=10 TO 0 STEP -1
20   INPUT A
30   PRINT A*COUNT
40   IF A=100 THEN COUNT = 0
50 NEXT
```

The **IF/THEN** statement in line 40 could cause the loop to exit early. To translate this properly into Modula-2 code, you must allow for this contingency. Although some Modula-2 implementations may allow this, some do not because of the way that the compiler generates code for the **FOR/DO** loop. For some compilers, after the **FOR/DO** statement has been compiled, the actual number of times that the loop iterates is fixed—even though you changed the loop-control value in the body of the loop! Therefore, you must be careful when you encounter this situation.

Some BASICs have a **WHILE/WEND** loop construct. In this case, you would use a Modula-2 **WHILE/DO** loop in a straightforward translation process. If the BASIC that you are using does not have the **WHILE/WEND** loop, or if you choose not to use it, then your job is more difficult because you must recognize a *constructed loop* that was built with **GOTO**s. This is also the case when a **REPEAT/UNTIL** type of loop is constructed in BASIC. These types of translations become nightmarish because you must actually understand how the code works so that you can recognize and translate the loop into one of Modula-2's built-in loop-control structures.

After you have found a constructed loop in BASIC, there is an easy way to tell whether you should translate that loop into a Modula-2 **WHILE/DO** or **REPEAT/UNTIL**. Remember that a **REPEAT/UNTIL** loop *always executes at least once* because the loop condition is checked at the bottom of the loop, whereas a **WHILE/DO** loop may or may not execute because its condition is checked at the top. Therefore, you must look carefully at each constructed loop in BASIC to determine where the loop test is applied. For example, this BASIC code is actually a **REPEAT/UNTIL** loop in disguise:

```
100 S=S+1
200 Q=S/3.1415
300 PRINT Q;
400 IF S <100 THEN GOTO 100
```

You should translate this into a Modula-2 **REPEAT/UNTIL** loop because it always executes at least once. After line 100 executes, lines 200 through 400 will execute also. If **S** is less than **100**, then the program loops back to line 100. In Modula-2, this code would be

```
REPEAT
   s:=s+1;
   q:=q/3.1415;
   WriteCard(q, 0);
   WriteLn;
UNTIL s=100;
```

In the following BASIC example, the loop test is performed at the start of the loop:

```
10 A=1
20 IF A>100 THEN GOTO 80
30 PRINT A;
40 INPUT B
50 A=A+B
60 GOTO 20
80 PRINT "DONE"
```

This dictates that you use the **WHILE/DO** in the Modula-2 translation, as shown here:

```
a:=1;
WHILE a<=100 DO
BEGIN
   WriteCard(a, 0);
   ReadCard(b);
   a:=a+b;
END;
```

Avoid placing any initialization inside the loop itself. In this example, the statement a:=1 has to be outside the loop because it is a start-up condition and does not belong in the loop itself.

Converting the BASIC IF/THEN/ELSE

Most BASICs have only the single-line **IF/THEN/ELSE** statement. This means that when a block of statements must be executed according to the outcome of an **IF**, you must use the **GOTO** or **GOSUB**. You must recognize this situation because you will want to structure the code into a Modula-2 **IF/THEN/ELSIF/ELSE** statement when you translate it. For example, consider the following BASIC code fragment:

```
120 IF     T<100 THEN GOTO 500
130        Y=W
140        T=10
150        INPUT A$
  .
  .
500 REM RESUME DISK READS
```

To achieve an **IF** block in a BASIC program, you must cast the **IF** condition in the negative: the target of the **IF** must not be the condition that causes entry into the **IF** block, but rather the target must be the condition that causes a jump around it. This is one of the worst problems with BASIC. Using **GOSUB** routines as the target of the **IF** or the **ELSE** eases the problem slightly but not entirely. If you translated the code fragment directly into Modula-2, it would look like this:

```
IF t<500 THEN (*do nothing*)
ELSE
  y:=w;
  t:=10;
  ReadCard(a);
END;
(*resume disk reads*)
```

You can now see the problem: the target of the **IF** is really an empty statement. The only way to handle this is to recode the **IF** condition so that, when it is true, the block of code is entered. Therefore, the code fragment becomes

```
IF t>=500 THEN
  y:=w;
  t:=10;
  ReadCard(a);
END;
(*resume disk reads*)
```

Now the code, as written in Modula-2, makes sense.

The differences between the way that the BASIC **IF/THEN** is used and the way that the Modula-2 **IF/THEN/ELSIF/ELSE** is used illustrate that the programming language often governs the way that you think about a problem. Generally, most people find the positive form of the **IF** more natural to use than the negative form.

Creating Modula-2 Subroutines from BASIC Programs

One reason that translating BASIC into Modula-2 is difficult is that BASIC does not support stand-alone subroutines with local variables. This means that if you translated a BASIC program into Modula-2 literally, you would produce a large main module with no procedures. This negates many of the reasons that you may want to translate the program in the first place: maintainability, structure, and ease of modification.

A better translation would create a Modula-2 program with a fairly small main module and many other subroutines, but to do this requires knowledge of the program and a keen eye for reading code. However, here are a few rules to guide you.

First, you should make all **GOSUB** routines into subprograms. Next, look for similar functions in which only the variables have changed and collapse those functions into one procedure with parameters. For example, this BASIC code has two subroutines—one at 100 and the second at 200.

```
10 A=10
20 B=20
30 GOSUB 100
40 PRINT A,B;
50 C=20
60 D=30
70 GOSUB 200
80 PRINT C,D;
90 END
100 A=A*B
110 B=A/B
120 RETURN
200 C=C*D
210 D=C/D
220 RETURN
```

Both subroutines do exactly the same thing except that they operate on separate sets of variables. A proper translation of this program into Modula-2 has only one function that uses parameters to avoid having two dedicated procedures:

```
MODULE x;
VAR
    a,b,c,d:REAL;

PROCEDURE f1(VAR x,y:INTEGER);
```

```
BEGIN
    x:=x*y;
    y:=x/y;
END f1;

BEGIN
    a:=10.0;    b:=20.0;
    f1(a,b);
    WriteReal(a,0);
    WriteReal(b,0);

    c:=20.0;    d:=30.0;
    f1(c,d);
    WriteReal(c,0);
    WriteReal(d,0);
END x.
```

This Modula-2 code approximates the meaning of the code to the reader more closely than the BASIC version, which confuses the reader by implying that there are actually two separate procedures involved.

The second rule is that you should make all repeated code into a procedure. In a BASIC program, you often will find that the same lines of code are repeated to make the code slightly faster. Because Modula-2 is a compiled language, using procedures instead of in-line code has little negative effect on the speed of execution, and the increased clarity and structure outweigh any gain in speed.

Getting Rid of Global Variables

In BASIC, all variables are global: they are known throughout the entire program and may be modified anywhere in the program. During the translation process, try to convert as many of these global variables as possible into local ones because it makes the program more resilient and bug-free. The more global variables there are, the more likely it is that side effects will occur.

It is sometimes difficult to know when to make a variable local to a procedure. The easiest ones to change are those that control counters in short sections of code. For example, in this code

```
10 FOR X=1 TO 10
20    PRINT X
30 NEXT
```

it is quite clear that **X** is used only to control the **FOR/NEXT** loop. Therefore you can make **X** into a local variable within a subprogram.

Another type of variable that is a candidate for becoming local is a temporary variable. A temporary variable is used to hold an intermediate result in a calculation. Temporary variables are often spread out in the program and can be hard to recognize. For example, the variable **C12** is used to hold a temporary result:

```
10 INPUT A,B
20 GOSUB 100
30 PRINT C12;
40 END
100 C12=A*B
110 C12=C12/0.142
120 RETURN
```

The same code in Modula-2, with **C12** as a local variable, would be

```
PROGRAM x;
  FROM RealInOut IMPORT ReadReal, WriteReal;

VAR
   a,b:REAL;

PROCEDURE f2(x,y:REAL):real;
VAR
   C12:REAL;
BEGIN
   C12=a*b;
   C12/=0.142;
   f2:=C12;
END f2;

BEGIN
   ReadReal(a);
   ReadReal(b)
   WriteReal(f2(a,b),0);
END x.
```

Remember that it is always best to have as few global variables as possible, so it is important to find good candidates for local variables.

Final Thoughts on Translating

Although translating programs can be the most tedious of all programming tasks, it is also one of the most common. A good approach is first to learn to use and understand the way that the program you are translating works. After you know how it operates, the program will be easier to recode; you will know whether your new version is working correctly. Also, when you know the program that you are translating, the job becomes more interesting because it is not just a simple symbol-substitution process.

Concurrency

CHAPTER 11

One of the most exciting and difficult features of Modula-2 is its support of coroutines and concurrent processes. A language rarely defines these concepts because, traditionally, they have been left to the operating system. However, Professor Wirth recognized the need to standardize a concurrent programming interface so that the interface could remain fixed and stable in a variety of environments.

Concurrency and coroutines are simple in concept but complex in implementation. Many books have been written about the subject—and many more will be. This chapter will only scratch the surface of concurrency and coroutines. One problem is that not all Modula-2 compilers support the entire concurrent programming environment that Wirth defined. Another problem is that, even in complete implementations, many slight differences are bound to occur because of the limitations of CPU and the operating system. Although most introductory books on Modula-2 explain concurrent processes, concurrency is so important that a review is necessary.

A Review of Concurrent Processes

A *process* is a task that you can think of as a program or a procedure. If two processes are executing simultaneously on the same computer, they are called *concurrent processes*.

Today, most computers have only one CPU. Thus, only *quasi-concurrency* is possible because the computer is simply switching between processes rapidly, which gives the appearance of concurrent execution. Some computers actually have two or more CPUs, which allow true concurrent execution of processes. For Modula-2, there is no difference because the interface will be the same.

An important concept that you should know is that a process can *suspend* execution and then restart. A suspended process is not terminated — it is only waiting for execution to begin again. A process, such as a command input module, might suspend because it is waiting for input. However, a process may be forced to suspend if a resource, such as a disk drive, that is needed for its further execution is not available. Remember: a suspended process still exists at least logically in the computer — the process simply is not executing.

Any environment that supports concurrency has software called the *scheduler* that monitors all processes. The scheduler restarts suspended processes and, in some systems, gives priority to certain processes based on a certain priority scheme.

Coroutines

Simply defined, coroutines are separate processes that are part of the same program. The primary difference between a procedure and a coroutine is in the way that control is transferred. When one procedure calls another, the called procedure always executes from the top. However, when one coroutine transfers control to another, execution is resumed at the last point of execution before the previous transfer of control, which may be in the middle of the coroutine. Figure 11-1 presents a diagram of this situation.

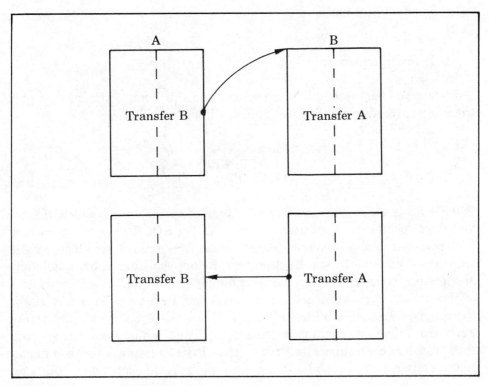

Figure 11-1. Transfer of control between coroutines

When one coroutine gives control over to another, the first coroutine is suspended, and no further execution occurs until the second coroutine returns control. In Modula-2, you can let the scheduler control what coroutine is actually executing at any given moment, or you can explicitly transfer control to various coroutines by using program control.

Creating Modula-2 Coroutines

In Modula-2, a coroutine has exactly the same syntax as a procedure. In fact, creating a coroutine is actually the transformation of a procedure into a process. The basic steps are as follows.

1. Create a procedure.

2. Designate it as a process.

3. Transfer control to it.

Before you can accomplish the second and third steps, you must import these new procedures and types from the library **SYSTEM**:

PROCESS
NEWPROCESS
TRANSFER

PROCESS is a variable type. You can think of variables of type **PROCESS** as holding pointers to various coroutines. **NEWPROCESS** is the procedure that transforms a procedure into a process. The procedure **TRANSFER** transfers control to the specified process. Before you learn about the details of these procedures, here is a simple example.

The following program creates two processes, **Proc1** and **Proc2**. Initially, the program transfers control to **Proc1**. However, if you press a key on the keyboard, the program transfers control to **Proc2**, which reads the key and then transfers control back to **Proc1**. After **Proc1**'s loop has finished execution, **Proc1** returns control to the main program and execution terminates.

```
MODULE Coroutine;

    FROM InOut IMPORT WriteLn, WriteString, Read, Write;

    FROM Keyboard IMPORT KeyPressed;

    FROM SYSTEM IMPORT WORD, PROCESS, ADR, SIZE, NEWPROCESS,
                       TRANSFER;
VAR
    ExitPoint, p1, p2: PROCESS; (* process variables *)
    work1, work2: ARRAY[1..1000] OF CHAR;  (* workspaces *)
    buf: ARRAY[0..100] OF CHAR;
    ch: CHAR;

    PROCEDURE Proc1;
      VAR
        i: CARDINAL;
    BEGIN
      FOR i:=1 TO 100 DO
        WriteLn;
```

```
      WriteString("In Proc1 at A ");
      IF KeyPressed() THEN
        TRANSFER(p1,p2);  (* go to other procedure *)
      END;
        WriteString(" In Proc1 at B");        .
    END;
    TRANSFER(p1, ExitPoint);  (* clean exit *)
  END Proc1;

  PROCEDURE Proc2;
  BEGIN
    LOOP
      WriteLn;
      WriteString("In Proc2 ");
      Read(ch);                    (* clear character buffer *)
      Write(ch);
      TRANSFER(p2,p1); (* terminate program *)
    END;
  END Proc2;

  BEGIN

  NEWPROCESS(Proc1, ADR(work1), SIZE(work1), p1);
  NEWPROCESS(Proc2, ADR(work2), SIZE(work2), p2);

  TRANSFER(ExitPoint, p1);  (* start up program *)

  END Coroutine.
```

As the program executes, it displays the messages

```
In Proc1 at A In Proc1 at B
```

continually on screen. However, if you type an X, for example, the program
displays

```
In Proc1 at A In Proc2 X In Proc1 at B
```

You should enter and run this program to understand its execution completely. Keep in mind these important aspects of the program. First, the program declares three variables of type **PROCESS**, which it uses to perform
the transfers between coroutines. In the main body of module code, the
statements

```
NEWPROCESS(Proc1, ADR(work1), SIZE(work1), p1);
NEWPROCESS(Proc2, ADR(work2), SIZE(work2), p2);
```

make **Proc1** and **Proc2** into processes. The general form of **NEWPRO-CESS** is

NEWPROCESS(*proc, workspace, WorkspaceSize, p*);

where *proc* is the name of the procedure that will become a process, *workspace* is the address of a region of memory that will be used by the process, *WorkspaceSize* is the size of the workspace, and *p* is a variable of type **PROCESS** that points to the process.

Another important consideration is the two complications that arise when you use **NEWPROCESS**. The first is where to get memory to hold the work space, and the second is how big that region of memory should be. You can resolve these questions by using two methods. First, in the program just given, the workspace was allocated by declaring an array of characters that was large enough to hold the local data and stack of the process, and then by using the **ADR** function to find its address. A second way is to locate a variable, through absolute addressing, at a specific location in unused memory and then find its address.

Sometimes, determining how big the workspace should be is difficult. In the program, 1000 was chosen because it is more than sufficient for the small demands of each process — in other words, you may need to do some guesswork. Some Modula-2 implementations may tell you how large each procedure is. Check your user manual on this point: there may be other factors that you should consider. For simple examples, you can make determinations with a little guesswork, but you should be careful in real programming tasks.

After the program creates both processes, the next line of code transfers control to **Proc1** by using its process pointer **p1**, as shown here:

```
TRANSFER(ExitPoint, p1);   (* start up program *)
```

The general form of **TRANSFER** is

TRANSFER(*from, to*);

where *from* and *to* are variables of type **PROCESS**. The effect of this procedure is to place a pointer to the current location into *from* and to go to the location that *to* points to. In this way, coroutines can continue execution at the next line of code after a **TRANSFER**.

Notice that **ExitPoint** is a **PROCESS** variable that the program uses to allow a final transfer back to the main module code for a clean termination. If you do not include a variable like this, your program will end with a run-time error that indicates that no processes are executing.

A Keyboard Buffer Example

To get a better idea of the way that you can use coroutines effectively, consider the following program:

```
MODULE KeyBuffer;

  FROM InOut IMPORT WriteLn, WriteString, Read, EOL;

  FROM Keyboard IMPORT KeyPressed;

  FROM SYSTEM IMPORT WORD, PROCESS, ADR, SIZE, NEWPROCESS,
                     TRANSFER;

  FROM Strings IMPORT CompareStr;

VAR
  ExitPoint, p1, p2: PROCESS; (* process variables *)
  work1, work2: ARRAY[1..1000] OF CHAR;  (* workspaces *)
  buf: ARRAY[0..100] OF CHAR;
  EOC: BOOLEAN;    (* End Of Command *)

  PROCEDURE Proc1;
    VAR
      i: CARDINAL;
  BEGIN
    REPEAT       (* run until KeyBuffer terminates program *)
      WriteLn;
      WriteString("processing");
      IF KeyPressed() THEN
        TRANSFER(p1,p2);  (* go to other procedure *)
        IF(EOC) THEN WriteString(buf); END;
        EOC:=FALSE;  (* reset *)
      END
    UNTIL CompareStr(buf,"quit")=0;
    TRANSFER(p1, ExitPoint);  (* clean exit *)
  END Proc1;

  PROCEDURE KeyBuffer;
    VAR
      count: CARDINAL;
      ch: CHAR;
  BEGIN
    count:=0;
```

```
      LOOP
        Read(ch);                    (* clear character buffer *)
        IF ch<>EOL THEN
          buf[count]:=ch;
          INC(count);
          EOC:=FALSE;
          TRANSFER(p2,p1); (* go on processing *)
        ELSE
          buf[count]:=CHR(0);   (* null terminator *)
          EOC:=TRUE;            (* end of command string *)
          TRANSFER(p2,p1); (* go on processing *)
          count:=0;
        END;
      END; (* LOOP *)
    END KeyBuffer;

  BEGIN

    NEWPROCESS(Proc1, ADR(work1), SIZE(work1), p1);
    NEWPROCESS(KeyBuffer, ADR(work2), SIZE(work2), p2);

    TRANSFER(ExitPoint, p1);  (* start up program *)

  END KeyBuffer.
```

This program uses **Proc1** to simulate a process that is performing some sort of real-time activity—such as monitoring the flight systems of a jet plane. **Proc1** can be terminated only when you type the command **quit** from the keyboard. Because **Proc1** should not stop processing while you enter the command, the program passes control to **KeyBuffer** for only one character at a time. When you enter a carriage return, the program then processes the command—in this case, the program displays the command on the screen.

You should enter and compile this code to understand its operation completely.

Processes: Using WAIT and SEND

In the examples given so far, you as the programmer have had explicit control over when each process was going to execute. In essence, you were bypassing the scheduler. However, you can allow Modula-2 to execute the processes on its own by simply specifying the condition upon which each process may execute or suspend. When a process suspends, the scheduler will automatically restart another process if that process is waiting to execute.

Having this form of concurrent programming requires that you use a new library called **Processes**, which contains the necessary routines that are listed here:

Routine	Action
StartProcess	Starts a process
SEND	Sends a signal
WAIT	Suspends a process until a signal is received
Init	Initializes a signal

In addition, the type **SIGNAL** is found in **Processes**.
   StartProcess has the general form

$$\textbf{StartProcess}(\textit{proc, WorkspaceSize});$$

where *proc* is the procedure to start and *WorkspaceSize* is the number of bytes that the procedure needs. As with **NEWPROCESS**, this number may be difficult to determine and (unfortunately) you may have to do some guessing. **StartProcess** immediately begins execution of *proc* —you do not need to use **TRANSFER**.
   Processes communicate with each other by using variables of type **SIGNAL**. To send a signal requires a process to use **SEND**, which has the general form

$$\textbf{SEND}(\textit{signal});$$

where *signal* is a variable of type **SIGNAL**.
   To receive a signal implies that a process is waiting for one. Therefore, you should use **WAIT**. It has the form

$$\textbf{WAIT}(\textit{signal});$$

SEND and **WAIT** work in the following way: When a process **WAIT**s for a signal, its execution is suspended while another process begins to execute. If there are no other processes that can be executed, the program terminates. **SEND**ing a signal either reactivates a process that is **WAIT**ing for it, or does nothing if no process is **WAIT**ing. In this way, you can use signals to synchronize two or more processes.

You must initialize all signals through a call to **Init**, before you use the signals. **Init** has a general form of

Init(*signal*);

Here is a classic example of concurrent execution and signals: the producer/consumer process pair. In this situation, one process produces something that the other process consumes. If you call the consumer C and the producer P, then C must suspend, or **WAIT**, until P has produced something. After P has produced something, P tells, or **SEND**s, C about it so that C can execute. Both C and P continue in this fashion. The program **ProCon**, shown here, implements a simple version of this: **Consumer** prints the strings that **Producer** reads from the keyboard. Only **Consumer** needs to be a process because **Producer** automatically waits while **Consumer** is executing; the execution of **Producer** does not depend upon a signal.

```
MODULE ProCon;

   FROM InOut IMPORT WriteLn, WriteString, Read, EOL, Write;

   FROM SYSTEM IMPORT WORD, PROCESS, ADR, SIZE, NEWPROCESS,
                      TRANSFER;
   FROM Processes IMPORT WAIT, SEND, StartProcess, SIGNAL,
                         Init;

VAR
   buf: ARRAY[0..100] OF CHAR;
   S: SIGNAL;

   PROCEDURE Consumer;
   BEGIN
     LOOP
       WriteString("waiting ");
       WAIT(S); (* wait until characters in key buffer *)
       WriteString(buf);
     END
   END Consumer;

   PROCEDURE Producer;
     VAR
       count: CARDINAL;
       ch: CHAR;
   BEGIN
     count:=0;
     LOOP
       Read(ch);                    (* clear character buffer *)
```

```
      IF ch<>EOL THEN
        buf[count]:=ch;
        Write(ch);
        INC(count);
      ELSE
        buf[count]:=CHR(0);   (* null terminator *)
        WriteLn;
        SEND(S);              (* allow other routine to execute *)
        count:=0;
      END;
    END;
  END Producer;

BEGIN

  Init(S);

  StartProcess(Consumer,1000);
  Producer;

END ProCon.
```

Cat and Mouse

As a second example of concurrent processes, here is a simple program called **CatAndMouse**. This program uses the random number generators **Ran1** and **Ran2**, which Chapter 8 developed, to simulate a cat chasing a mouse around a room. There are two possible conclusions to this situation. First, the cat catches, and presumably eats, the mouse. Second, the mouse escapes to its mouse hole and the cat goes hungry.

Two processes called **Cat** and **Mouse** implement this scenario. Each process generates a random number by using its own random number generator. The procedure **Judge**, which is not a process, moderates the chase and reports the winner. If the cat's number matches the mouse's number, then the cat wins; if the mouse's number matches the cat's number, then the mouse wins. The program begins by requesting a keystroke so that **Ran1** can begin generating numbers at some arbitrary point. If **Ran1** did not do this, the cat would always catch the mouse. Here is the entire **CatAndMouse** program:

```
MODULE CatAndMouse;
  FROM InOut IMPORT WriteLn, WriteString, Write,
       WriteCard;

  FROM Terminal IMPORT KeyPressed;

  FROM Processes IMPORT WAIT, SEND, StartProcess, SIGNAL,
                        Init;
```

```
VAR
  buf: ARRAY[0..100] OF CHAR;
  ch: CHAR;
  C,M: SIGNAL;
  a1, a2: CARDINAL;
  CatNum, MouseNum: CARDINAL;
  t: REAL;

PROCEDURE Ran1(): REAL;
  VAR
    t, Ran1Result: REAL;
BEGIN
  t := FLOAT((a1*32749+3) MOD 32749);
  a1 := TRUNC(t);
  Ran1Result := ABS(t/FLOAT(32749));
  RETURN Ran1Result
END Ran1;

PROCEDURE Ran2(): REAL;
  VAR
    t, Ran2Result: REAL;
BEGIN
  t := FLOAT((a2*1001+3) MOD 17417);
  a2 := TRUNC(t);
  Ran2Result := ABS(t/FLOAT(17417));
  RETURN Ran2Result
END Ran2;


PROCEDURE Cat;
BEGIN
  LOOP
    WAIT(C);
    CatNum:=TRUNC(Ran1()*100.0);
  END
END Cat;

PROCEDURE Mouse;
BEGIN
  LOOP
    WAIT(M);
    MouseNum:=TRUNC(Ran2()*100.0);
  END;
END Mouse;

PROCEDURE Judge;
BEGIN
 LOOP
    SEND(C);
    IF CatNum=MouseNum THEN
      WriteString("Cat caught mouse.");
      WriteLn;
      RETURN;
    END;
    SEND(M);
```

```
      IF CatNum=MouseNum THEN
        WriteString("Mouse escaped from cat.");
        WriteLn;
        RETURN;
      END;
    END;
END Judge;

BEGIN

  a1:=1;  (* init the random number generators *)
  a2:=203;

  CatNum:=0; (* init the numbers *)
  MouseNum:=0;

  Init(C);  (* init the signals *)
  Init(M);

  WriteString("Strike a key");
  WHILE NOT KeyPressed() DO
    t:=Ran1();  (* Randomize the first generator *)
  END;
  WriteLn;

  StartProcess(Cat,1000);  (* start the game *)
  StartProcess(Mouse,1000);
  Judge;
END CatAndMouse.
```

The program first multiplies the random numbers by 100 and then truncates them to produce a cardinal number between 0 and 100. An interesting variation to make to this game is to add graphics so that you can watch the cat and mouse movements.

Avoiding Deadlock

One of the most annoying and troublesome problems that you can encounter when you write concurrent routines is *deadlock*. Deadlock is a situation in which two routines are waiting for something that only the other can provide—hence, both routines are suspended and cannot run. These two procedures will deadlock:

```
PROCEDURE A;
BEGIN
    WAIT(S);
```

```
        SEND(T);
          .
          .
          .
        END A;
        PROCEDURE B;
        BEGIN
          WAIT(T);
          SEND(S);
          .
          .
          .
        END B;
```

A is suspended because it is waiting for signal **S**, while **B** is suspended because it is waiting for signal **T**! Neither procedure will ever send the signal that the other needs.

Although this simple situation is easy to see, deadlock is most "deadly" when it occurs through a combination of several processes and signals. Because you may not know the actual order of execution, it is difficult for you to determine why the deadlock occurred. For this reason, you must think through your routines carefully to avoid deadlock.

Final Thoughts
on Concurrency

To several types of programs, both coroutines and concurrent processes are extremely important. However, they are sources of trouble because the normal sequential execution of a program is no longer in force. Most people — including many programmers — have difficulty grasping the actual execution path of more than two or three concurrent processes. This makes program verification extremely troublesome when a program contains concurrent processes. Debugging time is also increased exponentially! Concurrent programming is best left to experienced programmers; you should use concurrent programming only when it is appropriate to do so.

Efficiency,
Porting, and
Debugging

CHAPTER 1 2

The ability to write programs that make efficient use of system resources, are transportable to other computers, and are error-free is the mark of a professional programmer. This ability transforms computer science into the "art of computer science" because so few formal techniques are available to ensure success. This chapter presents some of the methods by which you may achieve efficiency, portability, and program debugging.

Efficiency

When used with a computer program, the term *efficiency* can refer to the use of system resources, the speed of execution, or both. System resources include RAM, disk space, printer paper, and basically anything that can be allocated and used up. Whether or not a program is efficient is sometimes a subjective judgment that can change from situation to situation. Consider a program that uses 47K of RAM to execute, 2 megabytes of disk space, and whose average run time is 7 minutes. If this program is a sort program running on an Apple II, then the program is probably not very efficient. However, if it is a weather-forecasting program running a Cray computer, then it is probably very efficient.

Another point to consider when you are trying to make your program efficient is that optimizing one aspect of a program often degrades another. For example, making a program execute faster often means making it bigger if you use inline code instead of function calls to increase speeds. Also, making more efficient use of disk space means compacting the data, which can make disk accesses slower. These and other types of efficiency trade-offs can be frustrating—especially to the nonprogramming end-user who cannot see why one part should affect the other.

In light of these problems, you might wonder how efficiency can be discussed at all. There are some programming practices that are *always* *efficient*—or, at least, more efficient than others. There are also a few techniques that make programs *both* faster and smaller.

Avoiding Code Duplication

Even the best of programmers sometimes write *redundant code*. Redundant code does not refer to code that you could change into a subroutine; even very inexperienced programmers understand this. Rather, redundant code is the unnecessary duplication of similar statements within a routine. To get a better idea of what redundant code is, examine this code fragment:

```
ReadInt(a);
ReadString(y);
IF a<10 THEN WriteString('Invalid input'); END;
IF Length(y)=0 THEN WriteString('Invalid input'); END;
```

In this case, the statement

```
WriteString('Invalid input');
```

occurs twice. However, if you examine the code, it is apparent that the statement is not needed twice, because you could write

```
ReadInt(a);
ReadString(y);
IF (a<10) OR (Length(y)=0) THEN
  WriteString('Invalid input');
END;
```

Here, not only is the object code shorter, but the code actually executes faster because it executes only one **IF/THEN** statement instead of two; it is also faster because if $a<10$, **Length(y)=0** is not even examined.

The example just given is unlikely to occur in an actual program because the duplicate statements were close together, which makes them quite easy to see. However, because several lines of code often separate duplicated statements, redundant code occurs in most computer programs.

Redundancy sometimes happens because of the method selected to code a routine. For example, here are two ways to code a function that searches an array of strings for a specific word:

```
TYPE
    str80 = ARRAY [0..79] OF CHAR;
    StrArray = ARRAY [1..100] OF str80;

PROCEDURE StrSearch1(str:StrArray, word:str80):BOOLEAN;
(*Correct, non-redundant method*)
VAR
    t:INTEGER;
BEGIN
    FOR t:=1 TO 100 DO
      IF CompareStr(str[t],word)=0 THEN
          RETURN TRUE;
      END;
    END;
    RETURN FALSE;
END StrSearch1;


PROCEDURE StrSeach2(str:StrArray,word:str80):BOOLEAN;
(*Incorrect, redundant method*)
VAR
  t:INTEGER;
BEGIN
  t:=1;
  IF CompareStr(str[t],word)=0 THEN
    RETURN TRUE
  ELSE
    t:=2;
    WHILE(t<=100) DO
      IF CompareStr(str[t],word)=0 THEN
        RETURN TRUE;
      END;
```

```
        INC(t);
      END;
    END;
    RETURN FALSE;
END StrSearch2;
```

The second method not only duplicates the **IF/THEN** comparison statements, but also has two assignment statements, **t:=1** and **t:=2**, that are essentially duplications. The first version runs faster and will require much less memory.

In short, redundant code can be caused either by sloppiness in coding, or poor judgment in choosing the way to implement a routine. Either way, it is something to avoid.

Using Procedures

Always remember that the use of procedures with local variables helps to form the basis of structured programming. Procedures are the building blocks of Modula-2 programs and are one of Modula-2's strongest assets. Do not let anything that is discussed in this section be construed otherwise. With this warning, you should know a few features of Modula-2 procedures and their effects on the size and speed of your code.

Modula-2 is a *stack-oriented language:* all local variables and parameters to procedures use the stack for temporary storage. When a procedure is called, the return address of the calling routine is also placed on the stack. This enables the subroutine to return to the location from which it was called. When a procedure returns, this address—and all local variables and parameters—must be removed from the stack. The process of pushing this information onto the stack is generally referred to as the *calling sequence,* and the process of popping the information off of the stack is called the *returning sequence.* These sequences take time—sometimes quite a bit of time if several parameters are passed and temporary variables are used.

To understand how a procedure call can slow down your program, look at the two code fragments shown here:

```
Version 1                      Version 2

FOR x:=1 TO 100 DO             FOR x:=1 TO 100
     t:=compute(x);                  t:=Abs(Sin(q)/100.0/3.1416);
END;                           END;

PROCEDURE compute(q:INTEGER):REAL;
BEGIN
     RETURN Abs(Sin(q)/100.0/3.1416);
END compute;
```

Although each loop performs the same procedure, Version 2 is much faster because using inline code eliminates the overhead of the calling-and-returning sequence. To understand how much time is taken up, study the following pseudo-assembly code, which shows the calling-and-returning sequence for the procedure **compute**.

```
; calling sequence
move A, x  ; put value of x into accumulator
push A
call compute  ; the call instruction places
              ; the return address on the stack


; returning sequence
; the return value of the procedure must be placed
; into a register - we will use B
move B, stack-1  ; get value in temporary t

return  ; return to the calling routine
; calling routine then does the following
pop A   ; clear parameter use in the call
```

Using the **compute** procedure inside the loop causes the calling-and-returning sequence to be executed 100 times. If you really want to write fast code, then using **compute** inside a loop is not a good idea.

By now, you may think that you should write a program that has just a few large routines so that it will run quickly. However, in the majority of cases, the slight time differential will not be meaningful, and the loss of structure will be acute! But there is another problem: replacing subprograms that several routines use with inline code will make your program large because the same code is duplicated several times. Keep in mind that subroutines were invented primarily as a way to use memory efficiently. A rule of thumb is that making a program faster means making it bigger, while making it smaller means making it slower. It only makes sense to use inline code instead of a procedure call when speed is an absolute priority. Otherwise, the liberal use of procedures is definitely recommended.

CASE Versus ELSIF Ladders

The following code fragments are procedurally equivalent. However, one is more efficient than the other. Can you tell which one?

```
CASE ch OF              IF ch='a' THEN f1(ch)
  'a': f1(ch); |        ELSIF ch='b' THEN f2(ch)
  'b': f2(ch); |        ELSIF ch='c' THEN f3(ch)
```

```
    'c': f3(ch); |              ELSIF ch='d' THEN f4(ch);
    'd': f4(ch);                END;
END;
```

The code fragment on the left is much more efficient than the one on the right because, in general, the **CASE** statement generates tighter, faster object code than the series of **ELSIF**s.

The **ELSIF** arrangement, as shown in this example, is called an **ELSIF** ladder because program execution seems to "step" its way down the sequence. An **ELSIF** ladder is important because it allows you to perform multibranch decisions on a variety of data types that cannot be used in a **CASE** statement. However, if you are using scalars—**INTEGER**s, **CHAR**s, and enumerations—you should use the **CASE** statement instead.

Porting Programs

It is common for a program written on one machine to be transported to another computer with a different processor, operating system, or both. This process is called *porting* and can be very easy or extremely hard, depending upon the way that the program was originally written. A program is *portable* if it can be easily ported. A program is not easily portable usually because it contains numerous machine dependencies—code fragments that work only with one specific operating system or processor. Modula-2 has been designed to allow you to create portable code between all of its versions, but it still requires that you pay attention to details because of variations in the operating systems.

Porting code that originally was written with one Modula-2 compiler to another compiler can present problems because a different set of library procedures—with different names—may have been used. The reverse situation is also true.

This section examines a few specific problem areas and offers some solutions. You will also see ways to write Modula-2 programs so that they are portable.

Using CONST

Perhaps the simplest way to make programs portable is to make *every* system-dependent or processor-dependent "magic number" into a **CONST** declaration. These magic numbers include random-access record sizes for disk accesses, special screen and keyboard commands, memory allocation information, and anything else that has even the slightest possibility of changing when the program is ported. If you make the magic numbers into **CONST** declarations, then these definitions will not only make the magic numbers obvious to the person doing the porting, but they also simplify editing; their values have to be changed only once instead of throughout the program.

For example, here are two declarations of an array and two procedures that access it. The first version hardcodes the array dimensions, and the second places them into **CONST** declarations.

```
(*first version*)
VAR
    count:ARRAY[1..100] OF INTEGER;

PROCEDURE f1;
VAR
    t:INTEGER;
BEGIN
    FOR t:=1 TO 100 DO count[t]:=t; END;
END f1;


(*second version*)
CONST
    MAX = 100;
VAR
    count:ARRAY[1..MAX] OF INTEGER;

PROCEDURE f2;
VAR
    t:INTEGER;
BEGIN
    FOR t:=1 TO MAX DO count[t]:=t; END;
END f1;
```

The second version is clearly better if you want to port this program to a machine that allows, for example, larger array sizes. In this case only **MAX** would have to change, and all references to **MAX** would be automatically corrected. This version not only is easier to change, but also avoids many editing errors. Remember that there are probably many references to **MAX** in a real program so the gain in portability is often quite substantial.

Operating-System Dependencies

Virtually all commercial programs have code that is specific to the operating system. For example, a spreadsheet program might make use of the IBM PC's video memory to allow fast switching between screens, or a graphics package may use special graphics commands that are only applicable to that operating system. Some operating-system dependencies are necessary for fast, commercially viable programs. However, there is no reason to hardcode any more dependencies than is necessary.

When you must use system calls to access the operating system, it is best to do them all through one master procedure, so that you only need to change it to accommodate a new operating system and you can leave the rest of the code intact. For example, if system calls were needed to clear the screen and the end-of-line and locate the cursor at an X,Y coordinate, then you should create a master procedure, such as **OpSysCall**, shown here:

```
PROCEDURE OpSysCall(op,x,y:INTEGER);
(*Interface to operating system*)
BEGIN
    CASE op OF
        1: ClearScreen; |
        2: ClearEOL; |
        3: GotoXY(x,y);
    END;
END OpSysCall;
```

Porting a program that uses this method of access operating system calls would only require you to change the way that the procedures were implemented; you could leave the interface intact.

Debugging

To paraphrase Thomas Edison, programming is 10% inspiration and 90% debugging! Good programmers are good debuggers. Although you probably have good debugging skills, you should watch for certain types of bugs that can occur easily while you are using Modula-2.

Pointer Problems

A common error in Modula-2 programs is the misuse of pointers. Pointer problems fall into two general categories: misunderstanding of indirection and the pointer operators, and the accidental use of invalid pointers. To solve the first problem, you must understand pointers in the Modula-2 language; to solve the second, you must always verify the validity of a pointer before you use it.

Here is a typical error that Modula-2 programmers can make:

```
MODULE WRONG; (*This program is in error*)

TYPE
   pntr = POINTER TO object;

   object = RECORD
      x: CHAR;
      y: INTEGER;
      name: ARRAY[0..79] OF CHAR;
   END;

VAR
   p:pntr;

BEGIN
   p^.name:='tom';
   p^.x:='g';
   p^.y:=100;
END WRONG.
```

This program will probably crash—taking the operating system with it—beccause the pointer **p** is never assigned a value by using **NEW**! Rather, it contains an unknown random number, which could be pointing anywhere in the memory of the computer. This is certainly not what is wanted. To correct this program, you must add the line

```
NEW(p);
```

before the first use of pointer **p**.

"Wild" pointers are extremely difficult to track down. If you are making assignments to a pointer variable that does not contain a valid pointer address, then your program may appear to function correctly sometimes and crash at other times. Statistically, the smaller your program, the more likely it will run correctly even with a stray pointer, because little memory is in use. As your program grows, failures become more common, but as you debug it, you will be thinking about recent additions or changes, and not about pointer errors. Hence, you will tend to look in the wrong spot for the error.

A second, and more insidious, problem can occur when you use pointers: you can run out of memory during a call to **NEW** at run time. This causes a run-time error and execution will stop. Fortunately, Modula-2 has the procedure **Available**, which you can find in **Storage**, so that you can avoid this problem. You call **Available** with the number of bytes that you wish to allocate; it returns **TRUE** if that number is available and **FALSE** if not. Therefore, to correct the program completely, you should check for the existence of available memory before you attempt to allocate it. To do this, you must know the number of bytes needed for each data type that you are allocating. This number may change between processors and operating systems; however, you can use **SIZE** or **TSIZE** to determine the amount needed. The corrected program is shown here:

```
MODULE RIGHT; (*This program is OK*)
  FROM Storage IMPORT ALLOCATE, DEALLOCATE;
  FROM SYSTEM IMPORT SIZE;

TYPE
  pntr = POINTER TO object;

  object = RECORD
     x: CHAR;
     y: INTEGER;
     name: ARRAY[0..79] OF CHAR;
  END;
```

```
VAR
   p:pntr;
BEGIN
   IF Available(SIZE(p)) THEN
     NEW(p);
     p^.name:='tom';
     p^.x:='g';
     p^.y:=100;
   END;
END RIGHT;
```

One indication of a pointer problem is that errors tend to be erratic. Your program may work correctly one time and incorrectly another. Other variables may contain garbage for no reason. If these problems occur, check your pointers. As a matter of procedure, you should check all pointers when bugs begin to occur.

Although pointers can be troublesome, they are one of the most powerful and useful aspects of the Modula-2 language. They are worth whatever trouble they may cause you. Make the effort early on to learn to use them correctly.

Redefining Standard Procedures

Although Modula-2 does not allow you to redefine the keywords that make up the language, it does allow you to redefine the words that reference the standard procedures found in its library modules. Programmers sometimes think that it is a good idea to do this for various reasons; however, it can only lead to trouble. For example, here is a problem that is directly caused by redefining the standard procedure **Write**:

```
MODULE WRONG;   (*This program is incorrect*)

   FROM InOut IMPORT WriteString, WriteLn;

VAR
   t:INTEGER;

PROCEDURE Write;
BEGIN
   WriteString('try again');
   WriteLn;
END Write;

BEGIN
   REPEAT
```

```
      ReadInt(t);
      IF t<0 THEN Write; END;
    UNTIL t>=0;
    Write(CHR(t))
END WRONG.
```

In this example, the programmer thought that it would be "cute" to redefine the standard procedure **Write** but forgot that the reprompt message would be displayed instead of the character that corresponded to the number entered. The reason for this is that the redefinition of **Write** has replaced the built-in one.

Although the problem in this example is fairly easy to see, a worse redefinition problem occurs when a standard procedure or procedure is redefined but is *not* used directly in the program at that time. At some later date, when the program is modified, the redefined procedure is referenced as if it were still the standard procedure, as shown in this code fragment:

```
PROCEDURE Available: BOOLEAN;
(*See if room left in global array count*)
VAR
   t:INTEGER
BEGIN
  FOR t:=1 TO MAX DO
    IF count[t]=0 THEN  RETURN TRUE; END;
  END;
  RETURN FALSE;
END Available;
```

The redefinition of **Available** is fine as far as this fragment goes. The problem arises if the array **count** is changed later from a global variable to a dynamic variable that is allocated from the heap. In this case, if you tried to use **Available** to see if sufficient memory were left on the heap, your program would fail.

The only way to avoid these problems is never to give a procedure that you have written the same name as one in the standard library. If you are unsure, append your initials to the start of the name, as in **HSAvailable** instead of **Available**.

Unexpected Syntax Errors

Sometimes, your Modula-2 compiler may generate error messages that you cannot understand. For example, the syntax error that this code produces can be confusing:

```
(*This code will not compile*)
PROCEDURE F2;
VAR
    t:INTEGER;
BEGIN
    FOR t:=1 TO 10 DO WriteString('hi there');
END F2

BEGIN
    F2;
END X.
```

Here, the error is the omission of the semicolon at **END** in the procedure **F2**. However, Modula-2 will point to the error at the **BEGIN** that follows that **END**. Although this problem is easy to spot in this simple program, you may have to backtrack a bit in certain situations to find where a semicolon is missing.

IF/THEN/IF/ELSE Errors

Even very experienced programmers occasionally fall prey to the **IF/THEN/ IF/ELSE** error. For example, are you *sure* what this code fragment does?

```
IF count<100 THEN
    IF count>50 THEN F1
ELSE F2; END;
END;
```

Do not be fooled by the improper formatting! The **ELSE** is not associated with the first **IF**, but rather with the second **IF**: an **ELSE** is always associated with the closest **IF**. Thus, instead of executing **F2** if **count** is greater than 100, this example does nothing. Also, **F2** executes if **count** is less than 100, and then if it is less than 50. You can see this if the code is properly formatted, as shown here:

```
IF count<100 THEN
    IF count>50 THEN F1
    ELSE F2;
    END;
END;
```

If you wanted to have **F2** execute if **count** is greater than 100, you would need to use a **code** block, as shown next.

```
IF count<100 THEN
   IF count>50 THEN F1; END;
ELSE F2;
END;
```

Forgetting to Use VAR in Procedures

Sometimes, in the heat of programming, it is easy to forget that if a procedure will change an argument to that procedure, then you must specify it as a **VAR** parameter. Forgetting to do this can cause bizarre results and hours of frustrating debugging time. For example, consider this incorrect program:

```
MODULE Error;  (*This program is incorrect*)
  FROM InOut IMPORT ReadInt, WriteInt, WriteString;

VAR
   t:INTEGER;

PROCEDURE F1(x:INTEGER);
BEGIN
   WriteString('Enter a value: ');
   ReadInt(x);
END F1;

BEGIN
   F1(t);   (*get a value for t*)
   WriteInt(t,5);
END Error;
```

This program does not work because only the local variable **x** is assigned a value and, when **F1** returns, t is unmodified. To make this program work, you must declare **x** inside **F1** to be a **VAR** parameter. This modifies the calling variable t. The corrected program is shown here:

```
MODULE Fixed;  (*This program is correct*)

  FROM InOut IMPORT ReadInt, WriteInt, WriteString;

VAR
   t:INTEGER;

PROCEDURE F1(VAR x:INTEGER);
BEGIN
   WriteString('Enter a value: ');
   ReadInt(x);
END F1;
```

```
BEGIN
    F1(t);  (*get a value for t*)
    WriteInt(t,5);
END Fixed;
```

Although this simple program was easy to correct, when this error occurs in large programs, it can be one of the most difficult bugs to find.

General Debugging Theory

Everyone has a different approach to programming and debugging. However, certain techniques have proven to be better than others. In the case of debugging, incremental testing is considered to be the most cost-effective and time-effective method, even though it can appear to slow the development process.

In the early days of computers, programmers were taught to prepare their programs in advance, submit them for execution, and then interpret results. This process, called *batch programming*, was necessary when there were few computers. However, it is seldom used today because there are many computers that support an interactive programming environment. Batch programming helped give computers a bad image in the early 1960s because it required programmers to spend an enormous amount of time and mental energy to develop a program. Because all testing also had to be done in batch mode, it was difficult to try all possible conditions that a program could fail in. This lack of thorough testing led to the "computer-error" problems so common in many early computer installations.

Today, batch programming is virtually extinct because it cannot support an environment of interactive *incremental testing*. Incremental testing is the process of always having a working program: early in the development process, you should establish an operational unit, which is simply a piece of working code. As you add new code to this unit, you test and debug it. In this way, you can easily find errors because the errors most likely occur in the newly added code or in the way that it interacts with the operational unit.

You can compute debugging time, *DebugTime*, by using this formula:

$$DebugTime = (NumOfLines + X)^2$$

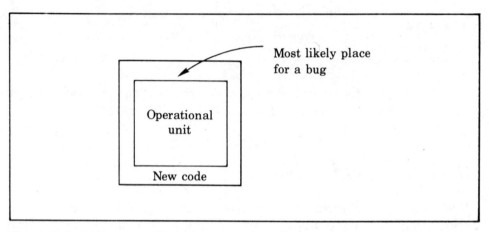

Figure 12-1. The most likely location of a bug when incremental testing is used

where *NumOfLines* is the total number of lines of code that can contain a bug, and X is some constant (which is programmer-dependent). As the formula shows, debugging time is a squared quantity. With incremental testing, you can restrict the number of lines of code to only those that are newly added—that is, those that are not part of the operational unit. Figure 12-1 shows a diagram of this situation.

Incremental testing theory is generally based on probability and areas. As you know, *area* is a squared dimension. Therefore, as your program grows, you must search for bugs in an n-squared area. While debugging, you as a programmer want the smallest possible area to deal with. Through incremental testing, you can subtract the area already tested from the total area, thereby reducing the region that may contain a bug.

Within a large project, several modules may have only mild interaction. In these cases, you can establish several operational units to allow concurrent development. In fact, Modula-2 is exceptionally well-suited for these types of projects.

Incremental testing is important for two reasons. First, it greatly reduces debugging time because errors are easier to find. Second, it speeds up the development process because design errors can be caught early in the project—before all of the code is written. (Of course, this should never take the place of a good design!)

Remember that incremental testing is simply the process of always having working code. As soon as you can run a piece of your program, you should do so, testing that section completely. As you add to the program, continue to test the new sections as well as the way that they connect to the established operational code. This allows you to concentrate any bugs to a small area of code.

Final Thoughts

Throughout this book, various algorithms and techniques have been discussed—some in considerable depth. Remember that computer science is both a theoretical and an empirical science. Although it is fairly easy to see why one algorithm is better than another, it is difficult to say what makes a successful program. When it comes to efficiency, portability, and debugging, experimentation sometimes yields information more easily than theoretical musings.

It has been said that the best programmers have an engineer's brain and a poet's heart. There is much truth to this statement because programming blends both art and science. It is a science because you must know logic, and understand how and why an algorithm works. It is an art because you create the total entity that is a program; the artistic side of the programmer can transform a lackluster program into something exciting and interesting to use. As a programmer, you really have one of the best jobs on earth—you walk the line between science and art, and get the best of both!

TRADEMARKS

CP/M®	Digital Research, Inc.
CP/M-86®	Digital Research, Inc.
IBM®	International Business Machines Corporation
IBM PC™	International Business Machines Corporation
MS-DOS®	Microsoft Corporation
PC-DOS™	International Business Machines Corporation
Turbo Pascal®	Borland International, Inc.
Turbo Prolog™	Borland International, Inc.
Wall Street Journal™	Dow Jones & Co.
ZIP™	United States Postal Service

I N D E X

A

Activation record, 154
ADDRESS, 34
ADR( ), 35
Again( ), 22
Algorithm
   n-squared, 50
   recursive, 105, 107
   sorting, 46
ALLOCATE( ), 32, 115
AND, 7
arctan( ), 28
ARRAY, 7, 153
Array, multidimensioned, 7
Arrays, 117
   differences in Pascal, 43
Artificial intelligence, 139-148
ASCII character codes, 237
Assembly code, inline, 157
Assembly code routine, external, 155

Assembly language
   8086/8088, 149
     interfacing to, 149-160
Assign( ), 33
AVAILABLE( ), 116
Available, 32, 360
Awaited( ), 30

B

Balanced trees, 109
Bar graph, 186
BASIC, 3, 6
   converting to Modula-2, 328-336
Batch programming, 365
BEGIN, 8, 36, 363
Bidirectional parameter, 153
Binary search, 70
Binary trees, 104-111, 122

The manuscript for this book was prepared and submitted to Osborne/McGraw-Hill in electronic form.

The acquisitions editor was Jon Erickson, the technical editor was Seth Pratt, the copy editor was Lorraine Aochi, and the project editor was Fran Haselsteiner.

Text body and display set in Century Expanded and Eras Demi. Cover art by Bay Graphics Design Associates; cover supplier, Phoenix Color Corp. Book printed and bound by R.R. Donnelley & Sons Company, Crawfordsville, Indiana.

Other related Osborne/McGraw-Hill titles include:

PC Secrets: Tips for Power Performance
by James E. Kelley

Power performance is at your command with these secrets for mastering the PC. This collection of shortcuts and solutions to frustrating and frequently encountered problems gives users of the IBM® PC and PC compatibles the inside edge. James Kelley, author of numerous books on the IBM PC, discloses his secrets for controlling hardware, peripherals, DOS, and applications software. You'll learn tips for keyboard harmonics, display enhancements, controlling fixed disks, managing the printer, and manipulating DOS routines that include batch files, directories and subdirectories, as well as system menus. You'll also find programs that help you use WordStar® and Lotus™ 1-2-3™ to greater advantage. With *PC Secrets*, you don't need to be a technical expert to become a PC power user.

$16.95p
0-07-881210-0, 224 pp., 7³/₈ x 9¹/₄

PC-DOS Tips & Traps
*by Dick Andersen, Janice M. Gessin,
Fred Warren, and Jack Rodgers*

Solve immediate problems and quickly perform specific business tasks on your IBM® PC or PC-compatible with *PC-DOS Tips & Traps*. Written for everyone using PC-DOS 2.1 or MS-DOS 2.11, Andersen provides an array of tips and discusses frequently encountered traps with their solutions. You'll find a broad range of helpful information from initializing your system and formatting disks, to controlling peripherals, and managing the DOS environment. Throughout the book Andersen shows you how to use the DOS Batch files to design your own commands and automate certain tasks. Tips for using DOS utilities including EDLIN for text editing and DEBUG for programming are also discussed. You'll save time and minimize the chance for error with Andersen's insights on the PC- and MS-DOS® operating systems.

$16.95p
0-07-881194-5, 250 pp., 7³/₈ x 9¹/₄

Your IBM® PC: A Guide to the IBM PC (DOS 2.0) and XT
by Lyle Graham and Tim Field

"Excellent reference for the IBM PC with PC-DOS version 1.0, 1.05 and 1.1. Provides a clear overview of IBM PC hardware and software, step-by-step operating instructions, and an introduction to BASIC programming, color graphics, and sound. Also includes a chapter on trouble-shooting and IBM's PDP (Problem Definition Procedure). Rating: A" (Computer Book Review)

$18.95p
0-07-881120-1, 592 pp., 6⁷/₈ x 9¹/₄

The Osborne/McGraw-Hill Guide to Using Lotus™ 1-2-3,™ Second Edition, Covers Release 2
by Edward M. Baras

Your investment in Lotus™ 1-2-3™ can yield the most productive returns possible with the tips and practical information in *The Osborne/McGraw-Hill Guide to Using Lotus™ 1-2-3.™* Now the second edition of this acclaimed bestseller helps you take full advantage of Lotus' new 1-2-3 upgrade, Release 2. This comprehensive guide offers a thorough presentation of the worksheet, database, and graphics functions. In addition, the revised text shows you how to create and use macros, string functions, and many other sophisticated 1-2-3 features. Step by step, you'll learn to implement 1-2-3 techniques as you follow application models for financial forecasting, stock portfolio tracking, and forms-oriented database management. For both beginners and experienced users, this tutorial quickly progresses from fundamental procedures to advanced applications.

$18.95p
0-07-881230-5, 432 pp., 7³/₈ x 9¹/₄

Financial Modeling Using Lotus™ 1-2-3,™ Covers Release 2
by Charles W. Kyd

Readers of Kyd's monthly "Accounting" column in *Lotus™* magazine already know how helpful his 1-2-3™ tips can be. Now his *Financial Modeling Using Lotus™ 1-2-3™* shows experienced users how to set up a data bank that can be used by everyone in the office to make more effective use of numerous financial applications. Kyd provides models for managing the balance sheet, controlling growth, handling income statements and management accounting, using Z scores for business forecasts, and more. Each model features a summary of 1-2-3 techniques, including helpful information for using the new Release 2, and explains the financial theories behind the application. You'll also find out how data for many of these financial models can be shared in the office data bank, creating an even greater resource for business productivity.

$16.95p
0-07-881213-5, 225 pp., 7³/₈ x 9¹/₄

The Advanced Guide to Lotus™ 1-2-3™
by Edward M. Baras

Edward Baras, Lotus expert and author of *The Symphony™ Book, Symphony™ Master,* and *The Jazz™ Book,* now has a sequel to his best-selling *Osborne/McGraw-Hill Guide to Using Lotus™ 1-2-3.™* For experienced users, *The Advanced Guide to Lotus 1-2-3* delves into more powerful and complex techniques using the newest software upgrade, Release 2. Added enhancements to 1-2-3's macro language, as well as many new functions and commands, are described and thoroughly illustrated in business applications. Baras shows you how to take advantage of Release 2's macro capabilities by programming 1-2-3 to simulate Symphony's keystroke-recording features and by processing ASCII files automatically. You'll also learn to set up your own command menus; use depreciation functions, matric manipulation, and regression analysis; and convert text files to the 1-2-3 worksheet format.

$18.95p
0-07-881237-2, 325 pp., 7³/₈ x 9¹/₄

Using dBASE III® PLUS™
by Edward Jones

Osborne's top-selling title, *Using dBASE III,®* by Edward Jones, has now been updated to include Ashton-Tate's new upgrade, dBASE III® PLUS.™ With Jones' expertise you'll be in full command of all the new features of this powerful database software. Learn to design, create, and display a dBASE III PLUS database, devise entry forms with the dBASE III PLUS screen painter, generate reports, use Query files, and plug into dBASE III PLUS networking. In addition, you'll find out how to install dBASE III PLUS on a hard disk, conduct data searches, and manipulate assistant pull-down menus. *Using dBASE III® PLUS™* is a thorough and practical handbook for both beginning and experienced dBASE III users.

$18.95
0-07-881252-6, 350 pp., 7³/₈ x 9¹/₄

Microsoft® Word Made Easy, Second Edition
by Paul Hoffman

Hoffman's top-selling *Microsoft® Word Made Easy* has been revised to cover Microsoft's latest version of this widely used word processing software. Both beginning and experienced users will find a clear presentation of Word's new features, "made easy" for immediate application. Hoffman covers text outlining, spelling correction, hyphenation, creating indexes and tables of contents, and laser printers. Word's new functions, style sheets, windows, and glossaries are described in depth, and you'll find extra tips for using the mail-merge function. In the tradition of Osborne's "Made Easy" series, all techniques are explained with practical hands-on examples and are illustrated with helpful screen displays.

$16.95p
0-07-881248-8, 300 pp., 7³/₈ x 9¹/₄
AVAILABLE: 8/86

Wordstar® Made Easy, Second Edition
by Walter A. Ettlin

"An excellent manual for the most popular CP/M-based word processor. The WordStar documentation is notoriously undecipherable. With WordStar® Made Easy, you can learn the essential commands within four hours."
(Computer Book Review)

$15.95p
0-07-931090-7, 132 pp., 7³/₈ x 9¹/₄

Advanced MultiMate® and MultiMate® Advantage™
by Mark Brownstein

Experienced users of MultiMate,® the powerful word processing package for the IBM® PC, get two books in one with this addition to Osborne's "Advanced" series. You'll have a fast-paced tutorial to both MultiMate® and Advantage™ (versions 3.5 and 3.6). High-powered techniques are discussed and illustrated in short applications and examples. Brownstein emphasizes the new features of Advantage, including its networking capabilities; multi-column documents; the On-File™ database program, which simulates an index-card file system; and the GraphLink™ program, which transfers graphics to MultiMate from Lotus® 1-2-3,® Framework,® and other popular software packages. Brownstein, the former editor-in-chief of *Easy Home Computer* magazine, is a free-lance consultant and author.

$17.95p
0-07-881247-X, 325 pp., 7³/₈ x 9¹/₄
AVAILABLE: 9/86

Advanced WordPerfect®: Features & Techniques
by Eric Alderman and Lawrence J. Magid

You can make this word processing software for the IBM® PC and compatibles work above and beyond the usual with *Advanced WordPerfect.®* Written by columnist and consultant Eric Alderman and Los Angeles Times syndicated columnist Lawrence Magid, *Advanced WordPerfect®* brings you application tools and concepts that greatly increase your productivity. After a brief review of basic functions, you'll learn how to apply macros to open, close, and resize windows; make document format changes; even control memo headers. You'll also find out about paragraph numbering and outlining, indexing and building tables of contents, using WordPerfect's mathematical capabilities, setting up printing formats, and integrating WordPerfect™ with other products, such as Lotus® 1-2-3,® dBASE III,® Sidekick,® and ProKey.™ *Advanced WordPerfect®* is the source for ambitious users who want information that exceeds the documentation.

$16.95p
0-07-881239-9, 300 pp., 7³/₈ x 9¹/₄
AVAILABLE: 7/86

Micro-to-Mainframe Links
by Ronald F. Kopeck

Here's a book that sorts out all the complex issues involved in linking microcomputers to mainframes for sophisticated, high-powered applications. With *Micro-to-Mainframe Links,* data processing and communications professionals can fully understand the major considerations behind PC-to-mainframe integration. A concise, detailed text thoroughly explains the planning and evaluation process used in determining how PC-to-mainframe linking fits into your office environment. Data transfer, security, and use of existing networks are also discussed. You'll find out about link products and the real and hidden costs of linking, as well as maintenance and service. And you'll learn about monitoring, the safe ways to begin the PC-to-mainframe link by establishing and evaluating tests and measurements. Kopeck, a widely-known consultant and editor of *Micro-to-Mainframe Link News,* draws on his extensive knowledge of this field to bring you the most comprehensive coverage possible.

$18.95p
0-07-881228-3, 300 pp., 7³⁄₈ x 9¹⁄₄

The Practical Guide to Local Area Networks
by Rowland Archer

Deciding which local area network is right for you doesn't have to be a difficult process. With *The Practical Guide to Local Area Networks,* you'll be prepared to evaluate and select the LAN that's best for your business needs. LAN specialist Rowland Archer guides you through the process of planning your LAN installation, pointing out the advantages and potential pitfalls every step of the way. Archer then applies the criteria he has developed to five of the most popular LANs available for the IBM® PC and compatible computers: 3Com Ethernet® Corvus Omninet® Orchid PCnet® Novell NetWare,™and IBM® PC Network and Token Ring.

$21.95p
0-07-881190-2, 250 pp., 6¹⁄₂ x 9¹⁄₄

Desktop Publishing From A to Z
by Bill Grout, Irene Athanasopoulos, and Rebecca Kutlin

As a desktop publisher, you can use your microcomputer to create your own newsletters, catalogs, conference brochures, news releases, and more. *Desktop Publishing From A to Z* helps you choose the software, equipment, and procedures you need to achieve professional results. Grout discusses software packages and hardware that are available for desktop publishing, from project-management programs to page makeup programs, from the Macintosh™ and the IBM® PC to the LaserWriter™ printer. You'll find out how to establish a publishing plan, control costs and profits, handle printing and binding, promotion, and distribution.

$17.95p
0-07-881212-7, 225 pp., 7³⁄₈ x 9¹⁄₄

Available at fine bookstores and computer stores everywhere.

For a complimentary catalog of all our current publications contact: Osborne/McGraw-Hill, 2600 Tenth Street, Berkeley, CA 94710

Phone inquiries may be made using our toll-free number. Call 800-227-0900 or 800-772-2531 (inside California). TWX 910-366-7277.

Prices subject to change without notice.